ALSO BY TAMAR E. CHANSKY

Freeing Your Child from Obsessive-Compulsive Disorder

Freeing Your Child from Anxiety

POWERFUL, PRACTICAL STRATEGIES

TO OVERCOME YOUR CHILD'S FEARS,

PHOBIAS, AND WORRIES

Tamar E. Chansky, Ph.D.

DIRECTOR, CHILDREN'S CENTER FOR OCD AND ANXIETY

Illustrations by Phillip Stern

BROADWAY BOOKS

NEW YORK   LONDON   TORONTO   SYDNEY   AUCKLAND

Broadway Books titles may be purchased for business or promotional use or for special sales. For information, please write to: Special Markets Department, Random House, Inc., 1745 Broadway, New York, NY 10019.

PRINTED IN THE UNITED STATES OF AMERICA

BROADWAY BOOKS and its logo, a letter B bisected on the diagonal, are trademarks of Random House, Inc.

Visit our website at www.broadwaybooks.com

First edition published 2004

Book design by Chris Welch
Illustrated by Phillip Stern

Grateful acknowledgment is made to Crown Books, Random House, for permission to reprint and adapt drawings from *Freeing Your Child from Obsessive-Compulsive Disorder.* T. Chansky. Crown Publishers, 2001. Figures 1, 9, 11, and 17.

Library of Congress Cataloging-in-Publication Data

Chansky, Tamar Ellsas.
Freeing your child from anxiety : powerful, practical strategies to overcome your child's fears, phobias, and worries / Tamar E. Chansky ; illustrations by Phillip Stern.
p.   cm.
1. Anxiety in children.   I. Title.
RJ506.A58C48 2004
618.92'8522—dc22
2003065208

ISBN 0-7679-1492-9

7   9   10   8

For Phillip, Meredith, and Mireilla

Acknowledgments

I am very grateful to my agent, Gareth Eserky, who welcomed me in the publishing world with my first book and continues to be a trusted source of guidance and encouragement for the work I do. Thank-you to Patricia Medved and her assistant Beth Datlowe for their enthusiasm and care in bringing this book to fruition.

I feel fortunate to be working in a time when there are so many gifted colleagues who are working hard on behalf of anxious kids. I appreciate the contributions of Philip Kendall and John March in advancing both the science and practice of treating childhood anxiety disorders. Special thanks to Jeffrey Schwartz for his inspiring work and for a vote of confidence at a critical moment. Thank-you to Sandy Pimentel and Amy Verstappen for their assistance with research and to Jodi Mindell, who is always there with great advice! For advance articles and helpful input I thank John Piacentini, Daniel Pine, Margo Thienemann, Amy Wilensky, Golda Ginsburg, Mary Lou Reaver of the PA-TSA, and Christina Pearson of the Trichotillomania Learning Center. Deepest gratitude to Kellie, Scott, Jessica, and the Childhood OCD Project for their support and collaboration.

I am grateful for all the encouragement of friends, siblings, and extended family. Special thanks to my parents, Elissa and

Norman Chansky, for sharing in the joy of our children and taking good care of our family. I am blessed to once again be able to thank Maxine Baylor for her loving care of our children. Without her it would be very tough to pursue my work. Special thanks to Crystal Baylor and Christopher Baylor for helping make all the connections happen.

Though writing a book is a significant undertaking, there are many days when, with the inspiration of my patients, the book at times wrote itself. My deepest respect and gratitude go to the children and families for sharing their stories and discoveries so that others may benefit from their experience. Their courage inspires me to work hard to make all this make sense. It is a pleasure to work with such gifted and committed people.

Finally, the ideas in this book have been running through my mind for over a decade. Committing them to paper is a wish that, at this stage of my life, could only be granted by my husband, Phillip Stern. Without your generosity, sacrifice, and devotion this project would simply not have been possible. You have made a home where creativity is prioritized, and the risks I take are by your example. You have laid eyes on every line of this book and once again brought the metaphors to life with wonderful illustrations. A heartfelt thank-you to my children for sharing their mom with this project. Meredith, you are wonderful company and wise beyond your years. I enjoy your sense of humor and all-around goodness each and every day. And Mireilla, your zest for life keeps our home buzzing and happy.

Contents

Acknowledgments   *vii*

Introduction   *1*

PART I ✳ ANXIETY DISORDER BASICS
What You Need to Know to Set Your Child Free   11

CHAPTER 1 "I Can't, I'm Too Scared"
Understanding Children's Fears and Worries   15

CHAPTER 2 Making the Diagnosis for Anxiety
Is It Just a Phase?   28

CHAPTER 3 When and Where to Turn for Help
Treatments for Childhood Anxiety   44

CHAPTER 4 Behind the Scenes in Your Brain
Anxiety Glitches, Rewiring Fixes   56

CHAPTER 5 Putting It All Together
The Master Plan for Managing Anxiety   83

PART II ✳ ALL WORRIES GREAT AND SMALL
Common Childhood Fears and Worries and Problem Anxieties 101

CHAPTER 6 From Everyday Worries to Generalized Anxiety Disorder (GAD) *107*

CHAPTER 7 From the Mini-Scaries to Real Phobias *122*

CHAPTER 8 From Shyness to Social Anxiety and Selective Mutism *146*

CHAPTER 9 From Clinginess to Separation Anxiety and Panic Disorder *164*

CHAPTER 10 From Superstitions and Rituals to Obsessive-Compulsive Disorder (OCD) and PANDAS *196*

CHAPTER 11 From Nervous Habits to Tourette Syndrome and Trichotillomania *221*

CHAPTER 12 From Acute Stress to Post-Traumatic Stress Disorder *238*

PART III ✳ ANXIETY
Beyond the Diagnoses 253

CHAPTER 13 Things That Go Bump in the Night
From Nighttime Fears to Sleep Anxieties 257

CHAPTER 14 Expanding the Focus
Anxious Children at School and with Friends and Family 269

CHAPTER 15 Worry Prevention in the Real World 285

CHAPTER 16 Freeing Yourself from Anxiety
Your Child Will Lead the Way 294

Appendix 299
Endnotes 307

Introduction

Our oldest, Tina has always been on the anxious side. She goes a mile a minute with her questions and can be a little bit the drama queen, but mostly gets through things okay. But every once in a while we hit a wall where she's afraid to try something new, or she's absolutely convinced that she can't get through something—a play, a test, a phone call—and we're stuck. She's stuck thinking things are impossible, and we don't know how to tell her that there's another way.

The day I found out that Dan had been eating his lunch in a bathroom stall rather than face the kids in the cafeteria, I died a thousand deaths. I knew he was shy, but I didn't realize how unbearable life had become for him. This can't be the story of his life. We've got to help him, but I don't know where to begin.

Kelly is an extremely serious kid; it's painful to see how life is such a burden to her. She worries about everything from catching the bus to catching a cold, getting good grades, not hurting anyone's feelings, not making a mistake. She never lets up; she's always on alert. She has a full-time job of "just making sure." How do we convince her that she can relax sometimes?

Marty has never been a worrier; he's a really put-together kid. I was stunned when he walked off the bus for his school overnight, and in front of all the kids said, "I can't do it." I know he has some trouble falling asleep, but this was so humiliating for him. How do I help him get over this?

> I speak for the trees, for the trees have no tongues.
> —*Dr. Seuss,* The Lorax

Children with anxiety suffer in silence. Today, there is an ever-growing forest of kids who desperately need our help. But be advised, they are probably not going to be flagging us down. Not overtly, anyway. To their peers, teachers, and even parents, anxious children appear to be fine much of the time. That is their goal, to their credit and their detriment. Some kids don't realize that they are worrying; it is just their way of life. Others know they are different from other kids but don't want anyone to find out. Perceived as competent and model students, their efforts to not stand out or be found out come at a great cost, since kids don't know that this is not a long-term solution. A child who is anxious and hiding anxiety is like the swan seemingly gliding across the surface of a pond but paddling like crazy underneath—the work is exhausting, and relentless. Stuck with a worry soundtrack playing in their minds, these children don't know there is a choice, that there are specific steps they can take to change the score. They need our help. When parents learn how anxiety works, they can make a world of difference in teaching these essential lessons to their children and save them from a worried way of life.

Though I conceived of this book many years ago, these ideas are more relevant than ever now that our tragic introduction to the new century has put us all on emotional overload. This has only made the concern for our children greater. When our emotional reserves are tapped, we are less available to respond to our children's needs. Anxiety doesn't go away on its own. And, unfortunately, anxiety-producing situations are not going to disappear. It is my firm belief that our future depends on our recognizing the essential need for anxiety prevention for our youth. When one considers what we already knew about anxiety *prior* to 9/11, the urgency of addressing the needs of anxious kids is undeniable.

Consider the facts:

- Anxiety disorders affect over 13 percent of children; they are the most prevalent psychiatric condition among children today. In fact, the typical schoolchild during the 1980s reported more anxiety than psychiatric patients did during the 1950s.[1]
- Anxiety does not go away without treatment, but in fact worsens over time and has adverse effects on cardiac, immune, and respiratory functioning.
- Anxiety disorders are the most prevalent psychiatric condition in adults. The majority of adults with an anxiety disorder report that their symptoms started in childhood.
- Anxiety disorders cost the country $42.3 billion each year in disability, hospitalizations, and medical care.
- Anxiety disorders are the most treatable psychiatric condition. Cognitive-behavior therapy is an effective, safe, empirically supported treatment for anxiety disorders.

We have more reasons than we can count to take on the job of teaching our children how to manage their anxiety. To start, we need to understand the lessons ourselves. That is the purpose of this book. Parents will find here the nuts and bolts of how worry works, and solutions for how to reduce it step by step. When parents learn the principles of how anxiety builds and resolves, they will feel prepared rather than overwhelmed by their child's fears and worries and can introduce simple strategies into daily life. This practice with the small stuff helps kids be prepared to competently handle the big stressors when they come along.

Taking this job seriously, however, doesn't always mean keeping a serious tone. As you will see in the pages of this book, it means using whatever creative means you need to reach your audience. Think of the ad campaigns for the war on drugs—they used clever, creative, even humorous ways of getting the information across. The war on worry should be no different.

The most important lesson is not to take worry at face value. Worry is not the calm, still voice of reason that we could really use on our side when we're in a pinch. On the contrary, worry is a relentless exaggerator, a distorter of the facts, and for anxious kids it is the *default first reaction*. To them, the worry sounds convincing, but in truth it operates independent of reality—there's no interface. Managing worry means challenging the credibility of those automatic thoughts and cultivating a strong *second reaction*—speed-dialing that voice of reason, connecting to some truth circuits, and in so doing, bringing that magnified risk down to a manageable size. By giving kids permission to play with their own thinking, a new possibility opens up—the possibility that kids can actually doubt and "boss back" the worry rather than being held hostage by it. This is what cognitive-behavior therapy looks like in practice, and many of the lessons can be implemented easily at home. To do this, your children need to know it is safe to come to you with their worries (even when they don't make sense) much as they would come to you with a math question.

The best news about anxiety disorders is that treatment works—these disorders are the most treatable psychiatric condition, and cognitive-behavior therapy is our most powerful tool. Hundreds of studies have supported the efficacy of treating anxiety disorders in adults, and more recently, in children.

Children are able to overcome their symptoms and maintain their progress long after treatment has ended. The lessons they learn are internalized for life. As anxiety experts Drs. John Walkup and Golda Ginsburg of Johns Hopkins describe, "It is dramatic to observe a child 'anxious since birth' or even 'in the womb' respond to treatment with what appears to be substantial changes in 'temperament and personality.' "[2]

In the past, anxious children were at best ignored and at worst boxed in—allowed to remain scared or shy, or told to get over it. No doubt, our view of anxious children often came from our blinders about our own anxiety. Parents in my office often remark that they didn't know that the "normal" worried way they lived their day-to-day life as kids is today considered an anxiety disorder. Not knowing that you were wired for worry and that your child might have inherited that predisposition leaves generations to cycle through the same territory. Today it is possible to break that cycle by recognizing worry as a dysfunctional voice and learning how to generate realistic alternatives.

Enlisting the Mind to Change the Brain

While this may be the Age of Anxiety, it is also the dawning of the Age of Neuroplasticity. Advances in the neurosciences are documenting the great capacity of the brain to change or rewire connections, given the right kind of practice. In *The Mind and the Brain*, Dr. Jeffrey Schwartz and Sharon Begley argue that brain circuitry operates on the principle of "survival of the busiest." In other words, whichever brain circuits we engage the most enlist the greatest numbers of neurons or brain cells. This concept has applications to many different brain functions, whether we are talking about recovering the use of functions after a stroke, contending with obsessive-compulsive disorder or tics, or countering anxiety. The more we engage in worry, the more, the faster, and the more easily the brain will be mapped to make those anxious connections. When we recognize our worries for what they are and begin to dispute and dispel them, we are actually harnessing the transforming power of the mind to reroute the brain's processing map. The more we invest our time and energy in connecting to healthy circuits, the more automatic that response will become.

DISCREDITING WORRY TALK AS A BRAIN GLITCH

How do we help kids extricate themselves from the worry so they can decide what to think and do? Rather than rushing to reassure or argue rationally, we must devalue the worry message in the first place. If your child came to you distressed about a telemarketer's insistence to buy new siding, you would likely respond by saying, *"That's just a telemarketer; his job is to make everything sound urgent. What does he know about what you need?"* Substitute the phrase "worry brain" for "telemarketer" and you've begun to understand how to enlist your child's critical thinking. For young children, it helps to give the worry a name—the buzzing of the Worry Bug. For older children, referring to it as the worry tape or the Exaggerator opens up the possibility of hearing the worry with an analytical ear. The mountain has now been reduced to a molehill, and kids are more willing to approach their worry situation and overcome it one step at a time.

Teaching Our Children by Starting with Ourselves

In this unstable world, we are all feeling the gaps in our ability to handle our own worry. Even more daunting is the task of helping our children who are burdened with their worry. If you feel unable to manage your fears, big or small, the ideas in this book will put you in a better position to encourage and teach your children.

We would do anything to take the hits of life for our children if we could. Whether it's the pain of their scraped knee, their diabetes, rejection by friends, or rejection from college, it hurts us less if we hurt for them. Sometimes the idea of helping our kids to manage their worry by facing it head on feels foreign, uncomfortable, and even mean. We want to keep them protected from fears instead. But in our efforts to shield our children, we turn away from teaching the very things that could prevent the suffering in the first place. When they encounter tough situations, they'll be stuck waiting for someone to rescue them if they haven't learned how to face them alone. No parent wants that. The first step is learning not to get overwhelmed by your child's distress, knowing that whatever they are facing is *uncomfortable*, not *unbearable*. If your child burns his mouth on soup, you don't stop serving him soup, you make the soup cooler, teach him to blow on it—eventually, he can handle soup.

Many a child, once they've begun to learn how fear works, will say, "If I don't start working on it, I'll never get used to it." This realization that things get *easier* when you approach them, rather than avoid them, will make the difference between having a life and standing on the sidelines watching everyone else.

The time has come to teach our children the ins and outs of handling fear and worry, like any other skill—math, reading, bike riding. It's like handing them an operating manual for their emotions, which lays out the steps they must take to reduce their fear—to "plug in" a picture of themselves coping and reach for ready-at-hand strategies to manage any situation. Like knowing how to change a tire, or dial 911, the time to learn these lessons is not in the heat of crisis. That's the premise of this book—that teaching our children the small steps of managing fears and worries is one of the greatest gifts a parent can give.

The best time to intervene is early. If you teach your children worry management skills when they are young, they will grow up knowing how to handle themselves more competently. Though it may be "normal" to worry about separations, or the dark, or going to sleep at night, if your child is clearly distressed *and* not progressing in his or her management of those so-called normal fears, get help. There's no justification for waiting till your child is unquestionably incapacitated before you get help. If your gut is saying *something isn't right*, listen to it. When you deny there is a problem or invalidate or dismiss your child's concerns, she has no one to communicate with and the problems deepen. Fear and worry may be universals, but recently it seems as if unexpected sources of worry are turning up with greater frequency. The question these days is not "Are kids worrying?" It is "How can kids get competent at managing their worry?" In this climate, all parents want to know how to steel their children against new sources of fears and worries.

This book is organized in three parts. In the first part, we explore the causes of anxiety, how to diagnose it, and what treatments are available for kids. We take a closer look at the mechanisms of anxiety and offer user-friendly ways to talk about them to your child. Part I ends with the "Master Plan," a set of six steps to implement in most anxiety situations.

The second part of the book takes a closer look at specific anxiety issues, including worry, phobias, social anxiety, separation anxiety, obsessive-compulsive disorder, and tics and habits. Applying the techniques introduced in Part I, these chapters illustrate how to adapt the strategies to address the particular concern your child is having. In Part III, we take a brief look at issues that impact anxiety level, such as contending with real-life fears, and at managing hot spots for anxious kids—including going to school, dealing with siblings, and going to sleep.

Whether you are a newcomer to the ways of anxiety in children or have indelible memories of trying to take your child out of the car at school or calm him when he was inconsolable, my hope is that through the examples of other families facing the same situations you'll be inspired to see that worry management is not only a skill, but a gift that you can work on with your child.

You will meet in these pages many children and families who know well what life with anxiety is like because they live it too. These generous families have agreed to share their stories—their struggles, and ultimately their triumphs—so that others may learn, and perhaps find the path a bit easier because they know that they are not alone. These are families who may have started out knowing nothing about anxiety, or have known the dark side of it from their own childhoods, but they have succeeded because they learned how anxiety works so that they could explain it to their children. They learned to not be afraid of their children's fears, and they have learned, as Schwartz and Begley encourage, to "use the mind to change the brain."

Remember the goal: it's not to talk your children out of their fears, it's to teach them how to talk themselves through their fears. Don't remove the hurdle, but teach them how to jump over it.

PART I

Anxiety Disorder Basics

WHAT YOU NEED TO KNOW TO SET YOUR CHILD FREE

Parents are excellent leaders when they know where they are going. Many parents feel so overwhelmed by their child's anxious distress that they get confused about where they are headed—are they trying to make their child feel better or are they trying to help their child feel stronger? Torn between these two options, parents often feel at an impasse. The chapters in this section will introduce parents to what they need to know to tackle both goals at once. By learning the fundamentals of how anxiety works, how to identify it, and how to successfully intervene, parents will competently help kids to overcome their fears and worries—nothing feels better than that!

In Chapter 1, we look at the potential causes and correlates of anxiety in children. When parents begin to see the "no-fault" nature of anxiety disorders, kids sense that their feelings are being accepted rather than called into question or judged. Understanding your child's anxiety means accepting your child for who he or she is. Accepting your child doesn't mean closing the door on change, it actually is the key to opening it. When your child doesn't have to act out or fight you to help you understand how he is feeling, this frees up that energy to focus on moving forward in making changes. Chapter 2 introduces the different types of anxiety disorders and provides descriptions to help you find the anxiety-disorder type that best fits the theme of your child's worry. Chapter 3 covers the when and how of treatment for childhood anxiety. In Chapter 4, the nuts and bolts of cognitive-behavior therapy are presented with exercises and illustrations to help you understand the concepts easily so that you can in turn use them when working with your children. The Master Plan in Chapter 5 pulls together the concepts presented in Chapter 4 in a cohesive plan which can be adapted for most fear and worry situations. Oftentimes parents struggle to find the right words to use in talking to their kids about anxiety. To address this, parents will find scripts in Chapter 5, some for use with young children, the others with older children.

✳

CHAPTER 1

"I Can't, I'm Too Scared"

UNDERSTANDING CHILDREN'S
FEARS AND WORRIES

From the children:

When I was little my mom worked the "graveyard shift" at the hospital. Every night I was so worried that meant she was going to die and I'd never see her again.

When people tell me to lighten up, that things aren't so bad, it makes me feel much worse. They must think I actually like being this way.

Views from parents:

It is very hard to see my daughter in pain and so scared. Before we got treatment, I felt there was nothing I could do to alleviate her pain. I felt so helpless, being the parent and not knowing what to do; that was the worst feeling.

Teachers think I'm nuts because my daughter is picture perfect at school. She's the model student—never a problem. But at home she totally falls apart, her anxiety is so intense, it makes normal life impossible for us. I wish they could see her at home so they would understand what I'm talking about.

Anxiety in Children:
Too Much of a Good Thing?

"Don't run into the street, stop climbing on that, careful, that will break." These are words that most parents have to say over and over again, but that most parents of anxious children will probably never have to utter. In fact, parents may find themselves kept in check by their worrying child—*"Did you lock the door? Is the gas tank full? Did you send in the permission slip?"* Though it can often be confusing or frustrating to parents that their child must feel every wrinkle in the day and race ahead to prepare for every eventuality, we must understand that anxious kids are just doing what their brain tells them to do. Anxious children are highly cautious, overcorrecting for the possibility of danger. In fact their wiring has them seeing danger when it's not there. Born with a mind that casts tall, scary shadows on ordinary things, they spend their days enduring great distress over things that their peers don't even notice. Anxious kids may recognize that they are different, but they don't know why, assuming that this is just how they are.

Because we don't see things as anxious kids do, we may be impatient, judgmental, and perhaps even overprotective, but not necessarily effective. The more that we can understand about what our children are seeing and feeling when they are anxious, distortions and all, the more we can empathize. If we don't empathize, we lose our audience. They won't stick around for the lesson, because they think you don't understand the problem in the first place.

Children's fears are a source of concern, distress, and even embarrassment for parents. When it's their child who is hiding in the corner at the birthday party, in tears at the school play, or unable to go on the school camping trip, parents are stuck. Rather than getting mobilized to help, parents often feel an urgent need to find the "off" button for those fears to simply stop. What fuels that concern further are two thoughts: first, "this shouldn't be happening, my child shouldn't be afraid," and second, "I don't know how to fix it." It is this two-part punch that fear delivers to parents, immobilizing their helpfulness response and leaving both them and their kids at a loss—or more often in a "you should," "I can't" contest of wills.

This chapter introduces the concept of fear—how it functions as an essential safeguard for survival. Fears and worries can help children put the brakes on in situations with which they are unfamiliar. Rather than hurling yourself into a swimming pool when you don't know how to swim, a good dose of fearful "what if?" can keep a healthy degree of caution in the picture until that is no longer needed. In addition, this chapter explores the differences between normal fears and anxieties, and takes an inside look at how anxiety shapes a child's experience. Finally, it presents different models for how fears and anxieties develop, exploring the influence of such factors as genetics, temperament, and experience. The bottom line is that children come by fears honestly. The more parents understand that fear is nothing for *them* to fear, the more they can be instrumental in helping kids out of these glitches.

Fear: A Normal and Necessary Part of Life

Fear is a necessary function for our survival. Because our natural inclination is toward growth and development, we would not survive as a species if it were not for our ability to hold back and appraise and avoid danger. It is a protective mechanism and a normal part of development.

The focus of anxiety changes for children over time as their world broadens and they encounter new experiences that they have not yet mastered. Babies are afraid of a loss of support and loud noises, toddlers who are learning to run away themselves are afraid of separation and things bigger than themselves, and young children are afraid of the results of their emerging imagination, especially at night—monsters, burglars, and other bad guys. Adolescents fear social scrutiny and begin to look beyond themselves to the world community and such abstract issues of safety as war, and success in the future. Fear can be considered

---

❋   **Typical Developmental Sequence of Fears in Children**   ❋

INFANCY: In response to a growing ability to differentiate familiar faces (parents) from unfamiliar faces, stranger anxiety (clinging and crying when a stranger approaches) develops around 7 to 9 months and typically resolves by end of first year.

EARLY CHILDHOOD: As a healthy attachment to parents grows, separation anxiety (crying, sadness, fear of desertion upon separation) emerges around one year of age and improves over the next three years, resolving in most children by the end of kindergarten. As children's worlds expand, they may fear new and unfamiliar situations and real and imagined dangers from such things as big dogs, spiders, or monsters.

ELEMENTARY SCHOOL: With access to new information, children begin to fear real-world dangers—fire, burglars, storms, illness, drugs. With experience, they learn that these risks can exist as remote rather than imminent dangers.

MIDDLE SCHOOL: Growing importance of social status leads to social comparisons and worries about social acceptance. Concerns about academic and athletic performance and social-group identification are normal.

HIGH SCHOOL: Teenagers continue to be focused on social acceptance, but with a greater concern for finding a group that reflects their chosen identities. Concerns about the larger world, moral issues, and their future success are common.

the emotional response that occurs in the interim between confronting a new situation and actually mastering it. In the same way that adults may be fearful of a new piece of technology until we have figured out how it works—and may entertain unrealistic scenarios of blowing up the computer by pushing the wrong button—kids' fears and anxieties are fueled by an active imagination trying to piece together an explanation for how the world works. A little information goes a long way. A four-year-old at the aquarium is afraid when she hears that she's going to see the sharks because she is old enough to learn that sharks are dangerous, but not old enough to understand that she will watch safely from outside the tank. An eight-year-old is beginning to understand about germs and disease but can't yet grasp how unlikely it would be to get sick just from engaging in normal activities. Temporary fears are part of life.

Anxiety is the tense emotional state that occurs when you can't predict the outcome of a situation or guarantee that it will be the desired one. Even in the best circumstances children experience some worry. Anxiety becomes a disorder when a child automatically exaggerates risks and underestimates the ability to cope with a given situation. Anxiety is debilitating to children, causing not only chronic fatigue and other physical complaints, but also decreased academic functioning and even school attendance, and strained peer and family relations.

Who Is the Anxious Child?

Anxiety has many faces. Some children appear visibly stressed, others keep their anxiety under cover and worry silently, still others are angry-anxious kids, reacting to their limitations with frustration. Demographically speaking, prevalence rates range from 5.7 to 17 percent of all children.[1] Rates of anxiety disorders tend to increase slightly with age; however, most studies of anxiety disorders draw from a sample of children over seven years old, so the prevalence of anxiety disorders in very young children is unclear. Girls tend to be diagnosed with anxiety disorders more often than boys, though more boys may be brought to treatment, as the outward signs of anxious behavior—crying, shying away, overt distress—may be less socially acceptable in boys than girls. The consensus across numerous studies of anxious children is that the majority of them have more than one anxiety disorder occurring at the same time, which is referred to as "comorbid." If left untreated, anxiety symptoms become more disabling over time, and the course is considered to be chronic with fluctuations across the lifespan.

Though children with anxiety disorders are as impaired as children with disruptive disorders, they will often stay below the radar of the adults around them and go undiagnosed because their symptoms don't interfere in the classroom, but rather are internalized. The seriousness of anxiety disorders is often downplayed by the public—anxious children may be seen as simply needing to lighten up.

The invisibility of the symptoms makes them no less detrimental to the child. Anxious children may have fewer friends because of social fears, or because their free time is consumed by worry or rituals. They may spend inordinate amounts of time preparing for an event, trying to fall asleep at night, getting their homework just right, getting reassurance about their safety. They may not go out for a sport to avoid the risk of being humiliated. They may not go to friends' houses, not consider college because of panic or separation concerns. At home, family life may lose its sense of spontaneity and fun, as participating in ordinary events may be too anxiety-provoking.

From morning till night, with little exception, worried kids are bombarded with a myriad of "what ifs." With so much on their minds, we might marvel at how well anxious kids are able to hold it together.

Causes and Correlates of Anxiety

All parents spend time worrying and wondering about what caused their child's anxiety. Many entertain the dark question of whether they somehow brought this anxiety on their child—either by their own behavior or by genetic transmission. The second issue is easier to address—as we'll see below, there is a strong genetic link for anxiety disorders, but as we know that genes do unto the next generation as has been done to the previous one, we have no choice in the matter. The genetic recipe folds the bad into the good. It does help to understand the physiological nature of anxiety, as it helps parents and kids maintain a no-fault approach to the problem. We would never blame our children for their asthma or diabetes—or blame ourselves for passing it on, and so it should be with anxiety disorders.

What we'll see in this section is that like any aspect of a child, anxiety is the result of the knitting together of multiple influences. No one factor accounts for all. "Bad parenting" can't cause these problems, and good parenting alone can't fix the problem. If there are changes you want to make, your child's difficulties may spur you on to turn over a new leaf, but understand that this will only help the process; it will not be the reason why there was trouble in the first place. In fact, what look like "strange parenting practices"—accommodating a child's fear—are often an *effect* of having an anxious child, not a cause.

Nature? Nurture? Our understanding of the causes of anxiety in children comes from an appreciation of the interaction of multiple factors. These include (1) genetics and brain physiology, (2) temperament, (3) parenting style, and (4) environmental factors including traumatic events. All of these inputs have both sensitizing as well as buffering influences.

GENETICS: BORN TO BE ANXIOUS?

It is commonly said that evolution selects for anxious genes—and when considering the survival of the species it's not hard to see why. Too many false positives are better than one fatal oversight, but when you scale that down to the individual child's narrow shoulders it doesn't make it comfortable for the owners of those anxious genes.

Genetics researchers have found some support for the genetic transmission of anxiety. Children of anxious parents are seven times more likely to develop an anxiety disorder than children of non-anxious parents.[2] Although the evidence for familial transmission is strongest for panic disorder, genetics explains about 30 to 40 percent of all transmission. Thus, while genetics make a significant contribution, the majority of children with anxious parents do not develop an anxiety disorder. Genetics determine your overall vulnerability or susceptibility to anxiety. Children may be born more sensitive and reactive, with lower distress tolerance, but other factors intervene to tip the scales. There are likely multiple genes that contribute to a child's anxiety disorder, not one identifiable gene for anxiety. The genes affect how different cells in the body's alarm system operate—the sensitivities, reaction times, and absorption rates. We now take a behind-the-scenes look at that system, and at some of the areas that have been identified as central to our processing and experience of fear, threat, and anxiety.

The Anatomy of the Brain: Wired for Worry

At the center of the brain's defense system—let's call it the "anxiety works"—an almond-shaped cluster of cells, the amygdala, operates within the limbic system, the system responsible for processing emotional experiences. The amygdala is a lifesaver—pulling us back from the curb to avoid a speeding car—fast, but not always accurate—alarming us over a stick that looks like a snake. Thus, it may also be the culprit when it comes to anxiety disorders, signaling us to jump to dire conclusions when there is nothing to fear. The amygdala is like a first responder—it quickly assesses the emotional significance of cues and activates nearly every system in the body to survive a perceived threat, whether that means to fight or run for your life. When the perceived danger has passed, the prefrontal cortex, which acts like brakes in the fear circuit, signals the amygdala that it's time to downshift so that the body can then return to its baseline or steady state. Evolution selects for cautious genes by favoring easy starts to the fear response, but not easy stops.

One area of ongoing anxiety research concerns the role of serotonin, a neurotransmitter, or brain messenger chemical. When danger and all-clear messages are not transmitting efficiently, excessive anticipation and prolonged distress may result. The Selective Serotonin Reuptake Inhibitors, or SSRIs, are the medications that are most prescribed for anxiety disorders. These are discussed further in Chapter 3.

TEMPERAMENT AND BEHAVIORAL INHIBITION

"Temperament," according to Ralph Waldo Emerson, "is the iron wire upon which the beads [of life] are strung." Many anxious children appear to be sensitized to change and risk *from birth* and as a result have a curbed approach to exploration. This predisposition is a blueprint for predicting children's needs and experiences in any given situation. Their extremely cautious style is no one's fault. Dr. Jerome Kagan, at Harvard University, identified this trait, which he calls behavioral inhibition (BI), in children as young as twenty-one months old. They react to even the most minor changes in their environment—a new mobile or cup—with distress, while other infants respond with excitement or delight to the same changes. Dr. Kagan found that these inhibited children had a higher than average likelihood of developing an anxiety disorder later in life.

ENVIRONMENTAL FACTORS: STRESSFUL EVENTS AND PARENTING FACTORS

Stressful Events. Not all children who develop an anxiety disorder have a traumatic event in their history—in fact most do not. However, in our world today, children and adolescents are commonly exposed to traumatic experiences. As many as 15 to 20 percent of children and adolescents will encounter a significant traumatic event during their youth.[3] Though many studies suggest that the majority of children who undergo trauma do recover without incident, a child who has experienced a traumatic event is twice as likely to develop some type of difficulty, whether this is anxiety, depression, or a behavioral disorder. All children faced with stressful or traumatic situations may go through periods of greater sensitivity, clinging, and regression. This is not only normal, it is adaptive. It enables them to get the nurturing they need to recover emotionally and physically from a trauma. In Chapter 15, we discuss factors that sensitize children to stress or help protect them from it, and how to handle stressful events in a way that enhances coping and serves as a buffer against adverse effects. In Chapter 12 we look at treatments for children who are experiencing a disorder known as post-traumatic stress disorder.

We would expect any child facing such stressors as illness, death of a loved one, being the victim of violence, losing a best friend, or facing parental separation, hospitalization, or divorce to have difficulties for a period of time. These events only compound an already heavy burden in an anxious child and may turn occasional anxiety into a full-blown anxiety disorder, or trigger some regression in a recovering anxious child.

Family Enhancement of Thinking Style in Anxious Children. At a recent visit to my daughter's dentist, as I sat respectfully at a distance, the doctor was complaining about those other folks who "parent by helicopter," hovering over the child, making sure they are okay, constantly asking, "Now, does that hurt?" While his concern was how these "pilots" get in the way of the equipment, the real concern is how this hovering impacts kids' experiences in stressful situations like the dentist's chair. Though we know that parent interaction/instruction alone cannot cause anxiety reactions, studies suggest that family interaction can enhance the anxious child's perceptions about a situation, which in turn dictate or at least influence the child's actions. While parents may be trying to protect kids from potential dangers, they may be inadvertently spotlighting them. To be sure, a child without anxious wiring will be able to shrug that information off and even think to himself, "There goes Dad, getting freaked out again," but to an already anxious child, this behavior reinforces the idea that these situations are scary. Rather than turning down the volume on that worry soundtrack, the child is now hearing it in stereo.

It may be that parenting by helicopter is a *reaction* to a child's anxiety, not a cause—a concerned parent's best attempts to respond to a child's worrying mind. In fact, there is a significant body of literature suggesting that several parenting factors are *correlated with* anxiety in children. What this means is that while we know that certain parenting styles accompany anxiety in kids, we don't know whether these are a result of or a cause of the anxiety. Studies have found that children with anxiety disorders describe their families as more controlling, less cohesive and supportive, and more conflictual than families of kids without a diagnosis. These studies always give me pause because parents may feel blamed by them. I see how very stable parents become understandably alarmed and distraught in *response* to distress in their child, not out of some bizarre desire to make their child anxious.

A paper released in 2002 by psychologists Golda Ginsburg and Margaret Schlossberg of Johns Hopkins University School of Medicine, summarized over twenty studies of parenting factors associated with anxiety in children.[4] With permission, a synopsis of these findings is given below, listing the factors that either reinforce or reduce anxious behavior in children. It is crucial to understand that these studies could show only the correlations between anxious behavior in children and certain parenting behaviors; they were not designed to indicate which came first. As you're reading the following lists, keep in mind a recent interaction with your child. Go through them and see what is going well and what you need to work on.

❄ Parenting Behaviors Associated with Anxiety in Children ❄

- PARENTAL OVERCONTROL: intrusive parenting, exerting control in conversation, limiting of autonomy and independence in conversation
- OVERPROTECTION: excessive caution and protective behaviors without cause
- MODELING OF ANXIOUS INTERPRETATION: agreeing with child's distortion of the risk in a situation, reinforcing the idea that normal things in the world are too scary to approach
- TOLERANCE OR ENCOURAGEMENT OF AVOIDANCE BEHAVIOR: suggesting or agreeing with not trying something difficult
- REJECTION OR CRITICISM: disapproving judgmental, dismissive, or critical behavior
- CONFLICT: (not as strong a factor) two out of five studies found fighting, arguing, and disharmony in family associated with high levels of anxiety

Positive Parenting Behaviors That Buffer Stress

- REWARD COPING BEHAVIOR: focus on means, not ends, reward taking on challenges, recognize partial successes
- EXTINGUISH EXCESSIVE ANXIOUS BEHAVIOR: reduce anxious behavior by not responding to it excessively, either with concern or anger
- MANAGE OWN ANXIETY: limit displays of distress, don't introduce parent's worries into the mix
- DEVELOP FAMILY COMMUNICATION AND PROBLEM-SOLVING SKILLS: open-house policy for positive communication and problem-solving opportunities
- AUTHORITIATIVE/DEMOCRATIC PARENTING STYLE: Authoritative/Democratic style—parents direct children's behavior while valuing independence—is associated with lower levels of anxiety (vs. Authoritarian style—parent's demand obedience, limit autonomy; or Permissive style—parents avoid any attempts to control behavior.)

CHAPTER 2

✳

Making the Diagnosis for Anxiety

IS IT JUST A PHASE?

Is this your child?

Six-year-old Matthew is taking swimming lessons for the first time. He has lots of questions: Is the teacher going to be mean or nice? Will he have to be in the water the whole class? Does he have to tread water? He doesn't want to tread water because that's what you have to do so you don't drown, and he doesn't like to think about drowning. He wants to know if the teacher will let him out of the water if he's cold. But he's excited about learning how to be a stronger swimmer and hopes that he will be allowed to try the diving board. He asks his mom if she can stay for the class.

At the end of class Matthew is excited that he's going to go on the diving board in a few weeks, he says his teacher is okay, and he thought that learning how to tread water was funny—they called it the doggy paddle! He did get cold and wants his mom to ask the teacher if he can get out of the water next time if he's too cold. Matt still wants Mom to be there for class in case he needs her.

Or is this your child?

Six-year-old Jason has always had a hard time with new situations. He doesn't want to try swimming lessons and has been crying and refusing to go ever since his mom mentioned it last week. He can't talk about why he's scared, he just doesn't want to go. On the day of the class he hides behind the chair in the living room, refuses to get dressed, and cries the whole time his mom is leading him out to the car. When he arrives at class he won't get out of the car and hangs on to his mom as she helps him up to class. Jason is unable to participate like the other children; he keeps looking to his mom when the teacher asks him to try something. The same scenario continues for two more weeks until Jason's mom and dad decide it would be best to drop the class.

Matthew might be considered temperamentally a "slower to warm up" child. He is cautious and needs more details than other kids. His imagination leads to some worries, but whatever it can dish out, he seems to be able to take in stride, given a little time and patience. Jason, on the other hand, is stuck. Not only does he go through much distress and upset anticipating an event, as do his parents, he also comes away with a sense of failure and a confirmation that the best way to deal with something hard is to avoid it. Unfortunately, this pattern plays out in multiple situations. It would make no sense for Jason's parents to keep bringing him to class and expect him to learn to swim. However, the situation could be salvaged by taking a few steps back. Jason could go to class as an observer for several weeks to see how things work, perhaps meet the teacher for a couple of one-on-one lessons—or even just a pleasant exchange at the snack bar—and eventually even try to participate in the "safest" five minutes of the class. Jason and his parents need help in learning how to get out from under the pattern of distress and avoidance.

This chapter will help parents sort out an anxious phase from a serious anxiety. We first review general red flags for problem anxiety, and next describe features of specific anxiety disorders. Sometimes anxiety isn't the only issue your child is contending with. We close the chapter with brief descriptions of other common diagnoses which may co-occur with anxiety.

When *You* Should Worry:
Red Flags for Anxiety in Your Child

We saw in Chapter 1 that there are normal and expectable fears and anxieties of childhood, which can make it confusing for parents to tell if or when their child's situation is diverging from the expected track. Even though your child's fears may be "normal" in *content*—dogs, shots, the dark—this doesn't mean that the *process* your child, and by extension your family, is going through is normal, tolerable, or desirable. Rather than thinking normal or not normal, ask yourself the following questions:

IS MY CHILD SUFFERING FROM HIS WORRIES?

Red flags

- Demonstrates excessive distress out of proportion to the situation: crying, physical symptoms, sadness, anger, frustration, hopelessness, embarrassment
- Easily distressed, agitated, or angry when in a stressful situation
- Repetitive reassurance questions, "what if" concerns, inconsolable, won't respond to logical arguments
- Headaches, stomachaches, regularly too sick to go to school
- Anticipatory anxiety, worrying hours, days, weeks ahead
- Disruptions of sleep with difficulty falling asleep, frequent nightmares
- Perfectionism, very high standards by which nothing is good enough
- Overly responsible, excessive concern that others are upset with him or her, unnecessary apologizing
- Demonstrates excessive avoidance: refuses to participate in expected activities, refuses to attend school

- Disruption of child or family functioning, difficulty with going to school, to friends' houses, religious activities, family gatherings, on errands, on vacations
- Excessive time spent consoling child about distress with ordinary situations, excessive time coaxing child to perform normal activities—homework, hygiene, meals

DO I HAVE A PLAN IN PLACE TO HELP?

You may be aware that your child is struggling with a worry or fear but not know how to help him move ahead.

- Are you able to communicate with your child about the problem, or does he refuse?
- Does your child understand what's happening to him and how to work on it?
- Is your child progressing, or is the situation worsening (more distress, more avoidance, more restricted life) despite your efforts?

If the answer is yes to any of the items in the first question and no to any of the items in the second question, it is time to address the situation directly.

Signs of Transitory Anxiety (A Phase)	Signs of Problematic Anxiety
Fears and concerns are reasonable and expectable	Fears and concerns are unreasonable, out of proportion with event
Child is responsive to suggestions for change	Child becomes overwhelmed and may regress in response to suggestions for change

Signs of Transitory Anxiety (A Phase)	Signs of Problematic Anxiety
Questions, though they may be plentiful, have answers that are accepted—child absorbs information and benefits from reassurance	Reassurance is never enough; no answer is good enough. Concerns are taken deeply to heart and create distress in the present and about the future
Symptoms diminish in intensity over time, and take up less time	Symptoms increase in intensity over time and the worry takes on a life of its own
Symptoms are limited to the situation	Symptoms generalize to increasingly more situations
Child understands why he needs to face the situation	Child more focused on how to avoid the situation than how or why to face it
Symptoms catalyze/ facilitate positive change	Symptoms interfere with growth and productivity
Themes are in synch with developmental stage	Themes are out of synch with developmental stage

Making the Diagnosis: Criteria for the Primary Anxiety Disorder Diagnoses

The descriptions below summarize the specific diagnostic criteria for each type of anxiety disorder. Each diagnosis will be presented here in snapshot form; in Part II, a chapter is devoted to each one.

GENERALIZED ANXIETY DISORDER (GAD)

GAD is the diagnostic category for excessive, uncontrollable worry. Children who suffer from it leave no worry stone unturned. Their first reaction to any stressor is to envision the worst-case scenario. Children with GAD spend their time making sure that they are doing the right thing all the time—looking ahead, planning, making sure that nothing goes wrong, and fearing the worst consequences for small actions. They often look stressed and have difficulties with headaches, stomachaches, and falling asleep at night. Symptoms must be present for *at least six months*. (See Chapter 6.)

SPECIFIC PHOBIAS

Phobias are what may be considered the "narrow-minded" brand of anxiety (one of the few examples where being narrow-minded is a good thing). Whereas other anxiety disorders tend to lead to anxiety in multiple situations, children with phobias involving a specific stimulus, such as bees, dogs, elevators, or injections, are generally without anxiety if they are able to avoid the feared object or situation. This is not to say that having a phobia is an easy situation. A child who is afraid of dogs may be unable to walk to school, play in her neighborhood, or go to friends' houses if there is a dog there. It may affect her willingness to play sports, go to the mall, or go anywhere else that dogs may be found. Similarly, fears of storms can lead to daily checking of the weather, or refusal to participate in activities if there is a risk of a storm. Symptoms must be present for *at least six months* and interfere with a child's routine or create significant distress about having the phobia. (See Chapter 7.)

SOCIAL ANXIETY

Social anxiety refers to a persistent fear of social or performance situations, where children feel under constant scrutiny by others. Not shy by choice, the socially anxious child feels instantly paralyzed by imagined or actual social encounters. Kids with social anxiety anticipate humiliation and ridicule and as a result are extremely focused on themselves and on trying to interpret if what they said was "stupid," or if people are making fun of them. Imagine life without a "backstage," and you begin to approach the feeling of exposure that the socially anxious child experiences. Symptoms are present for *at least six months,* and interfere with participation in social, academic, or family activities. For children these symptoms must occur with peers, not just in interactions with adults. (See Chapter 8.)

SEPARATION ANXIETY DISORDER (SAD)

Children with SAD worry about separating from their parents during school, work, a quick errand, bedtime, or even when they are in the next room. There isn't enough reassurance available that each day the parent will be fine, or that the child herself will be fine while she's away from the parent. Kids with SAD report a vague feeling that something bad will happen and they need to be near their parent either to prevent that from happening or just in case it does happen. It's common for these children to have difficulty attending school, make frequent calls home, and show unwillingness to play at friends' houses or go on field trips in order to stay on their watch. Although they feel tremendous relief if they are rescued from a situation—if they are picked up from school early, or if parents cancel plans due to the child's distress—it is only temporary relief, as the next separation is always around the corner. Even at home, some children aren't able to relax because of a separation on the horizon. In fact, the most unfair thing for kids with SAD is that the focus of their close relationships is about the *threat of loss,* thus preventing them from enjoying the security of their parent's love. Symptoms that are developmentally inappropriate must be present for *at least four weeks.* (See Chapter 9.)

PANIC DISORDER

Children with panic disorder suffer from recurrent panic attacks, sudden surges of anxiety symptoms that appear out of the blue and peak within minutes. During an attack, the child may feel unreal or fear that he is going to faint, die, or go crazy. Following a first attack, children become very fearful and avoidant of any situations or cues that were associated with the attack, often refusing to go places where escape may be difficult or embarrassing. Children with panic experience a very frightening surge in physical symptoms that they interpret as life-threatening in some way and feel they need to escape the situation in order to stop the symptoms. The most difficult aspect of panic is that until children understand that what is happening is a false alarm from the body they can be inconsolable with fear that something is actually wrong with them, and this only prolongs the attack and increases its severity. To meet the criteria for the diagnosis children must have panic attacks that are followed by *at least one month* of persistent concern about having another attack. (See Chapter 9.)

OBSESSIVE-COMPULSIVE DISORDER (OCD)

In contrast to the child with GAD who has unrealistic fears about things that basically make sense—doing well in school, being liked, being healthy—the more than one million children with OCD have fears that are senseless, even to them. They suffer from intrusive thoughts, images, and impulses that are bizarre and are diametrically opposed to the child's being (a loving child pictures stabbing a parent; a religious child fears that she hates God; an innocent child believes he was sexually inappropriate). Children engage in rituals or compulsive behaviors such as excessive washing, checking, redoing, counting, or tapping to relieve anxiety. In order to meet the criteria for the diagnosis, symptoms must cause distress, take more than one hour a day, or significantly interfere with a child's home life, school life, or social functioning. (See Chapter 10.)

POST-TRAUMATIC STRESS DISORDER (PTSD)

Children with PTSD have been exposed to a traumatic event that was perceived as life-threatening or resulted in death, and which caused them to experience intense fear, horror, or helplessness. They may suffer frightening and disabling residual symptoms such as flashbacks, nightmares, physiological reactivity, inability to sleep or concentrate, or emotional reactivity in situations that are similar to or remind them of some aspect of the traumatic event, and they may try very hard to avoid thoughts, feelings, conversations, and places that remind them of the trauma. Other emotional reactions include detachment, a sense of a foreshortened future, and a diminished interest in activities. Symptoms have been present for *more than one month* and cause significant distress or impairment in important areas of functioning. (See Chapter 12.)

Other Diagnoses to Consider

The following diagnoses share some symptoms in common with anxiety disorders but have a different focus. Children can have more than one diagnosis, which is referred to as a comorbid condition. They can also exhibit some anxiety as a result of another, nonpsychological problem they are experiencing. For example, when a child is having trouble understanding math and begins to avoid math tests, or go to the nurse's office during math class, the child's primary issue may be math; the anxiety is how the child is communicating that problem. While anxiety management techniques may go a very long way to clear away the haze of anxiety, they won't solve the underlying problem of a math issue or a learning disability. If your child exhibits the symptoms of these other disorders, you may wish to seek professional intervention to address your concerns. For further information, see the resource guide in the appendix.

TOURETTE SYNDROME (TS)

TS is one diagnosis in the category of tic disorders, relatively rare neurological conditions that involve involuntary motor and vocal activity. Only 1 in 2,000 schoolchildren has TS, but as many as 15 percent have tics that come and go. Motor tics can be simple such as eye blinking, face grimacing, or neck rolling, or they can be complex, such as pinching, kissing, or throwing things. Tics can be phonic or vocal; examples of simple vocal tics include throat clearing, squeaking, or clicking. Complex vocal tics are words—though not spoken intentionally, such as saying "oh boy" or "yep that's it" often at the beginning of a sentence. The most distressing example and most well-known symptom is coprolalia, or outbursts of foul language; it is also very rare among patients with TS, occurring in 5 to 30 percent of cases. OCD symptoms and tics can be difficult to distinguish from each other. Many times children with tics will get a "warning" before the tic, which resembles an obsessive thought; some children with OCD, especially young children, have compulsive behaviors such as tapping, which are not triggered by an obsessive thought. Tics in isolation are generally not TS—it is when motor and vocal tics are both present that the diagnosis is considered. Some children have what is called transient tic disorder, where tics last only a few weeks or months and may recur over the course of several years. In contrast, TS is diagnosed when motor and vocal tics are present for a year with no more than three consecutive months tic free. TS is typically treated with medication and a type of behavior therapy called *habit reversal*, which helps a child learn relaxation strategies and behaviors that are incompatible with the tic. The treatment of tics and TS is described in Chapter 11.

TRICHOTILLOMANIA

Compulsive hair pulling, or "trich," is what is known as an obsessive-compulsive spectrum disorder, as it shares some features in common with OCD, such as repetitive intrusive thoughts, urges, and behaviors that are difficult to interrupt. Like OCD, trich begins with a cycle of strong urges accompanied by tension that is relieved by engaging in the behavior. Unlike OCD, however, there is a temporary feeling of pleasure and/or relief associated with pulling the right hair. Immediately following that brief relief there is intense shame and embarrassment over one's actions, and the visible repercussions of the disorder. The treatment for trich, as with Tourette syndrome, is habit reversal, described in Chapter 11.

DEPRESSION

While all children have good days and bad days, when a child is depressed there is little hope that anything that a day could bring would make a difference. Instead most days are laden with a heaviness that won't lift or fade, or a struggle against an anger that won't break. Depression can be expressed either through sadness, despair, or extreme irritability, or by feelings of hopelessness or apathy and a lack of energy for life. Many children with OCD or other anxiety disorders may experience depression if their symptoms are not improving or they are not getting treatment for their anxiety and are becoming more and more disabled. Though we may think of depression as signaled by sadness and crying, children often express depression through irritability and low frustration tolerance. Additional red flags are changes in appetite, either overeating or loss of interest in food, and changes in sleep habits, either sleeping the day away or being unable to sleep. Children may drop out of circulation with friends, lose interest in sports or schoolwork, or lose themselves for hours at a time in television or computer games and be unapproachable.

Younger children express depression more through clinginess, irritability, and regression. If this constellation of symptoms is present for at least two weeks, reflects a marked change in your child's usual behavior, and is interfering with your child's functioning, it is time to pursue professional help.

ATTENTION-DEFICIT/HYPERACTIVITY DISORDER (ADHD)

While many symptoms of anxiety and ADHD overlap on the surface, the core reasons for the symptoms are quite different. ADHD, another no-fault wiring issue, concerns the child's ability to harness attention and focus on the demands of a situation. Kids with ADHD have wonderful, busy minds that can engage deeply in novel, exciting, or interesting information. This is why they can seem so distracted in school or at dinner, but focus for hours on something they like—the brain has found the right stimulation. In contrast, anxious kids' minds are busy anticipating risk, overestimating danger, fearing the worst. While anxious kids may be fidgety, restless, and inattentive, it is likely because they are worrying if their parents are okay, if it's going to thunder, if they'll remember all their books, and on and on. Kids with ADHD may be fidgety because the brain is not sufficiently engaged in the activity and gets up and wanders. In addition, ADHD doesn't develop late in childhood, it is typically noticeable in very young children. Anxiety disorders develop throughout childhood, so if an eight-year-old is suddenly exhibiting fidgety, distracted behavior in the classroom, when he hadn't before during his school career, he may be more likely exhibiting anxiety symptoms. Importantly, the treatment of choice for ADHD is medication along with behavioral interventions to maximize attention and focusing at home and school. Medications for ADHD, psychostimulants, can often increase nervousness in children with anxiety disorders. For children who have both anxiety and ADHD, ask your child's doctor for the best course of treatment.

Differentiating Anxiety and ADHD Symptoms

Symptom	Anxiety Cause	ADHD Cause
Inattention, easily distracted, doesn't seem to listen, doesn't follow through on instructions	Distracted by worries, rituals, and fears; may be afraid of hearing question wrong; may race through assignment, not follow directions, due to nerves	Distracted by kids and noises, may notice that teacher is saying something, but doesn't process the instruction; may rush to get unwanted task done quickly and go on to something more fun
Unable to concentrate on work	Afraid that work will be too hard or will have to be done perfectly so avoids; can't tolerate feeling of not being sure something is right	Difficulty sitting still due to boredom
Impulsivity; blurts out answers, interrupts, can't wait one's turn	Fear that he will forget answer; needs reassurance that he is right, unable to leave a mistake as is	Not enough processing available between idea and action—no mental brakes; unaware of interrupting
Hyperactivity; fidgety, gets up from seat; talking excessively	Fidgety from anticipation, tension, or worry—can't sit still, wants to go home, get the day over with Nervous energy; may be checking compulsions with questions; may be experiencing trauma flashbacks (PTSD)	Physical need to move, keep hands busy

BIPOLAR DISORDER

There has been increasing recognition of the presence of bipolar disorder in young children. As with ADHD, many symptoms overlap with anxiety disorders, including excessive separation anxiety or worry and difficulties sleeping. Some children have compulsive behavior and excessive activity, and distress when everything is not just so. However the cardinal symptoms of bipolar disorder include protracted, explosive temper tantrums or rages, usually triggered by limit setting (being told "no"); abrupt, rapid mood swings; irritable mood states; and periods of depression. Bipolar disorder can be diagnosed in young children and is treated by a combination of medication such as mood stabilizers, individual therapy, and family therapy to track and manage the course of the disorder.

SENSORY INTEGRATION DYSFUNCTION

Some children don't seem to be able to "go with the flow," feeling every bump in the road, whether it's the tag on their clothing, a strong food smell, or the seam on their sock. It's as if every piece of sensory input is registered as an obstacle to overcome. These children are described as having sensory defensiveness, a condition first identified by Dr. Jean Ayres in the 1960s. Though adults may perceive them as "picky" and "oversensitive," their experience is not a factor of their personality, but rather of the efficiency, coordination, and maturity of their central nervous system. Children with sensory integration dysfunction have to, in a sense, "hand process" each piece of sensory input that should have been processed automatically. In addition, how that "input" is registered is distorted either by the nerve endings being overly sensitive (a gentle brush is perceived as painful) or undersensitive (a child doesn't realize that it hurts you when he keeps bumping into you—he's not feeling it).

Because of inefficient processing of sensory information,

children with sensory integration dysfunction often get exhausted easily and are very prone to sensory overload even in seemingly low-sensory situations. Children may be unable to focus on the task at hand because their brain resources are largely occupied processing the minutia of sensory experience—the elastic is bothering my waist, my underwear isn't right, my hair isn't tight enough, this food is too soft. Motor coordination is typically affected, and children may appear clumsy, fidgety, or unable to sit still. Rather than coming from nervousness, this excessive movement is the body's way of trying to get the sensory feedback it needs. This dysfunction can be overcome by desensitizing and retraining children and providing them with an enriched sensory diet to aid in desensitization to common sensory triggers. Sensory integration dysfunction is treated by occupational therapists.

PERVASIVE DEVELOPMENTAL DISORDERS (PDD)

The category of developmental disorders has been receiving much attention in recent years. Children with these disorders have significant impairments in several areas of development including, negotiating social interactions or understanding the nuance of social situations, a narrow range of interests, and in the case of Autistic Disorder, language acquisition. The continuum of functioning in PDD is very broad. Some children with a developmental disorder are severely impaired and require a special setting that can address their needs. Many children (and adults) with PDD are in our midst, contributing richly to our daily lives. There may be an excessive focus on rules, black-and-white thinking, perseverative behavior, repetitive or stereotyped mannerisms, or an intense very narrow interest (knows everything about planes, a specific person, a cartoon character on TV), but otherwise the child is able to manage himself quite well in a traditional setting provided there are supports for transitioning from task to task. Children with PDD may have excessive social anxiety because they have difficulty with the ambiguous nature of social interactions. Without a script to predict what will happen in a situation they may feel quite nervous and not know how to manage their anxiety. While some anxiety management strategies may be helpful, it is best to focus on generating "new rules" or a formula for how to handle a given situation. Children with PDD may engage in repetitive behaviors, such as tapping, head banging, or repacking and redoing, but it feels right to them. There is not the subjective experience of senselessness and unacceptability of the action that one would see in OCD, nor is there necessarily the feared consequence of not performing the behavior. Still, many of the behavioral strategies used to treat OCD may be used with a child with PDD if adapted to his or her developmental level.

In this chapter we have seen that while all children may experience anxiety, it is the degree of distress and interference that distinguishes a passing anxiety from a disorder. We have previewed the different subtypes of anxiety disorders. Because each anxiety disorder requires a different approach in treatment, we will take a closer look at each diagnosis in Part Two. Once you have identified your child's area of difficulty, you are faced with many choices about the "who," "what," and "when" of treatment. These issues are explored in detail in Chapter 3.

✦

When and Where to Turn for Help

TREATMENTS FOR CHILDHOOD ANXIETY

I feel like for the first time someone actually understands what it's like to be me—what it sounds like in my head. It's such a relief. It makes me believe that there's hope that I can get better.

I'm afraid if I go for help that my child will be labeled, but I don't want my issues to get in the way of her getting help.

When to Go for Help

As we saw in Chapter 2, if your child is suffering and you don't have a plan to move through it, it's time to go for help. About one-half of adults with anxiety disorders report that their symptoms began in childhood. They will say (and if you are one of them, you know) how much they wish that their parents had gotten them help when they were young. With so much suffering that can be avoided, waiting and watching is not a prudent plan. You may recall from Chapter 2 that many diagnoses of these disorders are made when symptoms persist for a month. Use that as a rule of thumb. Even if your child doesn't meet all criteria for a diagnosis, err on the side of seeking consultation. Early intervention is the best strategy for keeping problems small and keeping your child growing.

Child psychologists are most often trained in cognitive-behavior therapy, the treatment of choice for child anxiety disorders. Later in the chapter you will find interview questions to help you find out a particular therapist's experience and qualifications. A child psychologist will ask questions of both you and your child to assess the type and severity of your child's anxiety, rule out other diagnoses, and make treatment recommendations. If medication is indicated, a child psychologist will refer you to a psychiatrist for further evaluation.

If you are not ready to bring your child in, consult a child psychologist yourself. Get information about how to work on the problem at home and learn what would signal the need to bring your child in for treatment. You will either gain the peace of mind of knowing that your child is only having minor difficulties due to temperament or developmental stage, or you'll learn what's wrong and how to help. If a child is suffering and we intervene early when the problems are small, then we can prevent that unfortunate moment when things have gotten so bad that everyone agrees beyond a shadow of a doubt that there's something wrong.

Parents are often concerned about the negative effects of bringing a child to treatment or putting a child on medication. Whatever risks you fear must be weighed against the negative effects of ongoing stress or anxiety for the child and the family. If you are worried about the stigma of your child going for treatment, weigh that against the costs and conspicuousness of your child running out of class, crying at school, or not being able to go to a dance or take a test. A skilled therapist will help your child feel comfortable, and empower your child to understand that these issues are entirely manageable when he learns the skills to overcome them. If your child's therapist is not doing this important cheerleading and taking this matter-of-fact approach to the problem, talk to him or her about it. Though therapy is often hard work, your child's coach shouldn't be the one making it harder.

Treatment Options: Cognitive-Behavior Therapy and Medications

If you ask doctors or even lay people to compare medications with therapy, many will say a combination works best. While this might seem like common sense—the broader the treatment, the greater the chances for improvement—the fact is that we don't have evidence to support that conclusion for all situations. Some parents feel that because an anxiety disorder is physiological, or no-fault, in nature, a child necessarily requires medication to treat it. Other parents believe that medications are necessarily harmful to their child and categorically refuse to use them. Neither belief is correct. In fact, in the case of OCD, for example, brain imaging studies using positron emission tomography (a PET scan), which measures metabolic activity in the brain, reveal that both cognitive-behavior therapy (CBT) and medication can lead to changes in brain circuitry that are reflected in a reduction in OCD behaviors. With child anxiety disorders in general, approximately 50 to 70 percent of patients respond to medications as compared to a 70 to 80 percent response rate with CBT. Some children may require medication in order to be ready to participate in CBT. There is no one-size-fits-all answer for anxious kids. You need to be informed about the issues and your options so that at the end of the day, you know that you are doing what's best for your child. In an ideal world we would have more precise information about what works best with the least cost physically, psychologically, and economically for kids who suffer from anxiety—and one day this may be possible. For today, be a good consumer: learn what you can about different treatments and their appropriateness for your child. The review below will serve as a starting point for learning what we know about the different treatments for anxiety.

COGNITIVE-BEHAVIOR THERAPY

Cognitive-behavior therapy, a practical, action-oriented treatment, is based on principles of anxiety acquisition and reduction that have been developed over decades of research. The goal of cognitive behavior therapy is to teach kids and parents how anxiety works so that they can combat it like an expert, with a specific set of skills to address the thoughts, physiological responses, and behaviors associated with anxiety.

The American Psychological Association (APA) has set stringent standards to determine the efficacy of specific treatments for specific disorders. Based on evidence from multiple studies, CBT is considered an efficacious treatment for children with anxiety disorders, according to the APA standards.[1] Well-controlled studies show significant reduction of anxiety symptoms in 50 to 80 percent of children who undergo this type of therapy.[2] Importantly, these improvements are maintained when follow-up studies are conducted over an average of three and a half years. Therefore, when a parent asks a therapist, "Will this work?" CBT-trained therapists can answer confidently that the scientific community considers CBT the treatment of choice for anxiety disorders.

The nuts and bolts of CBT will be described in detail in Chapter 4 and throughout the chapters on specific disorders, but in brief, CBT includes the following components:

Psychoeducation. The therapist demystifies the experience of anxiety for a child, teaching her how it develops and the skills she needs to reduce it.

Somatic Management Skills. The child learns techniques such as breathing and progressive muscle relaxation to counter the unnecessary triggering of the body's fight-or-flight response.

Cognitive Restructuring. With the therapist, the child identifies negative or anxiety-producing automatic thoughts and learns realistic, coping thinking.

Exposure. This includes practicing the new responses one step at a time in the target situations.

Relapse Prevention. The therapist identifies with the child the signs of a possible relapse and potential stressors and devises a plan the child can use to quickly address any setbacks that may occur.

One of the first studies to document the efficacy of CBT for anxiety disorders in children was based on a treatment program developed in the mid-1980s at Temple University in Philadelphia by Dr. Philip Kendall and Drs. Bonnie Howard, Marti Kane, and Lynne Siqueland, who were graduate students at the time. The fun, easy-to-implement treatment protocol that emerged at that time, now known as "Coping Cat" for children aged eight through thirteen, was shown to be effective with a variety of anxiety diagnoses. It earned the distinction of being "an empirically supported treatment" through independent testing in other settings as far away as Australia and Canada. In the initial study of this program, children who received CBT demonstrated significant improvement, with 66 percent no longer meeting the criteria for an anxiety disorder at the conclusion of treatment. Subsequent studies have yielded comparable results.[3] I was fortunate enough to have trained at Temple in the late 1980s and to have treated many of the children who were included in the initial treatment trial. As young therapists we were finding that kids could easily learn the nuts and bolts of anxiety management, the "FEAR Steps," as they were called, and apply them to increase their confidence and competency in approaching rather than avoiding a variety of situations where we did exposures.

In Chapter 4 we will take an in-depth look at the new lessons of CBT in plain language so that parents can be on the same page as their child's therapist as well as implement these techniques at home.

How Do I Find a Qualified Therapist Who Performs CBT? Many licensed psychologists have received specialized training in CBT. Some social workers and even psychiatrists are turning to CBT for training in effective, time-limited treatments for anxiety. You can ask your pediatrician or school counselor for a recommendation. In addition, many organizations keep lists of qualified therapists by geographical area. See the resource list in the appendix for organizations to contact.

When you are looking for a therapist, don't be afraid to ask questions. Let the therapist demonstrate her qualifications by describing her techniques and telling you how many children she has treated for your child's particular problem. Don't mention techniques first, see what the therapist says. He or she should specifically mention cognitive-behavior therapy, systematic desensitization, exposure treatment, and (for OCD), exposure and ritual prevention. Find out the ways parents are included in the treatment. Parent participation in some form is an essential component of treatment success. I have spoken to many parents who from their searching on the Web and reading up on their child's issues find that they are more informed than their child's therapist. If your gut tells you this is the situation, listen to it, and find someone who is going to teach *you*. Also gauge your own reaction to the clinician's personality. Is he warm, caring, patient, and confident in his ability to help you? Chances are, if you feel comfortable with the therapist, your child will. If you are not clicking, it is likely that your child will not either.

Remember that there are numerous specific techniques for challenging anxious thoughts and approaching anxious situations. If a therapist talks about helping a child get his mind off the anxiety, this may be a red flag that he or she doesn't understand how anxiety treatment works. Though distraction may be a strategy, it is not the one with teeth. It's also most likely the one your child has been using unsuccessfully up to this point, and the reason you are currently seeking professional services. Listen for new ideas, optimism, and a plan.

QUESTIONS TO ASK A PROSPECTIVE THERAPIST

- What is your approach to working with children with anxiety? (Let them tell you first.)
- Do you use cognitive-behavior therapy? What strategies would you use in working with my child?
- How many children with this type of problem have you treated, and what is your success rate?
- How do you explain anxiety and CBT to kids? Do you tell children the name of their diagnosis?
- How do you help kids get interested in and cooperate with treatment?
- How soon do you begin to address the issues?
- How do you work with parents?
- Who is in the room with you during sessions? Do parents participate?
- Is there an opportunity for parents to speak to you privately?
- Do you do exposure work outside of the office?
- Do you assign homework? How do you help us work on goals outside of sessions?
- Are there physicians you work with who can prescribe medication if needed?
- Do you have contact with the school?
- What is the best way to contact you in a crisis?
- What insurance do you accept?
- How long is the typical treatment? Are you available for periodic follow-ups?

Can Young Children Participate in Cognitive-Behavior Therapy?
There is a substantial body of literature documenting the effec-

tiveness of CBT in children as young as eight years old. Some of the earliest research on behavioral techniques was conducted with very young children. In daily life parents naturally use principles of reinforcement and desensitization with their very young children without even knowing it. Young children often have a great time in CBT—the structure, the hands-on experiential nature of the work, and the clear goals and rewards are right up their alley, and they feel very proud of their accomplishments. Excellent results can be obtained when younger children are guided through parent-directed exposures ("Let's just see what that doggy is doing now" "Let's peek out the window at the night sky") and parent-modeled coping skills ("That slide does look big, but I'm brave and I'll climb the steps one at a time" "I'm a little scared in the dark, but my eyes will get used to it and then I'll be able to see better"). Younger children may not be able to reflect on their thinking and how it makes them feel, but when you find the right venue for working on these things with them, whether it be role playing, making cartoons, or puppet shows, they learn how *they* can control unpleasant thoughts and feelings. Young children's abundant creativity, active imaginations, and righteous desire to be in charge easily compensate for any cognitive maturity they lack.

MEDICATIONS

When working with children with anxiety disorders, cognitive-behavior therapy is considered the treatment of choice, as it is least invasive and has no negative side effects. But sometimes children's symptoms are so disabling that they are prevented from being able to engage in CBT. Fortunately there is a wide range of medication options for children. A rule of thumb in treating obsessive-compulsive disorder, but one that can be applied more generally, is to begin with CBT and then consider adding medication if the child is not showing some response to CBT within approximately four to six weeks. In some circumstances, the use of medications is indicated from the start. If a child is suffering from depression, has not been sleeping for weeks, or is struggling with some other disruptive or intolerable symptoms, medication will likely be initiated early in the process. It is outside the scope of this book to provide a comprehensive review of psychiatric medications for anxiety. There are several excellent comprehensive guides to psychiatric medications for children; these are listed in the appendix. If your child is on medication, or if it has been recommended as part of his or her treatment, please do consult these texts for information about efficacy, side effects, dosages, and other pertinent topics.

By the time medications are considered, parents and/or kids are often at their breaking point and feel that things need to change immediately, but it is best to think about medication as part of your tool kit, not an instant fix. It may be one important component in a multifaceted solution. This is in part because most medications take time—days, weeks, or typically months—before their full effect is felt or achieved. Also, rather than eliminating symptoms altogether, medications act to reduce the severity of target symptoms so that your child will be better able to use other strategies such as CBT to bring the symptoms under control. Taking the sharp edge off disruptive or distressing symptoms, medications open up opportunities for parents (i.e., move out of crisis management mode and into therapeutic mode), and also for kids who can use their thinking and acting strategies to face the challenges in front of them. As one of my young patients described it, "Medications can open the door, but *you* still have to walk through." Just as with other physiological conditions, such as asthma or diabetes, medications are a part of the answer, but behavioral management issues, such as watching diet, exercise, or sleep, are equally critical in maintaining good health.

Is Your Child a Candidate for Medication? While some parents want to avoid medications due to safety concerns, others may look desperately to medications to quickly fix the painful situation their child is in. All medications have to go through FDA approval before they can be prescribed in this country. Often, however, medications that are used for kids have not been specifically FDA approved for use in children. This doesn't mean that the drugs are not safe, but certain types of testing have not been conducted on that age group. There are times when the risks or unknowns are outweighed by the potential benefits of the medication. If a child has not been sleeping for weeks, and is so overtired that he is not able to respond to behavioral or parent interventions, then goal number one is to get him sleeping again—here medications may make sense in the short term. Once he has recouped some sleep he will be more receptive to learning how to control his anxiety so he can calm himself into a reasonable night's sleep. Likewise if a child is significantly depressed and has OCD, medication may be an essential first step to relieve the symptoms of depression so that he may then have the energy and resources to devote to his OCD treatment. For certain disorders, such as ADHD, medications have been found to be the treatment of choice.

What Medications Are Prescribed for Anxiety? There are two primary categories of medication for anxiety, which have very different goals and operate on different systems in the brain. The most common medications used for anxiety disorders are a class of antidepressants known as Selective Serotonin Reuptake Inhibitors (SSRIs). These drugs, which include such medications as Prozac, Zoloft, Paxil, Celexa, and the generic form of Luvox, are slow-acting medications that take anywhere from two to twelve weeks to achieve desired results. They act to block the reuptake of the neurotransmitter serotonin so that with more chemical messengers available in the space between the neurons (called the synapse), brain messages will travel more efficiently. Though SSRIs are considered "antidepressants," they are used for separation anxiety, generalized anxiety disorder, panic disorder, obsessive-compulsive disorder, and social anxiety, as well as for depression and sometimes for Tourette syndrome and trichotillomania. While it can take a long time before you see an effect, they have a low side-effect profile and are not addictive in any way. Note that unlike dosages for many other medications, SSRI dosages are not necessarily determined by weight, but rather by the child's response to the medication. In some cases it is normal for a child to be on the same dose of medication that might be prescribed for an adult. Your child's doctor will determine the correct dose with feedback from you and your child.

Benzodiazepines are the second class of medications prescribed for anxiety disorders. They are anxiolytics, or anxiety-reducing medications. These include Xanax, Klonopin, and Ativan. Quite different from the SSRIs, which target serotonin receptors and act to regulate neurotransmission over time, benzodiazepines are fast acting (usually within an hour) and work by having a sedating effect on the nervous system. They slow down the excitatory or sympathetic nervous system, so that kids do not get so worked up, which in turn calms anxious thinking. They are temporary and have no lasting effects but may be an essential part of treatment, blocking anxiety and enabling a child to function better. For instance, they reregulate sleep patterns so that children get back on track with sleep, and reduce anticipatory anxiety so that a child with separation anxiety or severe school avoidance can attend school. Some doctors are hesitant to prescribe benzodiazepines for children because they can be habit forming, so consult your child's physician for guidance in this area.

The majority of medication studies have been conducted with adults, but recent large-scale studies of SSRIs have shown promise in their use in children. Further investigation of medications is needed to assess for efficacy and long-term safety.

Who Can Prescribe Medications? For any childhood concern, most parents start at the pediatrician's office. Pediatricians are qualified to prescribe medications for anxiety, and may feel comfortable doing so. Because pediatricians have a broad range of conditions to keep up to date with, often they will recommend that parents consult with a pediatric psychiatrist, a physician with special training in working with children who have psychiatric conditions. Child psychiatrists, given their specialized work, have expertise and experience in working these medications. Child psychologists do not prescribe medications at this time.

QUESTIONS TO ASK YOUR DOCTOR ABOUT MEDICATIONS

- What are the immediate and long-term side effects of the medication?
- How effective is the medication?
- How soon should I expect to see improvement?
- What is the target dose for this medication? In what increments, and how quickly will you increase the dosage?
- Are there any food or drug interactions I should know about?
- What do we do if my child misses a dose?
- Are there any blood tests that need to be conducted prior to starting medication or during the course of medication?
- How long will my child stay on the medication?
- How often will I need to come in for appointments?

In this chapter we looked at the basics of treatment options for childhood anxiety. We are fortunate to have powerful treatments in CBT and medications. Each child has different needs and responses, and your pediatrician or child psychologist will be able to advise you on the steps to take in guiding your child's recovery.

CHAPTER 4

Behind the Scenes in Your Brain

ANXIETY GLITCHES, REWIRING FIXES

NON-ANXIOUS BRAIN

ANXIOUS BRAIN

THOUGHTS FALL THROUGH

THOUGHTS GET STUCK

All kids tend to worry about the same types of things, but while some kids are burdened with worry thoughts that get stuck, other kids are able to process their worries, break them down into manageable chunks, and work through them. We know that the difference isn't a matter of preference, but rather of brain processing. Anxious kids can learn to process and dismiss their worries, but only if you teach them how the brain—with all good intentions—is tricking them into feeling frightened about things that are essentially safe. Anxious thinking—for all of us—is notoriously distorted, exaggerated, and unreliable; this is essential information that children need to

know. Much more powerful and longer lasting than reassurance, the goal for parents is to reveal the worry tricks, so that the child can see the situation more realistically and dismiss the worries on his own.

Without this information, children take their worry thoughts at face value and begin to look for evidence to support the possibility that their worries could be true. Before they know it, they are spinning in worry and so confused that they can't listen to reason. The body starts to react to the stress with racing heart and accelerated breathing. Your child feels he has no choice but to heed the worry in order to survive the situation, all because no one showed him the ins and outs of the worry brain, letting him know that it was a false alarm in the first place. You can help your child understand that there is a choice, so that he can get off the wheel of worry and get on with his life.

A second fundamental concept is that anxiety is reduced by *approaching* rather than *retreating from* the source of discomfort—by breaking down the situation into manageable chunks. When kids are asked to explain how they got over a past fear, they almost always say that they just "got used to it" (GUTI). In cognitive-behavior therapy terms, this translates as *graduated exposure and systematic desensitization,* the benchmark of state-of-the-art anxiety intervention. I prefer to use the kid's term, and will refer throughout the book to the idea of GUTI exercises. Anxious kids should neither be kept away from new input nor be inundated, but encouraged to keep on trying things that their nature would have them avoid altogether. A child encounters static shocks on a slide at school and refuses to go on the slide again. Without intervention, situations like this, often imperceptible to adults, tend to become the model, or template, for every situation that the child faces. Someone needs to give the child the opportunity to approach his feared situation—have a successful experience with the slide, one step at a time until he masters it. So for instance, engaging the powers of modeling, observation, and experimentation, we would say, *"Let's watch someone else on the slide—did they get a shock? Let's send your favorite stuffed animal down the slide, walk up the slide, and come back down."* As time goes on, intervention can make the difference between getting on or staying away from the playground of life.

In this chapter we will explore the components of what is known as the Anxiety Triad—cognitions, physical symptoms, and behaviors—which interact and set an anxiety reaction in motion. The strategies in this chapter are based on sound cognitive behavioral principles that have proven their effectiveness in study after study. The metaphors and illustrations throughout will help you to better understand the principles and explain them to your child.

With the right strategies your child can reverse that anxiety spiral and bring his or her worry temperature right back down. Remember that your child's first reaction is a default response. It's as natural as flinching when someone bumps into you. The threat interpretations happen instantaneously. It's simply the expression of the anxious wiring. The key to rewiring the anxious brain is learning to build in a second, more realistic reaction. You will learn here how to talk to your child about the tricks that the brain can play, and the many options you have to fight back. When your child challenges that automatic worry thinking, a new, healthy circuit is set in motion, and is made stronger and more available each time the challenge is repeated.

THE ANXIETY FORMULA

Overestimation of Threat + Underestimation of Ability to Cope = Anxious Response

How Worry Talk Leads to Worry Walk

The fundamental premise of CBT is that what we think or believe in a situation dictates how we feel and behave. Therefore at the helm of our anxiety are our worrying minds. Our internal commentary, what is referred to as "self-talk," is filled with worry thoughts and distorted appraisals of a situation. When we perceive a threat, the brain sends a message to the body to mobilize against the threat. Like a revving engine, the body amps up to either stay and fight or run. The final component—our behavior—is what we do to "survive" the situation. In the best scenario, we may constructively ask for help, but when push comes to shove, we feel scared and want to flee. On the other hand, if we begin at the helm *to change* how we look at a situation—by verbalizing and analyzing—with more accurate appraisals of the risk, this sends us down another track and leads to different conclusions, feelings, and actions.

Brain Train

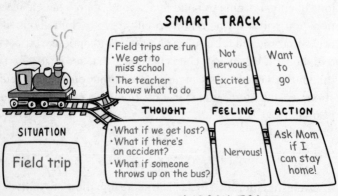

SMART TRACK

THOUGHT: • Field trips are fun • We get to miss school • The teacher knows what to do

FEELING: Not nervous / Excited

ACTION: Want to go

SITUATION: Field trip

THOUGHT: • What if we get lost? • What if there's an accident? • What if someone throws up on the bus?

FEELING: Nervous!

ACTION: Ask Mom if I can stay home!

WORRY TRACK

TEACHING YOUR CHILD ABOUT THE BRAIN TRAIN:
LOOK FOR THE FORK IN THE ROAD!

In this example of the brain train, we see that one situation can lead to very different outcomes depending on how your child is thinking about the situation. The two-track model of the brain train reflects the two tracks that run through your child's mind. The worry track is the first reaction or automatic path for an anxious child, but in working with your child on exercises like these, you can point to the fork in the road and begin to develop a second reaction, the other more constructive direction your child's thinking can take.

Down Dog Down! The challenge of teaching kids about worry is that they are by definition so distressed that they are unable to sit for the lesson. They need to see an example of how worry works "on someone else" before they can apply it to themselves. With this distance from their feelings, they are more able to think about the situation with their smarts, rather than react with their worry. You might, for example, imagine how worry works for man's best friend, as in the following script.

"Let's explore the brain train by looking at how a dog reacts to a situation. Let's say that the situation is a knock on the door. The dog barks every time someone comes to the door. What's in that dog's thought bubble [like in the cartoons]? You can imagine it's 'Uh-oh intruder,' which then sets off what? His body responds by getting keyed up. The dog barks and jumps up and down. He judges that there is a danger and behaves accordingly by defending himself. But if we could communicate with dogs we would say, "Hey Fido, it's just the mailman." If Fido could understand, he wouldn't jump. Instead he'd think, 'Oh, the mailman again,' and would remain at his post, scratching, enjoying a bone, waiting for a real alarm instead of a false one. What was the difference in those two tracks? Fido's very different interpretations of a simple knock on the door."

Now that your child has the basic idea, run another situation down the track, one that's slightly closer to home, but not something scary for your child. An easy way to remember the order of the brain train is to work your way down the body— head (thoughts) to stomach (feelings) to toes (do your feet run away or stay?). Take something your child is good at that other kids might be afraid of. If she loves cats or dogs, you can remind her that other kids are afraid of dogs and imagine how those other kids must see cats and dogs as dangerous, mean animals, while she has the inside story and knows they are safe. See where those very different thoughts lead in terms of feelings and behavior. If your child is a skateboarder ask him to imagine how someone else might view skateboarding and how that would affect their feelings and actions. Anything can be run down the brain train track—riding a bike, skiing, taking the train, doing algebra. How would someone think, feel, and act if they were afraid? How is your thinking different? See how that thought leads down a different track.

The critical point is to ask your child what changed. Was it the situation that changed, or the way you were thinking about it? That's the power of suggestion, the power of our thinking. You have taught the fundamental lesson of CBT—the split in the track—the choice we can make in how we experience life, simply by *not* taking our automatic worry thoughts at face value as the indisputable authority, but instead questioning them. With this opening many other changes can follow.

When I was explaining the brain train to seven-year-old Isabel, I asked her, "Which thoughts would make you feel better—the worry thoughts or the smart thoughts?" She answered, "Do you mean which ones would I rather think?" Then she asked, "Do I get to choose?" "Yes!" I said, "but you have to remind yourself you have a choice because your worry brain probably won't give you that information itself." I suggested, "Remember that you have two hands. How about the worry goes in one hand, and the calm thoughts go in the other? That should be easy to remember—when you go into a situation, just remember to take both hands!!"

Operating Instructions

Smart Brain™	*Worry Brain*™
SPEEDS	**SPEEDS**
■ Challenging (but I can do it)	■ Scary
■ Manageable	■ Scarier
■ Watch me go	■ Scariest
FUNCTIONS	**FUNCTIONS**
■ Accurate, realistic thinking	■ Jumps to conclusions
■ Evaluates needs in situations	■ Underestimates your abilities
■ Reminds you of your skills and strengths	■ Exaggerates risks
■ Stores your knowledge	■ Races ahead
■ Keeps you focused on what you can do	■ Catastrophizes
	■ Generates negative thoughts
Fine Print: I'm always available if you can turn down the volume on your Worry Brain	Fine Print: We guarantee that product does not tell the truth.

Cognition: How Worry Gets the Story Wrong and How You Can Fix It

Anxious thinking, generally speaking, is characterized by an overestimation or magnification of risk and an underestimation or minimization of coping ability. There's nowhere to go, you're boxed in. What follows is a series of essential lessons about the specific thinking glitches associated with anxiety. These glitches or thinking errors don't show up in red, or distinguish themselves from other thoughts; rather, they hide out as errors in disguise. Familiarizing yourself with the common types of thinking errors that occur in anxiety will help you identify them in your child's thinking and rather than asking the question *"Why are you thinking that?"* You can instead say, *"We know why you're thinking that—it's automatic, it's that worry glitch. Now let's do our worry work to correct the errors. What do you really believe will happen? What would you like to think? What would others think in that situation?"*

LESSON ONE: THE POWER OF SUGGESTION: USE IT TO YOUR ADVANTAGE

To help kids see the power of their thoughts, try the following exercise yourself, then try it with your child. Does your foot itch? Well, it probably didn't two seconds ago, but now that I mention it, you might be feeling a little persnickety sensation in the arch of your foot. If I stop there, you will forget about it, but if I persist about that very itchy sensation, you'll start thinking that you've just got to get to it! You'll be feeling pretty itchy. What happened? It's the power of suggestion. Thoughts dictate how we feel and what we do. Craving a hot fudge sundae? The kind with swirls of chocolate and whipped cream that melts in your mouth? Enough said. When we think itchy, we feel itchy; when we think food, we feel hungry; when we think that the creak in the floorboards is a robber instead of the settling of an old house, we feel scared. Use these examples with your child. Unveil worry's secret weapon, then use the power of suggestion to your benefit. The worry brain makes us feel scared just by suggesting a risk or threat.

So when your child says, *"I'm scared because I think someone might break in the window,"* you can say, *"Yes, anyone thinking that might feel scared. Worry brain is using that power of suggestion trick on you—you're scared because you had the thought, not because it's true!"*

LESSON TWO: FIGHT ALL-OR-NONE THINKING

At the base of all anxiety is some risk—*will I get laughed at if I raise my hand, will I get sick if I touch the doorknob, will I have a panic attack if I go to the movies?* The problem is that with anxious thinking the risk is all or none—there are no shades of gray, no scale of relative risk. Help your child to see that the worry brain is turning a maybe into a definite. Identify other situations where your child is able to take risks without a problem. Highlight that the reason he is able to do so is that his brain is working properly in those situations, keeping the risk in proportion to the likelihood—you let others borrow your belongings even if they *might* break, you run a race even though you *might* fall or lose, you play on the computer even though it *might* crash. Help your child see that anxiety warns, "if there's any risk, don't try," whereas your child can decide that small risks are manageable.

The new self-talk would go like this: *"This is a risk, but it's a small risk. I can handle it. Possible doesn't mean likely. My brain shouldn't be bothering me with the small risks, only the big ones. I'm pushing this one through the net!"*

LESSON THREE: WHEN ESTIMATING RISK, GO WITH THE FACTS, NOT WITH YOUR FEELINGS

Though your child may be feeling scared, if you ask the right questions, you can help her access her smarts about a situation. Work on getting the facts. For example, Anna is afraid that if she goes to school, something terrible will happen to her mom. She thinks every morning that her mom will get in an accident, faint, or get sick. On a feeling level, Anna feels awful, 100 percent. But when you pose the question *"If you had to take a test on what you think will happen today, what would you say?"* you see that Anna knows the facts. She would mark the thinking part right, and the feelings part all wrong.

Help your child to separate his feelings from the facts by

asking him the following questions: How much of you feels scared something bad will happen? How much of you really *believes* it will happen? You won't have to convince your child that the risk is low because by doing this exercise, putting his feelings aside, he discovers it for himself. Over time your child will learn that when the facts are in charge, he's in charge, when his scared feelings are in charge, worry is calling the shots.

LESSON FOUR: CONFUSING OUTCOME WITH LIKELIHOOD: DON'T THINK ABOUT HOW AWFUL SOMETHING WOULD BE, THINK ABOUT HOW UNLIKELY

If any one us thought about something sad, difficult, or tragic we would feel upset. That's our nervous system and humanity working properly. But just because we can imagine how bad

HOW BIG IS THE RISK?

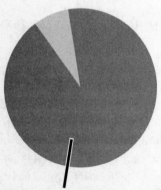

How much of you really thinks something bad will happen?

How much of you feels something bad will happen?

When the facts are in charge, you're in charge.

something could be, that doesn't mean it's any more likely to happen. That's the trick of confusing a bad outcome with the increased likelihood of that outcome.

Research on risk perception suggests that in general people are more inclined to focus on outcomes than probability. So, for example, we may think that flying means a terrorist attack, even though the risk of that is very low. We hop in our cars every day though the risk of an accident is hundreds of times greater. What slows down this trick are the questions *"Just because something could happen, how likely is it that it will?* and *What is more likely to happen?"* The first goal is to get better at estimation, but an even more important goal is to choose where to focus your thinking—on imagining how terrible something would be if it happened, or on assessing what is most realistically going to happen in that situation (nothing!). So when your child comes to you in tears because she is afraid that you'll forget to pick her up at school, rather than reassure her immediately, tell her, *"Yes, that is a scary thought, anyone would feel upset thinking about being left at school, but your brain is playing a mean trick by focusing on how awful that would be, and forgetting the most important fact, which is how absolutely unlikely that is—parents don't forget about kids, worry brain! That's not how it works!"*

LESSON FIVE: THOUGHT-LIKELIHOOD FUSION (TLF): MAGICAL THINKING INCREASES MISERABLE THINKING

Thought-Likelihood Fusion (TLF) occurs when a child *feels* that something will happen just *because* he was thinking about it, or that he *must want* something bad to happen because he just thought of it. It is, in short, a very unfortunate and very quick way of taking responsibility for something that's not your fault and making yourself feel miserable. *I thought about my mom dying, that means it's going to happen, or that I want it to happen. I'm a terrible person. I saw an ambulance, that means that someone in my family is going to die.* It's also a way of becoming alarmed by coincidental occurrences. A child with separation anxiety hears an ambulance while at school and believes that it must be rushing to his house for his mother.

Parents experience TLF all the time, but we wouldn't think of it that way. You hear a siren go by, you think how awful it would be if that was for your child—you wish you hadn't thought that because then you worry that somehow the likelihood is greater because you've thought about it, or you blame yourself—why would I have thought of such a terrible thing? But this is where the idea "It's not the thought, it's what you do with it" is most important. Our brain may make the erroneous connection between coincidence and catastrophe, but we can be smarter.

One fix is to help your child track the logic and look for signs of TLF. Sure, when we think something scary like *what if that ambulance is going to my house?* we have an automatic first reaction of fear, and that is normal; but the intensity of your emotions isn't any gauge of how likely something is, it's simply a result of entertaining the thought. Feeling something, or picturing something—even really vividly—can't make it happen; it doesn't change real life. Coach your child not to fall prey to TLF. Tell him, *"Feeling scared doesn't mean you are in danger. Go for your second reaction—think about the probability and realize that what you're warned about is no more probable now than it was before you thought it. Use good, smart thinking to boss back the worry brain, and teach it a lesson about how things work."* Here are some more examples of how to empower your child to reduce the power of the worry thoughts:

- That's not how the world works, that's just TLF.
- Just because you thought it doesn't make it true.
- You can think anything, it's just a thought, you decide what to do with it!
- Thoughts aren't magic, they only have the power you give to them.

- The only thing those thoughts can do is make you nervous—say no thanks!
- Tell your worry brain: if thinking something makes it true—then how come I'm not on a major league baseball team right now?

LESSON SIX: ANXIOUS THINKING IS FUTURE THINKING: SNAP BACK TO THE PRESENT—SET LIMITS ON WORRY

Quick, what will you be doing five years from now? When we are thrust into the future in our thinking, we naturally feel uneasy. We can't know exactly how things will be, and frankly, we're not supposed to know for sure. Life is full of surprises, some good, some bad, but the element of change is the one thing we can count on. Therefore predicting the future *for sure* becomes a very anxiety-provoking venture. If you listen to kids' worry talk, it is filled with "what ifs." Usually these "what ifs" get strung together, and what started out as a question about a sixth-grade math exam quickly leaps to *"what if I can't get into college?"* So instead of your anxiety reflecting your feelings about how you'll do on the math exam, it gets supersized to figuring out the rest of your life. Every time you "what if" about a situation, you are trying to predict the future; it's bound to lead to more worry, especially since we don't tend to "what if" about good things happening, only bad things. Worry is stretching your responsibility and the consequences for your actions far into the future. Snap it back. Non-anxious thinking is more present-oriented. Encourage your child with the following:

- Don't supersize your worry, just stick to what you need to think about now
- Put your worry on a "what-if diet"—feed it the "what-elses" instead
- If a friend told you that worry story, would you believe it?

One important fix for "what if" thinking is to put up stop signs and limit your child to thinking through the situation at hand. In the present we can *solve* problems, in the future we can just get *worked up* about them. If your child insists that those bad things *could* happen, let him know that they could, but they are not happening now. Worry is making him feel that he has to solve problems right now that, chances are, will never even happen. Let him know he has permission to keep the time frame small. Just because worry is flipping ahead in the book of his life doesn't mean he has to.

To further set limits on worry, teach your child how not to give it endless amounts of time and attention. Spending more time worrying doesn't protect you; rather, like listening to a sales pitch that preys on your fears, it only leads to more worry. Decide how much time your child will devote to worry and schedule it. For example, decide on a five-minute block that is "worry time." Then the rest of the day when worry thoughts come up, she can tell them it's not time yet and they'll have to wait. At worry time, she should start with the worry story. She can talk about her concerns or write them down on one side of the page. Next she should rate how likely they are to happen, from 0 to 100 percent (or simply low, medium, and high), then write in what the logical alternatives are. Write those more realistic conclusions on index cards. She can carry them with her and refer to them as needed during the day when worry tries pull her back to the scary story.

The Body Electric: Physical Symptoms of Worry and Anxiety—How to Teach an Old Brain Some New Tricks

Thank goodness for our body's early-warning system. It saves us from danger—anything from touching a hot stove to darting into traffic—but there are some downsides. Back in the day, way back in prehistoric time, when the brain's defense system was set up, life-threatening physical danger was a daily reality. We needed to be ready to mobilize virtually every system in a split second in the face of venomous snakes, saber-toothed tigers hiding in the brush, enemies lurking in the shadows. But now, thousands of years later, we are still operating with the same equipment. Our worries are now more benign, such as a test at school, saying hi to someone in the hallway, walking down the basement stairs. The problem is that our body has too much power for the job. When we see ourselves overreacting so automatically to these risks, it scares us more. Though we can't do a system upgrade for our antiquated emotional equipment, there are many things that we can do. What follow are some lessons in how to be smart about the machinery we've got.

LESSON ONE: WORRY'S FALSE ALARMS—PROTECTION THAT BECOMES THE PROBLEM

When the body's alarm system is mobilized without any immediate threat, you have anxiety. Unless you have been told that your body can create false alarms, you will continue thinking that there's a real danger. In other words, if the situation doesn't scare you, your body's reaction to it will. When kids understand why certain symptoms happen in the body, they are no longer afraid that those symptoms signal a problem, but understand that they signal a solution (your body is amping up to protect you, although you weren't in danger in the first place). Kids are fascinated to learn why their heart races, and their palms sweat. They find the antiquated functions funny, they see the worry logic, and most important, the next time they start panicking, they have a new circuit to engage—*"that's just my brain sending out the wrong signal, false alarm!"* Learning about the physiology of anxiety also reassures children that as anxious as they may feel, their symptoms are not dangerous; the body knows to cool down and reset. That's the confidence created by the fear extinguisher.

Breathe slowly — it's a false alarm.

Your imagination is spinning on its own.

Think how unlikely, not how awful.

You feel scared but you're not in danger.

The nervous system is made up of the sympathetic nervous system (SNS), which mobilizes the fight-or-flight mechanism, and the parasympathetic nervous system (PNS), which restores the body back to normal. When the SNS is going full tilt, kids and adults experience a lot of strange and sometimes uncomfortable symptoms, described briefly below.

Racing Heart. The SNS makes your heart beat faster. Why? To speed up the blood flow to the legs and arms in order to run or fight, and away from the fingers and toes (peripheral locations that can be punctured most easily). Kids may notice that their hands and feet feel cold, prickly, and numb, and that their skin looks pale when they are afraid.

Dizziness. In preparation for protecting you, breathing speeds up. You may feel like it's hard to breathe, even that there's a tightness in your chest. You may feel dizzy because the blood supply to the head is slightly (but safely) decreased.

Sweating. We sweat so that the body won't overheat. It's like a cooling system. But when we sweat our skin also gets slippery. Back in prehistoric times, slippery skin would make it tougher for an enemy to grab hold of us.

Stomachaches. The digestive system shuts down because when you're under attack is no time to think about food! Unfortunately, the result can produce nausea, stomachaches, or even constipation.

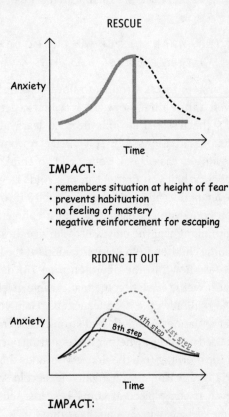

RESCUE

Anxiety

Time

IMPACT:
- remembers situation at height of fear
- prevents habituation
- no feeling of mastery
- negative reinforcement for escaping

RIDING IT OUT

Anxiety

4th step
8th step
1st step

Time

IMPACT:
- remembers success that allows habituation
- learns that anxiety passes on its own
- willing to approach increasingly challenging situations
- feeling of mastery
- positive reinforcement—feeling of pride for hanging in

Trembling. The big muscles, such as arms and legs, are tensing up, ready to fight; this can result in an aching feeling in the extremities and even trembling.

Next time your child comes to you afraid because his heart is racing and his stomach feels funny, help him to take a deep breath and reset the system back to normal. There is no emergency, it's just a turbocharged overreaction to an uncertain situation.

LESSON TWO: WHAT GOES UP MUST COME DOWN— ANXIOUS FEELINGS WILL PASS

Our nervous system reacts strongly to novel experiences and changes. Given a little time, however, it will also get used to things. That's the lesson that kids need to learn about approaching anxious situations. At first it will feel uncomfortable, but then it will get easier. Ask your child to think about a swimming pool. When you first get in, it's cold! Does it stay that way forever, or does it get more comfortable? If you stay in the water you know you get used to it, but if you get out you will be stuck thinking that the only way to survive the cold is to get out. Rescuing children from scary situations at the height of their anxiety (as shown in the figure on page 73) doesn't let them see that it would have become manageable given a little time, and also reinforces the need for escape. Help your child think of other situations where he had strong reactions at first and then got used to things, whether it was getting out of a nice warm bed in the morning (it's the first few seconds that are the toughest) or a nice warm shower (which feels cold when you get in), or even trying a piece of gum—it seems too spicy at first, but if you keep chewing it's not as strong.

Just like a roller coaster, you will find that anxious feelings go up, but they always come down. Ask your child if he ever had a time when his anxiety didn't come down. With the "Get Used To It" or GUTI exercises that you will find throughout the book, you are giving his nervous system a chance to get used to anxiety.

An important tool in the GUTI process is using a "fear thermometer" to track changes in your child's degree of anxiety. Taking your child's fear temperature every few minutes while he is approaching a tough situation will enable him to witness a decrease in his anxiety as he hangs in with the situation.

LESSON THREE: WHAT TO DO ABOUT YOUR NERVOUS SYSTEM: BREATHING AND RELAXATION TECHNIQUES

Because hyperventilating through over-breathing or sighing and yawning keeps the body in a state of tension, train your child to do normal breathing. Coach him with the following script: *Lie on your stomach, chest flat against the floor. Breathe in and out, slow and low. In this position you will be doing belly breathing, which is the kind of breathing we do when we are relaxed. After you get good at doing this lying down on the floor, you'll be able to find those same muscles when you are sitting up. Make sure that when you breathe in you don't hold your breath. Keep it even; breathe in through the nose counting 1–2, and out through the mouth (1–2). If you say the word "relax" or "calm" when you exhale, even picture the letters floating in front of you, this will be an additional cue to your body that when you hear those words your body will more quickly get to that state.*

Encourage your child to practice a couple of times a day, and within weeks she will be able to do this belly breathing inconspicuously whenever needed. She can focus on a pleasant scene—a serene, gentle waterfall, a beautiful spring day, or her cozy bed. Your child can imagine the sights, sounds, smells, and textures of that scene. Thus focusing on the present enhances relaxation and reduces distraction. If your child is distracted by other thoughts, rather than despair or fight the thoughts, just tell him to set those thoughts on a sailboat, let them pass, and know that he can pick them up later when the exercise is over.

THE FEAR THERMOMETER

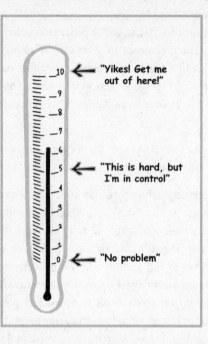

"Yikes! Get me out of here!" — 10

"This is hard, but I'm in control" — 5

"No problem" — 0

Some kids have difficulty relaxing—it isn't active enough for them, and they need a more structured exercise to guide them. For these children, the following script can be used:

In bed, start your breathing and imagine that with each breath you are blowing up a balloon, then track the flight of the balloon, watch it fly up above the treetops, above the buildings, into the clouds. Then "blow up" another balloon and track its ascent. Watch as the sky fills up with balloons, a rainbow of different colors, one by one. Your child can choose whatever repetitive image suits him best.

You can teach young children how to take in a relaxed breath and exhale by blowing soap bubbles through a wand. They can look in the mirror to see how their chest and shoulders stay relaxed (i.e., not jumping up with each breath).

Some children are so physically tense that it shows. They wiggle, they shake, they look like they could break. Maintaining their bodies at that level of tension adds to their feeling of anxiety—being braced for the worst translates to a feeling of unease in the mind. A daily exercise creating a pleasant, relaxed physical state will bring their baseline anxiety level down a few notches. If your child starts his day with an anxiety temperature of 4 out of 10 instead of an 8 out of 10, little things won't put him over the edge so easily. Below are some ideas for relaxation. There are also many commercially produced relaxation products available, and some children may find that yoga classes or videos offer similar lessons.

While we may store tension in many parts of the body, opening up the chest muscles may be the fastest way to loosen things up. At home or discreetly in class or even in the bathroom, kids can learn to stretch—first stretching their arms over their head and letting them drop slowly, then stretching them out to the sides but slightly behind them (picture a bird spreading its wings behind it), then letting them drop slowly. Just this easy two-second stretch will likely enable kids to do deeper, calmer breathing and will give them an instant reduction in their stress temperature.

The idea behind progressive muscle relaxation (PMR) is that in order to relax a muscle you have to first "locate" it by tensing it up. Relaxation is more passive and is best done after tensing, which is more active. Rather than relax his hands, PMR instructs a child to make a tight fist, and then by letting the fist go, his hand naturally relaxes. A young child can imagine that he's a cat or his favorite animal and can play Simon Says or Follow the Leader, imitating the stretches that you do. For older kids, a straight focus on muscle groups is the best tactic. So, for example, you can coach your child: "Begin with your toes, first stretch your toes, feel the tension, give it a color of tension—is it red? Then hold the tension to a count of three, then let the tension go—feel the relaxation in your feet, see the tension break up and dissolve. What's the color of relaxation for you? Is it a silvery blue, a healthy green, a warm yellow like from the sun? Choose a color."

As you continue up the body and repeat this sequence through legs, pelvis, stomach, back, chest, shoulders, arms, fingers, neck, face, eyes, and finally head, make sure that your child is seeing the tension color dissolve like sand and blow away and be replaced with the color of relaxation. For younger children, it may help them to picture a fairy sprinkling magic dust on each body part to help them relax, or the friendly king of sleepland who leads the relaxation exercise by pointing his scepter. The sky is the limit. You and your child will come up with the story that works best.

Behavior Plans: Alternatives to Escape or Fight—Opportunities for Action

As we saw in our brain train illustration, once the worry thoughts get going, the body gets on board, and we are looking for the quickest exit. Though our behavior is a consequence of thoughts and feelings, we actually have more control over our behavior than over our thoughts and feelings, which are more automatic and chemically produced. In this section we'll look at the behavioral principles that wield the greatest power for mastering an anxious situation.

LESSON ONE: EXPOSURE AND PRACTICE: THE BEST PROTECTOR OF YOUR NERVOUS SYSTEM, YOUR IMMUNE SYSTEM, YOUR MIND!

What's your first instinct about how to prevent colds and pet allergies? You might say, keep your babies away from pets and sick kids. However, scientists are learning that gradual exposure to such things as germs and allergens is the best way to build good "muscle tone" in the immune system. These small exposures help make sure the immune system is prepared to do its job when it's time. The same principle applies to dealing with fears, worries, and frustration. If you want to protect your child from being overwhelmed, you can help her to build up her "worry management muscles" a little at a time. It may take longer to approach anxious situations gradually, but speed is never a determining factor in overcoming anxiety.

Systematic Desensitization with gradual exposure is a process where a child gets gradually closer to a feared situation either by picturing himself approaching it *(imaginal exposure)* or by actually approaching it *(in-vivo exposure)*. The child uses breathing, relaxation, and realistic thinking to break the anxious association with the situation. Using the fear thermometer as a guide, the child stays in the situation until the fear comes down at least *two degrees* (out of 10), but preferably 50 percent. When an exposure becomes boring or too easy, the child is ready to climb to the next challenge on his list. Always take care to end an exposure on a good note, so if the exposure your child has embarked upon is too difficult, break it down. Do the challenge that is one step below it.

How do you start this process? You find your child's starting point with the question *"What part of this are you ready to do now?"* Anything can be broken down into smaller steps. Find the step that is just outside your child's comfort zone and begin the slow, steady climb toward the goal. Make a hierarchy of fear challenges, ranking them from easiest to toughest using the fear thermometer discussed earlier. If your child is having trouble with this, you can ask him, *"What would you like to do that you can't do now because you're scared or worried?"*

Often these challenges should be practiced first by role playing how the child will handle the situation. The parent or therapist models for the child ideas on how to cope with the challenge. GUTI exercises are best done frequently. Fear muscles, just like other muscles, are built best with regular practice. If a child has infrequent exposures, he is likely to forget his success in the situation, and instead revert to his previous fearful association.

LESSON TWO: BURN OUT YOUR WORRY WITH
COMPETING EMOTIONS—ANGER, RELAXATION, HUMOR

There is a popular mortgage commercial that says, "When banks compete, you win." Well, when emotions compete, you win too. It's a process called *reciprocal inhibition*. When other feelings or states compete with anxiety, such as relaxation, amusement, or even some righteous annoyance, they win out because feeling mad, relaxed, or goofy inhibits your ability to feel scared. Basically you can't be in two places at once emotionally, and fortunately the brain will favor the positive over the negative emotion. What can your child do? Encourage him to make a rap song out of his fears, stick his tongue out at the bugs that bother him, or play catch with a shoe that feels "contaminated." Switch the emotional tone out of scare mode and into something that feels more familiar—goofy, righteous fun.

Note that this fun is at the expense of the worry, and it should never become making fun of your child. Sometimes kids are not ready to poke fun at the anxiety. Follow your child's lead, because you don't want your solution to become part of the problem. When your child is ready to use some healthy humor and sarcasm, he'll let you know.

LESSON THREE: DON'T JUST DISTRACT
FROM WORRY, DISMISS IT ALTOGETHER

Many well-meaning people have told your child to simply distract himself from worry. Any child will tell you it doesn't work, and he is right. *Distracting* yourself from a bat in the room won't reduce your anxiety. Seeing that that bat was really just a shadow all along will. You must help your child to identify his worries as resulting from mistakes his brain is making that are not worth his time, making it much easier to discredit them, dismiss them, and get involved with what matters more. Because it will take a few minutes for the anxiety to pass (while he recovers from thinking he was dealing with a real threat), it is best to get busy with other things. The best choices are active ones when you are fighting worry. Sitting and reading or even playing a computer game still leaves your child's mind a captive audience for fear. Play a fast game of catch or hot potato with a softball, walk the dog, sing, or dance—all these activities help your child move out of worry mode and engage a healthier part of his brain.

LESSON FOUR: RELAPSE PREVENTION— DON'T LET A SLIP TURN INTO A SLUMP

Once your child overcomes a fear situation, she should celebrate her success, but be prepared for anxiety to try to sneak in again, particularly at times of stress. It will be different this time, because your child knows how to handle the problem. If you see anxiety and avoidance returning, don't wait till the problem gets out of control; revisit the fear strategies at the first signs of a problem. Pull out the fear hierarchy and redo the necessary steps to get that fear-fighting muscle back in shape. Catch the problems when they are small, and they will never have to get big.

Exercises for Parents and Children

First, ask your child to create his own version of the Operating Instructions on page 63. He can write out how he thinks his worry operates and even draw a picture of the worry machine. This will ensure that you both know the tricks your child's anxiety tries to play. Next, ask your child to draw his Fear Extinguisher: together you can identify statements and strategies that he wants to use to fight back his fear and cool down his anxiety. Make copies—post one on the fridge, or keep it private in a drawer, but now both you and your child will be clear about the nature of the problem and the solution.

In this chapter we've explored the tricks that the mind and body can play when worry starts, and learned how to outsmart those tricks with powerful fixes. In Chapter 5 we bring these lessons together into an action plan that can be used in most fear situations. Also included are ways to introduce these ideas to your children, with scripts for very young children all the way up to teenagers.

CHAPTER 5

✴

Putting It All Together

THE MASTER PLAN FOR MANAGING ANXIETY

*K*nowing what to do for Steve turned a hopeless, helpless situation into one where I have a plan. Now I don't get overwhelmed by Steve's worries. I feel like I am back in my comfort zone as a parent.

I would feel so guilty telling my daughter to just forget about it and go to sleep. I knew that wouldn't work, that's what my parents told me to do when I was a kid! I hated to see her so stressed and wanted her to stop because I didn't know what to do for her. When I learned that worry was something we could work on—verbalize and analyze—it was like someone just threw me a lifeline. How different my life would be if I had learned about this when I was ten!

In Chapter 4, we laid out the nuts and bolts of cognitive-behavior therapy—how to challenge anxious thinking, manage physiological reactions, and use gradual exposures to begin to approach fearful situations. This chapter organizes the principles into a step-by-step action plan with scripts to guide you in the process of rewiring your child's anxious thinking. Rather than trying to convince and reassure your child that his fears are unfounded, this plan helps you guide your child to reach that conclusion on his own. The Master Plan puts your child back in charge, helping him reconnect with how he would see the situation if worry weren't calling the shots. In the short run, this plan will build your child's competency and confidence. In the long run, your child will have a foundation of anxiety management skills that will be there, ready at hand, whatever comes her way.

When your child is steeped in worry, there is no benefit, no extra protection from harm, there's just fear. In fact, according to Dr. Jeffrey Schwartz and Sharon Begley, authors of *The Mind and the Brain,* a worrying mind just leads the brain to annex more space and resources for worry. The brain allocates neurons—brain cell messengers—to the busiest circuits. So if you are busy with worry, those circuits will get extra support.

If instead your child reroutes his thinking, breaking the invisible web of connections between ordinary experiences and anxiety, he will learn to build and busy up *new* circuits, healthy networks that are based on realistic thinking. The key is knowing that there is a difference between worry thoughts and reasoned thoughts, and in order to accomplish this, he needs you to help him identify the source right away. Like activating caller ID, identifying the source of the thoughts *beforehand* will help your child respond to those thoughts appropriately. Rather than setting off a contagion of fear when your child comes to you with a worry, you and your child will learn to recognize the sound of worry, and when you receive that call you will take a stance that says, *"Yeah, worry, what are you trying to sell me this time?"*

The Master Plan is presented here in practical detail with ideas and scripts to implement for three age groups, very young children (under 6), those in middle childhood (7–11), and adolescents (12 and up). Without a doubt, once you've done Step Two, relabeling the thoughts as coming from that unreliable, jumpy worry brain, it changes everything. Once you've devalued the thoughts, you are suddenly free to dispense with them. Just as we don't take copious notes on telemarketing calls, or pull out our highlighter pen when we're reading our junk mail—do we even read it?—recognizing that anxiety thoughts have little to offer us is half the battle. This notion of recognizing symptoms for what they are and relabeling them was introduced in *Brain Lock,* Dr. Jeffrey Schwartz's groundbreaking work on OCD, and was the basis of my book *Freeing Your Child from Obsessive-Compulsive Disorder.* These ideas have equal currency when applied more broadly to the array of situations that anxious kids face.

The Master Plan for Anxiety

Step One: Empathize with what your child is feeling

Step Two: Relabel the problem as the worry brain

Step Three: Rewire and resist: act with your smarts, not your fears

Step Four: Get the body on board—turn off the alarms

Step Five: Refocus on what you want to do

Step Six: Reinforce your child's efforts at fighting!

STEP ONE: EMPATHIZE WITH WHAT YOUR CHILD IS FEELING

It's difficult to approach a worrying child. He's stuck, he doesn't want to be feeling the way he is, but he doesn't know how to break out of it. He may even lash out at a helping hand. The best way to enter the system of a worrying child is with your empathy. It's no less than what we would want for ourselves. When we are already upset the last thing we want is for someone to be angry with us or to tell us that we are foolish for worrying in the first place.

So, resist the temptation to tell your child to stop worrying, or to reassure her there's nothing to worry about. The first step, which paves the way for any further communication, is to acknowledge what's going on for her. This can be done with words, with a gesture that lets her know you are on her side: a hug, a knowing look that says—on behalf of your child—I know you are sick of this. Kids will appreciate your candor, so if something "really sucks," don't be afraid to say so in so many words—either yours or theirs.

Words to Reflect Your Child's Feelings

- This is making you so upset
- You are working so hard, this is so unfair for you
- It's hard to do anything when your mind is so busy and making so much noise about everything
- Everything seems like a struggle

Help your child see what's in it for him. The fact is that kids don't want to be patients. They just want to feel better. Empathizing means seeing what your child is *losing* as a result of the anxiety. Help your child identify what he doesn't like (or hates) about worrying—how it is interfering with what he'd like to do. As a result, he can then focus on what he stands to gain by working on these problems.

STEP TWO: RELABEL THE PROBLEM AS THE WORRY BRAIN

If only worry thoughts came clearly labeled "unreliable" and "unrealistic," life would be so much easier. Then, like junk mail, they could be sorted out, ripped up, and thrown away. Since they don't, there's only one way to get enough distance from the anxiety to actually see it for what it is. When parents relabel and demote the validity of a worry thought, kids will feel freer to do the same. *It's a technical glitch, a false alarm, a worry brain jumping to conclusions, it's a sticky "what if" thought.*

Don't trust it! It is not mean to relabel instead of reassuring, it is helping your child to see the problem for what it is.

Relabeling won't make the thoughts go away—that takes a while—but it will help you and your child to dismiss them. You can't always stop telemarketers from calling, but you can control how long you stay with them on the phone. Just because worry has your number, and will try to talk your ear off, doesn't mean you have to listen. Hang up the phone! Relabeling makes a clear distinction between the worry voice and your child's own thoughts. Help your child to sort out his brain mail. When your child is stuck in a spin of worry, rather than responding directly to those thoughts, try to locate your child: *"Who is asking me that question—worry, is that you again? Michael, I know you're in there—come on out—I hear what worry is saying, but what do you think about this situation?"* Another advantage of relabeling is taking your child out of the hot seat of being the problem and instead making the *anxiety* the problem. This lets your child know that you know he is not doing this on purpose. With anxiety as the common enemy, parents and kids can join forces to fight back the anxiety instead of fighting each other.

Relabeling Techniques

- Give the worry a name, like *Brain Bug, Mr. Panic, Mrs. Watch-it* (let your child choose): It helps your child to externalize the problem, have a target for his frustration, and distinguish his rational thoughts from worry thoughts.
- Draw a picture of the Brain Bug.
- Make a puppet, doll, or figure you can use to act out the Brain Bug.
- Give the fears a voice of their own—when you voice them, say them silly or sarcastically to keep them from sounding scary. Sing them like Elvis, or Britney, say them like Homer Simpson, feel no obligation to respect the voice of anxiety.

- Stage an impromptu worry talent show. Do impersonations of the worry voice. Which version is it easiest for your child to dismiss?
- Invite your child to poke fun at the worry brain; have your child do some healthy teasing of how Brain Bug operates, think of some healthy accusations to throw Brain Bug's way.
- Use any of a number of metaphors to help them speak about the problem: Help your child to identify the caller—*it's a mechanical glitch, it's not my fault; it's the worry brain, it's not me. It's junk mail, don't take it personally, it doesn't know you or even the situation. It's a false alarm, jumping the gun, it's the worry mosquito—annoying but completely useless.*

Relabeling with Very Young Children. Parents can use puppets, stuffed animals, drawings, or a silly voice to differentiate worry thinking from regular thinking. In the context of a game or role play, worry can be a bug buzzing around, scaring a stuffed animal, say an elephant. The elephant is afraid of everything, but only because the Worry Bug keeps saying mean things in his ear, such as "you can't play with the doggy, you are too afraid, doggies bark and are too scary." Then you can turn to your child and say, "Wow, that Worry Bug is mean, and bossy, and I don't think he's right. He says that all doggies are mean. Let's think if we can prove him wrong. What about that doggie that we saw in the park running after the frisbee—did he look mean? No, I don't think so. He didn't want to hurt anybody; he was a nice doggy. Let's teach the Worry Bug a few things about dogs. Let's use a strong voice and boss back the Worry Bug—'*Hey Worry Bug, doggies are the best friends of lots and lots of children. They bark when they are happy or surprised, but that doesn't mean they want to hurt me!*' Let's sing a song—Worry Bug go away, I just want to go and play!—next time when we see a dog, it will be easier because you won't feel so scared." Repeat the role play letting your child decide if he wants to play the Worry Bug, or the brave child bossing him back.

Relabeling with Older Children. When you worry, it's your body's alarm system starting to backfire, setting off false alarms about situations that maybe aren't stressful at all, or at least not as risky as your brain junk mail is telling you. What do you want to call the brain trick? How do you want to think of your worry? It helps to give it a name—Brain Bug, Worry Glasses, Exaggerator Man, Repeater Reptile, Tricky Guy, Question Man, Bratty Brain, you decide—so that you can start to boss it back. The more you start to talk back to your worry, and correct the mistakes it makes, the more you will actually help your brain learn not to bug you with the little stuff, to only alert you to the real risks.

Let's draw a picture of your Worry Guy and do some role playing to practice bossing him back.

Relabeling with Teenagers. You can learn to label your worry talk and treat it differently from your rational thoughts. This is your brain overreacting. It's just a worry tape playing in your head, and because it's in your head rather than on the radio, it takes a little more work to recognize the distortions. Worry thinking plays on vulnerabilities. It is no voice to trust, but you have a choice: think of it as comedian Adam Sandler doing one of his funny voices or songs rather than as Peter Jennings on the nightly news. If you're thinking that Adam Sandler has no authority in this situation, that's exactly the point—your worry thoughts have no hold on the truth! You can turn down the volume, cut the cord, and change how much of that kind of communication comes your way. Over time you will help those overactive brain functions calm down, and you will have a direct line to more calm, analytical thinking. You'll have a more confident, realistic picture of your abilities and what you can handle.

STEP THREE: REWIRE AND RESIST:
ACT WITH YOUR SMARTS, NOT WITH YOUR FEARS

Rewire. In order to change your child's thinking, you have to start with the thinking you want to change. *Always* start with the worries or fear thoughts first, because that's where he's stuck. Once you've heard the "what ifs" ask your child to listen to his thoughts, check out if they really make sense, verbalize, and analyze. Then let him be the teacher, and give a true/false test on his worry thoughts—*"Are you going to get sick when you touch the paper from the doctor's office? Is something bad going to happen if you're the last one up?"* Separate the feelings from the truth. You know the truth, but the feelings are getting in the way.

It is important for you to find out what your child is really worried about. Let him tell you. Ask him what he is afraid would happen in the situation. Be careful about guessing—you may guess wrong and inadvertently introduce a new worry angle on the problem, one he hasn't even considered yet. Witness the following presumably reassuring comment on a child's fear of bats: "Listen, bats are safe, they don't usually have rabies." To which your child replies, "What?! Rabies! Isn't that fatal, bats have it too? Oh no! I was just worried about them getting caught in my hair. Oh my gosh, do you think I might have rabies?!"

While rewiring has to do with reconnecting to more realistic circuits, it also means kids taking back the power from their anxiety, and making it clear to the worry brain that they will not tolerate or be intimidated by worry intrusions. Children need to find their "boss back" voice, the strong voice inside of them they use to let people know they can't be pushed around. In order to tap into this mindset of defending their emotional turf, older kids can be asked to think of the voice they use when a bully or a younger sibling is trying to mess with them, take their stuff, or boss them around. Younger children can think of what a favorite superhero would say in that situation—because, after all, as one very vocal five-year-old recently told my husband, "Superman never worries!"

Examples of Boss Back Talk

You are not the boss of me! I decide what to think!

Be quiet, I'm going to smush you, Worry Bug!

If this were really important, my parents would be helping me worry, not helping me stop!

You don't know anything about this Brain Bug, go back to school!

You are just a false alarm, you don't know what's going to happen!

I don't have to listen to you; I'm changing the channel.

I don't need to worry about this; my friends don't so I won't.

SPAM alert—I'm blocking this message.

It's worry—my brain is overreacting, but I don't have to.

My parents would never let me be in danger—so this must be safe!

The goal is to help your child challenge that *first response* information he is getting from the brain, and come up with a smart, realistic *second response* to counter it. While anxiety will choose the most frightening scenario, help your child choose the most likely scenario. In order to gain confidence in that second response, have your child say it many times, write it down, or even make a tape recording of her realistic thoughts. Worry thoughts have dominated the airwaves in your child's mind; hearing herself say the confident, realistic thoughts is a powerful new experience.

Resist. Once your child has the story straight, it is time to resist the rules and warnings of worry and act on what he knows to be true instead. This means finding a starting point with the fear or worry situation and beginning the gradual approach and desensitization.

Make a list of feared or avoided situations, take the fear temperature for each challenge, then rank the steps to be overcome in dealing with each fear on a hierarchy or staircase of learning (see figure below), putting the easiest on the bottom step and the final goal at the top. Plan a series of small exposures or GUTI exercises. Your child can start from the easiest, right outside his comfort zone, and then, with frequent practice, begin to conquer that specific fear by approaching the sit-

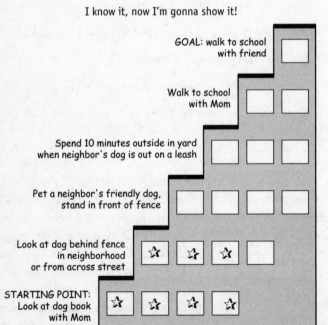

STAIRS OF LEARNING
I know it, now I'm gonna show it!

GOAL: walk to school with friend

Walk to school with Mom

Spend 10 minutes outside in yard when neighbor's dog is out on a leash

Pet a neighbor's friendly dog, stand in front of fence

Look at dog behind fence in neighborhood or from across street

STARTING POINT: Look at dog book with Mom

uation. Help your child choose a challenge that is not too big, but not too small. If it's too hard he will fail; if it's too easy, he won't have a sense of accomplishment. Your child can progress to the next step when he no longer feels significant anxiety from the current challenge.

In Chapters 6 through 12, you will find sample GUTI exercises for your child's particular fear or worry. There are some common variables that impact the degrees of difficulty for exposures (for example going somewhere new versus somewhere familiar, going somewhere at night versus during the day). Older children may be able to articulate these factors, younger children may not. Consider the factors illustrated in the Anxiety Equalizer on page 96, and see which ones are relevant to your child's fears.

✳ Getting on the Right Track with Very Young Children ✳

- Using stuffed animals, drawings, or puppets, act out the situation with a worry animal and a brave animal. Help your child to participate in the role play, eventually giving him the opportunity to play the role of the brave.

- Demystify the scaries: learn the facts. Monsters are made up—how many have you seen? Let's make up our own monster, how about a monster who doesn't know how to say "boo," but says "broccoli" instead? Maybe the monster is afraid of his shadow because it's so big! The monster wants to play the guitar, but no one will teach him. Help your child to boss back the scaries: "You're mean, you're not true, I'm brave." Give your child a sticker or small treat for practicing her "boss back" talk.

- If your child is not ready to approach a situation directly, she can do "research" and watch how other kids manage in that situation.

Getting on the Right Track with Older Children and Teenagers

- Draw stick figures with thought bubbles like in a cartoon. Have your child imagine what two different characters would think when looking at the same situation. What does Worried Walter think? How about Smart Samantha?

- Have your child draw two pairs of glasses (or even make them!). Describe the situation when looking through the *worry glasses;* how does the same situation look when you put those aside and put on your *smart glasses?* Look at the differences—which one do you really trust? (See figure below.)

WORRY GLASSES

SMART GLASSES

We're doomed!
What if the basement floods?
What if the house catches fire?
What if the lights go out?

We are safe.
Thunder is loud but not dangerous.
Rainstorms are part of life.
I can handle it.

Fear temperature ___10+___   Fear temperature ___3___

- Use the brain train illustration (see Chapter 4) to talk about how the worry thoughts lead to certain feelings and behaviors.

- Use the pie charts in Chapter 4 to color in how much your child *thinks* the worry will come true versus how much he *feels* afraid of the worry. Feeling something doesn't make it true. Feelings change, the facts stay the same. Help your child put his thinking part in charge. Remind him that when something is a small risk, he doesn't have to plan around it. (Isn't there a risk that he might get hurt in sports, but doesn't he still play? That's when he is in charge and the worry brain is quiet.)

- What is the worry expecting will happen? Write it down. Pull out your red pen and grade the worry paper. Which answers are true? Which are false? Rewrite the story with a more accurate and likely ending.

- Make a list of the "what ifs." Next to each item, make a list of the "what elses." What is more likely to happen in the situation? What would your child expect to happen if she didn't worry? Have her write "what ifs" on slips of paper and place them in a hat; pull out the "what ifs" and then take turns coming up with "what elses" to counter them.

- Ask your child to write her worry thoughts on cards and put them in a hat, then she should pull out a card and name two coping thoughts that will reduce the anxiety of that thought. Then parents take a turn doing the same.

- Have your child imagine she is a detective, or a lawyer in court, and she has to prove her worry case with the facts. Ask her to explain how she would go about it. Could she prove any of the worries, or are they really unlikely?

- Ask your child to imagine interviewing his friends about a worry situation. How would they handle it? How would they assess the risk? What would they say is the truth?

ANXIETY EQUALIZER
Common Variables that determine anxiety levels and degrees
of difficulty for exposures

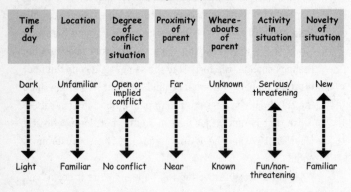

Time of day	Location	Degree of conflict in situation	Proximity of parent	Whereabouts of parent	Activity in situation	Novelty of situation
Dark	Unfamiliar	Open or implied conflict	Far	Unknown	Serious/ threatening	New
↕	↕	↕	↕	↕	↕	↕
Light	Familiar	No conflict	Near	Known	Fun/non-threatening	Familiar

STEP FOUR: GET THE BODY ON BOARD

Remind kids that when they are thinking worry thoughts, the body automatically gets in gear—worry gear—and that revving up only makes them feel more like the situation is an emergency and distracts them from being able to think straight. Use the balloon breathing exercise from Chapter 4. If your child is in the throes of an anxiety moment, he may not be able to start slowing down his breathing right away. Put out the expectation and suggestion that in a few minutes when he is ready he will be able to slow everything down. With younger kids you can hold their hands and have them match their breathing to yours. For older kids, have them focus on counting, breathing in 1–2, and out 1–2, without holding their breath at any point. Kids' bodies also get revved up when their behavior becomes agitated, regressed, or disorganized. Calmly but firmly instruct them that their job is to try to slow things down, *when they are ready.* Not forcing them to do it that second, but putting out the expectation and suggestion that they can, helps them to feel that they are making a choice to improve the situation.

- Help your child to slow things down.
- Remind him that anxiety always passes, but he can help it go faster by slowing himself down.
- Take your child's worry temperature on a scale from 0 to 10, or simply have the child rate her fear as low, medium, or high. This will help your child see that even though she may still feel anxious a few minutes later, the anxiety actually has *decreased* through her own efforts.

STEP FIVE: REFOCUS ON WHAT YOU WANT TO DO— WHAT WOULD YOU DO IF YOU WERE IN CHARGE, NOT THE WORRY?

Once you have bossed the worry back and corrected its mistakes, your child is ready to dismiss the worry and move on. Because the anxious feelings take several minutes to pass, it is best to get busy with something else. With this step you are not simply distracting your child—rather you're showing him how to pick up his mind and put it where he wants it to be. The stance is *"Don't stand there and let anxiety bully you, pick yourself up and move on to what you want to do. It's your time, you're the boss, you choose what to do with it."* Physical activity is best; for example, throw a ball back and forth (a pair of socks will do in a pinch), go for a run with the dog, dance, sing, or play tag. If physical activity isn't possible (i.e., if you are in the car), play a quick game of categories. Name all the movies you saw in the last few months, name all the foods that begin with the letter *P*—do something that gets your mind busy thinking and is a fun and better use of your time. Sedentary activities—reading, even playing computer games—will likely not be as engaging or offer as much relief to your child as he may double-task and still be thinking about the worry while doing the activity.

Ask your child, *"What would you want to be doing if you weren't anxious? Let's get busy with that and your brain will learn to jump the worry track and get back to calm thinking."*

STEP SIX: REINFORCE YOUR CHILD'S EFFORTS AT FIGHTING!

Praise your child for getting through a tough situation, for strengthening those good circuits! Use tangible reinforcers and rewards to increase a child's interest in and willingness to fight the worry. Rewards such as stickers, small treats, special time with parents, and yes, even toys, are not bribes but acknowledgments for a job well done. Make sure that you convey that to your child. Don't say, "If you stay in bed and don't call out for the next five nights, I'll buy you a new doll." Instead say, "You are going to work hard on staying in bed and using your "boss back" talk and your nighttime journal if you are scared. Is there a special treat you would like after you've had five nights where you met your goal?" Another advantage of rewards is that they change the tone of the work from serious and fearful to something positive—working toward getting pancakes for breakfast, a free pass from doing the trash, or borrowing the car.

Incentives/rewards

- In general it takes about three weeks to establish a new behavior, so continue rewarding your child until the new behavior is established.
- Highlight successes in coping, don't dwell on unsuccessful moments.
- Be specific about the target behavior: specify the amount of time, or specific behavioral challenge. For example, *stay in bed for ten minutes without calling out or crying out; go to the convenience store and ask one question; retie shoes one time instead of five; make calls to three friends.*
- Reward any behavior that is in the spirit of coping—don't

just look at the bull's-eye, reward anything that hits the board. Change the reward to an agreed-upon compromise if the child is able to partially complete the task.

- Don't look for consecutive successes (e.g., staying in bed five days in a row)—go for cumulative successes (a total of five days). Progress is often two steps forward, one step back.
- Practice, practice! One time does not mastery make. Children should repeat the same exposure until they have demonstrated mastery—little or no anxiety in the situation.
- Gradually fade out rewards for a given behavior as the task gets easier, then switch the reward to the next challenge on your child's worry list.
- Beware the Extinction Burst: If you have been reassuring your child about his worries for months or years, expect that there will be an initial backlash of resistance when you begin to approach the situation from a new angle. If you make sure that the goals are reasonable for your child, and hold steady, this initial burst of protest will pass and your child will be over the hurdle.
- Remember that behavior changes before thoughts and feelings. Kids say, *"I can't, I'm scared."* Don't wait for anxious feelings and thoughts to go away as a sign that your child is ready to change his behavior. Know that the thoughts will be there, encourage your child to correct them, and then work on what he can control—the behavior.

General Do's and Don'ts

- Do let your child know it's okay to be afraid.
- Do get your child's input—what's on her worry list, why does she want to fight it?
- Do help your child define his comfort zone and move out of it step by step.
- Do talk your child through the situation with pleasant, calm language.

- Don't avoid the feared situation.
- Do reinforce and encourage any interaction with a fearful situation—talking about the situation, drawing it, reading about it, role playing with it.
- Don't aim too high or your child will feel overwhelmed and will either resist or not learn.
- Do give kids a feeling of control, let them help you decide what steps they are ready for. The more they are involved in the planning, the more likely they will cooperate with the implementation.
- Don't force your child into a situation that is too scary; see what variable you can change to make it feel safer. Remember, kids grow from a place of security, not from a place of fear.
- Do at least some of the challenge in order to end on a good note. Remember it's not a race!

In this chapter we've laid out the steps to follow in teaching your child to reduce the amount of time, distress, and brain circuitry devoted to worry and anxiety. By learning to relabel worry, kids begin to devalue its logic (or lack thereof) and develop more realistic ways of looking at fearful situations. Over time, through these reasoned thoughts, healthy circuits will become more accessible to your child. The path to tempered thinking, greater options, flexibility, and more accurate reasoning will be paved by your child's practice and skill. With pride and relief you will step back and watch your child go!

PART II

All Worries
Great and Small

COMMON CHILDHOOD FEARS AND WORRIES
AND PROBLEM ANXIETIES

No two children are exactly alike in any respect, and anxiety is no exception. Children's anxieties are a unique combination of genetics, temperament, and experience in the world. What can be very reassuring to children and parents alike is that it is possible to find common underlying themes and patterns in the way children's anxiety manifests itself, supporting the idea that these glitches are nobody's fault. They are simply a bug in the system, a brain bug, that can be dealt with effectively with cognitive-behavioral strategies.

In this section we will examine common fear themes and diagnoses. As we saw in Chapter 2, anxiety disorder diagnoses are made based on the degree of distress and interference that the child experiences as a result of his symptoms. Even if your child does not meet the criteria for a diagnosis, the strategies in these pages will give you ideas about what to try at home and a behind-the-scenes look at what these symptoms are all about. It is not possible to address every worry or anxiety situation in this book (though believe me, I've tried!), but you will at least find close cousins of your child's situation and be able to apply the principles outlined here to your child. Familiarizing yourself with how worry works and how to best address it will prepare you to be a wonderful coach for your child.

In nearly every case, you will find that anxiety involves a distortion—the sensationalizing, exaggerating version of a story that puts *feelings* in charge. Your job is to help your child identify the mistakes and come up with a more realistic, scientific version that puts your child's smart side back in charge. Though you may be tempted to go right for the truth, always let your child explain the worry story first. Picture your child with his arms full of parcels of worry. There is no room for him to take in other perspectives until he's dumped out the worry first. Though each chapter will offer specific strategies for a particular type of anxiety, you will always do well if you keep in mind the steps of the Master Plan outlined in Chapter 5.

The key is to weave these ideas into your daily life. Anxiety isn't something that will go away—that would be dangerous. We need to have our wits about us, but in proportion to the actual risk in our lives. Though at first it may seem like it is *more* work to confront your child's anxiety rather than to simply accommodate or reassure, soon you will get fluent in these strategies and they will come to you easily. The families who do best with anxiety management treatment take some risks with it, and use creative means to show their child that they are not afraid of the anxiety.

Each chapter in this section describes aspects of a specific diagnosis and ways that it is treated. If your child has symptoms of multiple diagnoses, as many children do, you can jump around between chapters to get the information you need. While some diagnoses, such as PTSD, OCD, and Tourette syndrome, have specific strategies that differ somewhat from the Master Plan, the underlying ideas are the same: first understand the brain glitch, know about the mistake the brain is making and why, and learn how to retrain your brain to not send you unnecessary signals.

Remember that it is never too early to teach your child to manage her worry thinking, and likewise it is never too late.

Try these strategies on yourself when you recognize your worry racing ahead or find yourself spinning in a wheel of "what ifs." Verbalize, analyze, and get your smart brain working to rewire your anxious moments. You'll be that much calmer when your child comes to you for help.

CHAPTER 6

✳

From Everyday Worries to Generalized Anxiety Disorder (GAD)

A good imagination is good, too much imagination . . . that can be really awful!

A six-year-old with GAD

*N*ina *worries about everything. Sometimes I think that the world is just not made for anxious kids. People say things all the time that they don't mean, but Nina takes it all to heart. Her teacher says to the class, "You'll never go home unless you quiet down." She immediately starts worrying about staying at school forever, but these things happen all day long. I don't think she really believes it, but the wheels just start turning and she gets so stressed thinking, "What if that happened?"*

Max is so concerned about others, he would never want to hurt or offend anyone in any way. I know that sounds like that's the way you want your kid to be, but it's too much. I think his worry eats away at him. I'm afraid that he's internalizing all that pressure and it's going to be too much for him someday.

The Worry Factor: No Degrees of Separation Between Catastrophe and You

While many kids have worries that they manage, children like Nina and Max have worries that take on a life of their own. This debilitating burden of uncontrollable worry is likely *generalized anxiety disorder* (GAD) a condition that afflicts anywhere from 2 to 19 percent of children and adolescents. For someone to be officially diagnosed with GAD, the worry and associated symptoms must be present for at least six months. Children with GAD wiring struggle with a system that is over-programmed to find the element of fear or potential for problems in any situation. Rather than there being six degrees of separation between kids and any catastrophe, the worry telescopes down and places monumental weights on even the broadest shoulders. These are not just children who *wonder* "what if?"; they are braced for it every day. A key sign of GAD is that the worry is many steps removed from the initial situation. A child gets a ninety-four on a test and is worried about how this will affect her college career and future employment; when the grill chef at a Japanese restaurant is poised to "throw" food, she's sure she will go to the hospital choking, or maybe even die.

Setting limits on the distance of the worry is essential. When faced with a potential risk, most kids can do a quick worry calculation and dismiss a remote possibility as such. Kids with GAD do the long division. Powered by a supersonic imagination—by the idea that possibility means probability and that without a guarantee of safety there is a guarantee of high risk—the worry radar stays on all the time. Whereas kids with fears and phobias have excessive fears about a *specific* situation—dogs, insects, thunder—for kids with GAD worry is pervasive. It is a free agent that can latch on to any passing situation. A birthday party may evoke not fun, but rather fearful anticipation—*will there be enough cake, what if the candles catch someone's hair on fire, what if I don't like my presents, what if it rains?* Children with GAD, much to their detriment, can pick up the weakest signal, the most inconsequential aberration, and then misinterpret that signal as something urgent and inevitable.

Parents of kids with GAD find themselves alternating between feeling great sorrow at seeing their child struggling and feeling frustrated and even judged by their children, who can't seem to let anything go. Though you may feel controlled by your child's worry, remember they are being controlled too. They suffer daily from feelings on a par with what we might feel when we receive bad medical news, or a surprise tax bill, when no amount of reassurance can release us. Fortunately, worry can be curbed by following several key steps. In this chapter, you will learn that rather than talking your child out of his fears, you can direct him to tap into his own realistic thinking and do the job himself.

IN THE THICK OF IT: NOT EVERY BELL TOLLS FOR THEE

Kids with GAD live on "borrowed worry," spending endless time struggling with concerns that really belong to other people. Take Elizabeth, for example, a straight-A student in school with impeccable behavior, who wouldn't so much as blink an eye if it were against the rules. Yet she sits in front of me, wringing her hands, explaining why she is up until midnight every night worrying. The answer is that she is deathly afraid of the principal. Even saying the word sends her fear temperature climbing. She can't stop worrying about school because she doesn't want to go to the principal's office. She explains, "He has a mean face, when he gets angry he yells until he turns red." But it's not just the principal, it's also the teacher. "She's stressed, she gets mad a lot and yells; and if we don't finish our work in school, we'll have to stay after. If we talk in class, we miss recess. If we get in trouble more than once, we'll have to go to the principal and we'll get detention. If we don't write our name on our papers, we don't get credit. If we put it in the wrong box, we get an F. And cheating—don't even ask, we get our tests taken away." At night Elizabeth is so keyed up that she spends from 9 P.M. to midnight trying to figure out what she did wrong at school to make sure that she won't find out the next day that she's in trouble. She is beside herself with worry.

We could say that Elizabeth has had her worry wires crossed with the proverbial kid "in the back of the class," the child who goofs around, doesn't listen, who breaks the rules. This is the child who the teacher is really directing her comments to and maybe even upping the ante a bit to get his attention—not to the Elizabeths in the class. If only the teacher could flash the message that Elizabeth's brain is missing—*"this isn't about you."*

Red Flags for GAD

- Always has a list of worries—topics can change daily; needs to know details ahead of time, has pressing questions about logistics
- Takes offhand comments literally and seriously
- Future orientation: elementary school kids worrying if they will be good drivers, high school kids worrying about a job after college
- Performance fears: perfectionistic, very afraid of doing the wrong thing, always seeking reassurance, afraid of getting in trouble; fears about failure, and consequences of less than perfect performance
- Social/interpersonal fears: fear that friends don't like them

or friends are mad at them; worried about tests or reports—*"I'll fail the class, my teacher will be mad at me; other kids will think I'm dumb; my parents will be mad, and I'll get grounded."*

- Concerns about family: keeping constant tabs on the status of parents' marriage—worrying that anything other than the sunniest day could mean parents are fighting or are going to get divorced

- Fears about illness: an insignificant symptom may be a sign of a serious disease: *"My mouth tasted like pennies today—is that a sign of a stroke? I saw it on TV."* Concerns about finances and financial repercussions, how much things such as groceries, household repairs, doctor's visits cost

- Consequences of stress: always on edge, looks tense, is difficult to reassure, has difficulty concentrating and sleeping, headaches, stomachaches, is distractible, unable to enjoy things; overwhelmed by schedule

Key Interventions in Treatment: Don't Go by Your First Reaction, Fight Back with a Second, Realistic Reaction

When kids with GAD learn that a very useful and powerful process—the risk detector—is being engaged at the wrong time, they can begin to reassure themselves that the risks are really not what they seem. Only then can they respond to those worries with skepticism, sarcasm, and maybe even a touch of condescension—*"Yeah, worry, that story is really likely"*—rather than reacting with their fear. They are smarter than their worry. And that is a greater relief than any reassurance can deliver. When well-meaning parents, teachers, and even therapists take the worry at face value and rush to reassure, they are missing the point.

RELABEL THE WORRY VOICE: IT GIVES YOU A CHOICE!

If a child thinks that the worries are equal to her sensible thoughts, she will have trouble dismissing them. If she can instead start to sort her brain mail, get some distance from her worries, call them silly instead of serious, and recognize the tell-tale exaggerating signs of the worry brain (see Chapter 5 for illustrations to help with this distinction) then it will be easier to bring the risk down to size, and she will learn to dismiss it.

COGNITIVE FACTORS: RIGHT THE WORRY WRONGS— "WHAT IFS" BECOME "WHAT ELSES"

Children need to see the choices. Rather than immediately assuming that worry has the story right and getting distressed, they have to decide whether something is really a risk, and to size up the risk. There are a variety of methods for generating the thinking alternatives. Have your child tell you his fears about a particular situation, and write them down on one side of a page. Then help him come up with a second reaction to or story about what he really thinks will happen in that situation. See Chapter 5 for ideas and activities that enhance realistic thinking. Be creative—stage a debate between worry and your child, or sing the worries and say the truth. All of these interventions access your child's second, realistic reaction, reinforcing the idea that he has thinking choices.

Once you and your child have set up these thinking options, analyze the worry thinking and identify the brain trick—the way that it's getting the story wrong. When your child sees the trick, he will be confident that it really is safe to let the worry story go. The two most common thinking mistakes are focusing on how awful a situation could be rather than how unlikely that scenario is, and letting your feelings about a situation color the facts. For instance, after the teacher talks about gangrene, your child worries that the cut he got last week might become infected and that his arm will have to be amputated—then how would he play piano, write, or drive a car? Give your child a chance to tell you how likely that is these days. If he gets stuck, you can fill in the blank, but you may be surprised to hear how much he really does know when you take the microphone away from worry and give it to your child.

You can remind your child of the risks he does take without knowing it by turning the spotlight off his fears and on to someone else's, maybe even yours. My patient Ellie is very afraid of dogs, but when I role played being afraid to go out on a boat—*I'm going to capsize, I'll get soaked, my swimming isn't all that great, what if I can't get up, I'd be stuck in the water, who would help me, what if I didn't make it?*—she started to smile. I asked her why. She said, "Because it's not going to happen. First of all you wear a life jacket, you might get wet, but so what!" Ellie loves to go kayaking and has no problem taking the risks associated with it. We agree that in terms of kayaking her worry brain is behaving, not pushing the panic button *just because the risk exists*. We were then able to apply this discovery to her fear of dogs.

The second way that worry gets the story wrong—confusing facts with feelings—can be analyzed and corrected using risk assessment. Look again at the pie charts from Chapter 4. Your child needs to map a circle representing how much she *feels afraid* that something will happen—a robber will break in—and then another circle showing how much she actually *believes* that the bad thing will happen. Let her know that she will feel as scared as her feelings dictate, but feeling scared doesn't make the feared occurrence any more likely. If she sticks with the facts her anxiety will begin to come down. And, in accordance with the Master Plan, encourage your child to move her thinking where she wants it to go. What would she prefer to be thinking or doing now?

GETTING WORRY UNDER CONTROL:
PUTTING YOUR CHILD BACK IN CHARGE

Scheduling Worry Time. Kids with GAD have a running worry dialogue throughout the day. Help them get more control and increase worry-free times and zones by compartmentalizing the worry to a given time each day. See Chapter 4 for instructions on worry time. When worries come up at other times, the child can either jot them down, or simply chide them as they would another child, "It's not your turn, you have to wait!" If worry time is scheduled after school or in the early evening it will ease the tension at bedtime, which is often the default worry time. If a child is worrying about things far into the future, usually imagining how awful they will be—going to high school, having a baby, or paying bills, all from the vantage point of third grade—set a date or year when it would make sense to start *thinking* about these things.

Talking Back. Another way for kids to feel more control over their worry is to be able to talk back to it and even get angry at it. Kids with GAD often feel very frustrated from all the tension they hold in. Practice using "boss back" talk, as described in Chapter 5, and this will give them a great release. Let them tell their worry how they really feel about it. Give your child a chance to hear worry out loud—do a role play where you play the worry: *"You can't take that chance, listen to me I'm tricking you, oops, I mean helping you."* And your child can reply, *"You're not helping me, worry doesn't protect me it just takes up time and energy. I can live with these risks, but I can't live with you!"* Reverse roles and revive your child's feelings of being in charge of his feelings.

REDUCING PHYSIOLOGICAL SIGNS OF STRESS

Even if kids with chronic worry don't complain of headaches or stomachaches, you can usually read on their faces or their

rinc

37565003606885
Freeing yo

rinc
JORD - 4795

bodies that they are tense and on edge. Because the mind and body can play off each other, it helps to get both working toward greater balance. Look at the breathing and relaxation exercises in Chapter 4.

GETTING USED TO IT—GUTI EXERCISES FOR GAD

For children with GAD, the GUTI exercises are about *not* taking precautions they fear they should. Sometimes that means not doing things perfectly and other times it means not apologizing or asking people if they are mad at them because of a funny look. As with all other fears and worries, the child should generate a hierarchy of situations on their worry list. These situations are then placed on the "stairs of learning" to be practiced starting with the situations that generate the least anxiety and fear, climbing step by step to exposures that generate the most anxiety. When a child has repeated the exposure enough times so that it becomes manageable, maybe even easy or boring, she is ready to move up to the next step. Rewards and incentives can be used to mark and celebrate the child's accomplishments. The hierarchy below is an example of what a child with GAD may need to address. The goal is to be able to deal better with imperfection or mistakes so that worrying about them doesn't run the child's life.

When school-related challenges are involved, the teacher should be told that the child is under a tremendous amount of stress from anxious thoughts and that she needs some practice making small mistakes, to ensure that she can handle those situations. Having the teachers reinforce the idea that everyone makes mistakes will support the child's GUTI challenges and make these exposures more manageable. The chart below is an example of one child's challenges to work on not being so stressed about everything going right. Note that these challenges are listed from the easiest on top to the hardest on the bottom.

Challenge	Fear Temperature
Don't double-check homework assignment with Kimmy	50
Don't ask a friend if she's mad at me	60
Don't recopy notes that were sloppy	65
Forget a book at home	78
Forget part of gym uniform on purpose	80
Forget to do one homework subject on purpose	100
Make an annoyed face in class when teacher is looking at me	100

On the Homefront

"Did you write that note to the teacher?"

"For the hundredth time, I'll write the note after breakfast, stop worrying!"

"But what if you forget, then she won't know that you're picking me up early. You are picking me up early, right?"

"Peter, you know the answer—yes, I'm picking you up early!"

"But you might forget—just write it down so you don't forget."

"That's it, Peter—stop worrying!! It's fine, just like it's been every time!"

"But what if you do forget, can't you write it down?"

"Peter, stop it, that's enough, I'm the mother and I'm in charge!"

As the dialogue above illustrates, worry leads to overplanning. Parents see kids trying to control them. Kids with GAD don't necessarily have a premeditated plan to drive you crazy by controlling you, but they do have a pressing need to know what's going to happen next. The more you take it personally, the more your child will dig in. It's really the worry that is controlling your child. The greatest challenge for parents is to not lose patience with their worrying child. Try to remember that your child is in a sense being held hostage by the Worry Bully, so you can be unified against a common enemy. When your child leans over and wants to know how much is in the checking account, who is calling on the phone, and what were you just talking about, try to use some levity while relabeling what is going on: *"Who wants to know—you or your worry?"* Let your child know that he is off duty, and tell him to let the Worry Bully know that he isn't allowed to start worrying about those things until he is an adult.

The other challenge for parents is to not dismiss the worries. Just because the situations don't seem scary to you, that doesn't mean they can't be scary to your child. Worry and fear are in the eye of the beholder. Children suffer greatly when no one knows they are worrying. Needless time is spent getting very frightened. Listen carefully to your child's fears and worries because hidden within there may be some misconceptions that you can correct or some problem solving that you can do.

Six-year-old Will was having difficulty going to school. Each morning he would cry, delay getting dressed, try to hide, and do anything not to go. His parents were confused and concerned, but as any parent would do, they thought that these were just some school jitters, or maybe even plays for attention, and moved him along to school. When Will's mother, Sydney, was able to ask him what was in his worry "thought bubble" when he got ready for school, the story came tumbling out. He was very afraid that an older girl at school was going to kill him because she had said so (jokingly) when they were playing a game at recess. Will was thinking, *How is she going to kill me? Is she going to strangle me? Is she going to do it in the closet at school?*—far beyond what another child would make of that situation. Though killing clearly is frightening, and should not be joked about, instead of this thought passing through Will's worry net it was stuck, and the longer it stayed, the more it consumed him. With the kernel of the story uncovered, Sydney could help Will understand what had happened, reassure him that he was okay, and help him to put some new information in his thought bubble—the truth!

Taking Back Control: Elizabeth's Story

Elizabeth, whom we met earlier in the chapter, has been anxious since she was a young child. Elizabeth's mom knew this was somehow out of her daughter's control when at age four Elizabeth balked at getting into a rental car after theirs had broken down, because it "smelled different"—to the point of refusal and crying hysteria. Elizabeth's "scaries" were bigger than she was, and she needed help. Among Elizabeth's many fears was the constant dread that she was going to get sick or throw up and fears that she had done something wrong, or that something bad was going to happen. She would stay up until midnight each night dwelling on all the potential problems in her life. Elizabeth was afraid to be apart from her mom. She wouldn't go to friends' houses, on school trips, or anywhere other than to school when her mom was at work. At age ten, Elizabeth began to be upset with herself for having to make excuses all the time about why she couldn't do things. She rarely could play with her friends or go neat places she was invited. She had a school camping trip coming up in four months that she was supposed to go on, and she wanted to be able to do it. She felt nervous all the time. If kids misbehaved in class, she was afraid that everyone would get in trouble. She felt responsible for keeping everything calm. Her fear radar went off with every possible "what if." If she went to a friend's house she thought, *What if there is a fire?* In a friend's car, *What if I hear a noise? Something might smell bad? What if her dad isn't a good driver?* Invited somewhere for dinner, she thought, *What if the food isn't good?* We worked on turning off the worry tape, deciding that all it does is look for trouble—it finds tiny risks and turns them into huge risks and takes the fun out of everything. Elizabeth began to understand the tricks of the worry voice. She could spot them more easily and realized that when she bossed it back she felt better, not because the situation changed, but because her thinking changed.

For the trip she worried that she would forget something, that she wouldn't like the food or any of the activities—*I might not like the people in my cabin. What if I can't fall asleep and everyone else can?* We worked through the worry thoughts and worked out a plan for each of the concerns. She knew that the trip was only three days long, she wouldn't starve, that even if she did stay up, she could live with that, that her teacher would be there to help—and overall, that her Worry Bug was making all of this seem like an awful situation, when truly if she turned down the volume on that, it was a great chance to be out of school for a few days, be with her friends, and prove to herself that she could do this.

This is how we laid out her Stairs of Learning (see Chapter 5):

STAIRS OF LEARNING
I know it, now I'm gonna show it!

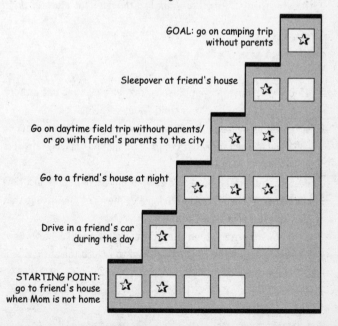

GOAL: go on camping trip without parents

Sleepover at friend's house

Go on daytime field trip without parents/ or go with friend's parents to the city

Go to a friend's house at night

Drive in a friend's car during the day

STARTING POINT: go to friend's house when Mom is not home

E-mail: October 12, 2002

Hi Tamar! How are you? Guess what?! I went to a sleepover!!!!! I went to my friend Terrie's house. She is one of my good friends. At night I was feeling a little worried about whether I would fall asleep or not. But eventually I fought it down. In the morning I felt very proud of myself! I feel a little more confident now that I can face Victory Camp now.

See you soon! Elizabeth

E-mail: October 18, 2002

Dear Tamar, I DID IT! I have completed my mission, defeated my worries, conquered them! I went for 3 days 2 nights at Victory Camp—NO PROBLEMS!!!!!!!!!!!!! I am truly proud of myself! Guess what? I didn't call home either! I am proud!   *Elizabeth*

Elizabeth feels that working on her fears has helped her with everything. *"I used to think bad thoughts too much of the time*

Idea Box

- Overplanners: Be spontaneous, change a plan, go out without a destination, give your child "wing-it" points.
- Certainty seekers: Won't take maybe for an answer, practice "maybe" tolerance, get points for handling "maybe" answers (vs. definite answers).
- Catastrophizers: Develop a code or phrase to denote just how "far out" the worry is—Flying Pig Alert, or Brain Bug that one's out of the ballpark.
- Chronic worriers: Sing the worries to a tune like "Row, Row, Row Your Boat" that is guaranteed to reduce the authority of those thoughts.

about everything! Now I've learned to push the bad thoughts away. Just because they are there, doesn't mean they are right, in fact they are basically always wrong. And thinking them just ruins my time. I basically forced myself to do things that were hard and proved to myself that I am capable. It feels really great."

CHAPTER 7

From the Mini-Scaries to Real Phobias

I wish they would just build a bug house outside for all the bugs so they would all stay in one place and never bother me!

It's gotten to the point with my son where I don't even know how to answer his questions. Sometimes I'll lie to him—"no, there won't be any dogs on our walk"—just so he'll stop asking. I know it's wrong, but how else can I get him out the door?

Some children become paralyzed with fear in the face of a situation that their peers wouldn't even register as a challenge. How can it be that one child clutches at you for dear life at the mere sight of a dog on a leash, while another happily pets the friendly animal? We could say that with the worry glasses on, anxious kids are seeing a different dog. They are focusing on and magnifying the most potentially frightening aspects of the situation (*look at the dog's sharp teeth, he is going to bite me*) while other crucial information (*the dog is on a leash, look at his tail wagging happily*) is entirely overlooked. With that exaggerated estimate of risk racing through their minds, anxious kids go into survival mode and insist on avoidance. One mistake that parents often make is to overlook the opportunity to make the situation manageable by making the picture more realistic. The other mistake is that often parents either keep kids completely away from the feared situation—so they never learn that they could handle it—or insist that they face the fear at full throttle, which usually sensitizes a child so much that she is even more adamant in her refusal to approach the situation than she was before the "intervention." In this chapter you will find the formula for success in treating fears: first bring the risk down to size with cognitive exercises, and then approach the situation with small, manageable GUTI exercises. First we will look at the ways in which children's fears are acquired and reinforced. When parents understand where their child's distortions are coming from, they will be in a better position to correct them. After a review of general treatment strategies for working with fears and phobias, the remainder of the chapter provides specific techniques for different phobia subtypes.

In Chapter 1 we reviewed the normal developmental sequence of fears. These fears are acquired and resolved as a child's development unfolds. The difference between normal fears and problem phobias is not the *content* of what a child fears, but rather his *reaction* to the fear. The content may be identical *in kind* to "normal fears" of childhood, but the intensity of these fears and their impact on a child's day-to-day life are disruptive, embarrassing, and constraining. To officially be diagnosed, a phobia must be present for at least six months. Rather than waiting for six months to identify the problem, however, it is best to address fears when they first surface and prevent them from taking on phobic proportions.

Approximately 10 percent of all adults and 2 to 4 percent of children experience a specific phobia—a circumscribed, unreasonable, and persistent fear of a particular object or situation. Common examples include heights, small animals, medical procedures, the dark, and thunder and lightning; less common examples include birds, newspapers, menstruation, and in one study I read . . . yogurt. While there are some idiosyncratic examples, it is interesting to note that those many varieties of phobias can be distilled down to a handful of themes: animals, situations (elevator), blood or injury, and nature (tornadoes). These common themes may reflect evolution hedging its bets on our survival by wiring the brain to be very sensitive to certain stimuli. Primitive fears like those of snakes or spiders may have just outlived their biological necessity as the fears remain while our actual exposure to those stimuli is generally limited. While there is a high prevalence of children with phobias, many do not get treatment. In addition to avoidance, and to interference with normal activities, other red flags for phobias include:

- Fears that are out of synch developmentally: Your child is struggling with issues that are typically resolved at an earlier stage (a teenager afraid of the dark, a ten-year-old afraid of dogs)
- Loss of perspective despite knowledge: Your child loses perspective about the feared situation and her ability to cope. *Bees* want *to sting me, I'll have to go to the hospital.*
- Sensitization with exposure: Your child becomes increasingly distressed and disorganized when you try to work through the fear, rather than being reassured.
- Anticipatory anxiety (planning ahead): Your child asks too many questions ahead of time—will there be a dog there? do we have to eat outside (fear of bees)?—refuses to go places without guarantees

Pathways to Children's Fears and Phobias

Understanding how a fear developed for your child typically reveals the path you need to take to undo your child's faulty or coincidental learning.

COINCIDENTAL LEARNING

Children's fears may not make sense to you until you get down to the child's point of view. Why would a child suddenly develop a fear of bridges, seemingly out of nowhere? It might be a simple matter of a suddenly changed point of view: the family has just traded a car for a minivan, allowing her to see the water below the bridge you are driving on for the first time. You help her see that she is just as safe in her higher perch as she had been in your old car. The worry glitch—*if I can see water, I'll fall in*—needs to be challenged with multiple bridge crossings. An eighteen-month-old suddenly becomes afraid of a tall uncle whom she had adored from the safety of her parents' arms when she was eleven months old. Now, at eighteen months, she's walking, and he's a giant. GUTI in this situation means bringing the uncle back down to the child's level—lying on the floor and playing friendly games so the child can forge a new association, *big uncle is fun,* instead of *uh-oh, big uncle!* The uncle can in successive encounters sit on the floor, then kneel, and finally stand. A child is afraid of monsters in her bedroom, and insists he can hear them breathing. After getting more of the story the parent learns that it's the forced-air heat coming through the vent, and shows the child what happens when the heat is on or off. Having learned the truth, he can begin to rewire. When he hears the heat now, he says, *"heater is on now"*—nothing too scary in that!

DIRECT EXPERIENCE AND MODELING

Some phobias are learned through actual unpleasant experiences, which then carry negative associations, or captions. Every time one of these situations comes up, the brain pulls up the picture and caption, and the circuit is connected. A child who briefly choked on a pretzel at a party worries about birthday parties because *birthday party=pretzels=choke=avoid,* and over time, she may become afraid of eating any hard food, or any food at all. Other incidental aspects of direct experience get encoded as well, such as the location of the event and what immediately preceded it. For example, getting stung by a bee on the patio may lead a child to avoid that patio. Or, if a child throws up after eating toast, she may assume that it was the toast that was the reason, but in fact it was just a coincidence and she was going to throw up anyway because she was sick. It is best if parents keep in mind the possibility of temporal associations, and then by citing a more comfortable example, they can help their child see that the logic doesn't hold. *"If your Gameboy broke in the living room, would you not want to play in the living room ever again, or would you know that the Gameboy would have broken anywhere? How many times didn't it happen in the situation—how many times was everything fine?"*

Some phobias may be learned by seeing or hearing how others respond in a situation. Modeling or imitation is a primary pathway to learning. Spend a minute with any toddler and you will know why. When you squat to be at her level, she squats to imitate you, if you whisper, she whispers, if you scream and jump up and down when you see a spider, you will likely have an understudy mapping your moves. Since experiences are free agents looking for a label, remember that your kids are watching you as a model of competency or fear. Try to remain calm in these situations, or, if you do overreact, go back later and explain what happened. Fear of vomit may in part be influenced by the look of horror on adults' faces when kids throw up, snatching them up to race them to the bathroom as if saving them from an oncoming car.

Finally, the power of the picture can lead to phobias. Seeing a plane crash on television, vivid and tragic, may make a lasting impression because you feel like you are there. Children may acquire intense fears of fires, hurricanes, or large animals by seeing them portrayed on television. The news and other programs may lead children to believe that disasters are a common occurrence—that fires happen easily, that regardless of where you live, weather is *always* devastating. Sadly, many children exposed to the rebroadcasts of the September 11 tragedies believed that each viewing of a falling tower was another tower falling and therefore thought that planes were crashing into towers everywhere. As a picture can overpower a thousand realistic thoughts, be careful what your children watch and make sure you deprogram afterward. Find out what they think of the show, and correct any misconceptions.

The Basic Strategy for All Fears and Phobias: Cognitive Restructuring and Systematic Desensitization

STEP ONE: COGNITIVE RESTRUCTURING

Imagine if you were afraid of choking on dry foods and your first step in treatment was someone forcing you to eat. You would be so busy protecting yourself from perceived harm that the only thing you would learn is that you couldn't trust your therapist! When it comes to fears and phobias, you can't "just do it." Because the underlying belief in phobias is that *contact with the feared situation will cause physical harm,* this belief first needs to be verbalized and analyzed. Then with a more realistic thought in mind—for instance, *choking is rare and the body is built to handle it, eating isn't dangerous for us, if we can relax, our bodies basically know how to do the rest*—you will be more able and willing to approach and interact with your fears. Think about this the next time you suggest that your child "just do it."

First Say the Worry Story, Then Correct It. We saw in the Master Plan that your child needs to right the wrongs of his worries. But before you can correct the misperceptions, your child needs to tell you exactly what he fears. Write out the fears in a worry thought bubble (or role play them with young children), and see if your child can identify the tricks her brain is playing. Look at the suggestions in Chapter 4 for building realistic thinking: run the thoughts down the worry track, look at the outcome pie charts, grade the worry papers, stage a debate between the worry brain and the smart brain, use accurate thoughts to rewire the brain. Other points to consider include:

- If there has been a previous negative encounter with the experience, have the child walk through the pages of that story. Don't stop in the middle at the tough part, and make sure your child tells you how things ended up. Teach him that *once* doesn't means *always*. Did he also learn something helpful from that experience?
- Every fear has some grain of truth. But just because a risk exists, that doesn't mean the worst is likely to happen. Always do research about the fears: look at books, talk to experts—such as vets or pet owners—and learn the facts about how to be safe in the situation. Observe how other children cope with the situation; do they not care about getting hurt, or is their brain giving them different information?

STEP TWO: REAPPROACHING THE FEAR: SYSTEMATIC DESENSITIZATION

Systematic desensitization through gradual exposure is the treatment of choice for phobias. This means breaking down the fear into approachable, manageable chunks, finding your child's starting point—what he is ready to do first—and then using his fear temperature as a guide and working your way from the easiest to the toughest challenge. Starting points vary, as do end points. Many children with phobias are so sensitized to their fear that they even cover their ears at the mere mention of the phobic situation, and for them the starting point isn't an encounter with a spider, it's several steps back. It may mean covering one ear when the word spider is said, then hearing the word without earmuffs, writing the word, saying it in pig-latin, saying it in English, looking at spiders in books, drawing pictures, gathering information, teaching a lesson to an adult about it, practicing breathing and boss back talk with a fake spider, and eventually getting closer and closer to the real McCoy (a spider in a jar with holes poked through the top).

Some fears lend themselves to imaginary exposure. Make an audiotape in which you describe your child facing the fear. Make the tape relevant and realistic by using the information your child gives you about his fears, e.g., an episode of throwing up (*you feel hot and chilled, there's pressure in your throat, you run to the bathroom*) or an encounter with choking (*you eat a piece of candy, it gets stuck and you feel like you're choking, you relax, you cough the candy up, you're okay*). Your child can then listen to the tape several times a day. It will be anxiety-provoking at first, but in essence your child will "wear out the worry tape," it will no longer bother him, and desensitization will be complete. You will know he's listened to it enough when the tape starts to sound boring or silly to him (and he has it memorized and can spoof it).

The end point is also negotiable. Some kids want to be able to just coexist peacefully with their feared situation; in that case the ultimate goal would be to sit and watch TV or read in a room with a spider without paying attention to it. Other kids want to be able to interact with the object; that would mean having spiders crawl on a stick that they hold, or escorting an indoor spider back to its natural habitat via a cup or jar. Remember that as your child progresses with this, his fear will decrease, so he may be able to set a more ambitious goal after he has a few steps under his belt.

How Does Systematic Desensitization Work Best? Think Reciprocal Inhibition. We learned in Chapter 4 that you can't be in two feeling states at once: when a different emotion competes with fear, it chips away at the fear and your child feels less anxious. Relaxation—taking deep breaths while looking at a spider, or making silly faces at the spider—and emotions like anger or bossiness can be used to compete with fear. Humor at the child's level is very effective: for instance Jak tackled his fears of throw-up by pretending to throw up on family members and *planting* fake vomit around the house, to see who got faked (or grossed) out! Working on fear of the dark doesn't have to be gloomy. Kids can have fun by playing flashlight tag in your basement or going on a scavenger hunt for glow-in-the-dark toys. Bottom line—making "worry work" fun doesn't just make it more inviting, it makes it physiologically more effective. Don't be afraid to have fun!

GUIDELINES FOR GUTI EXERCISES

- Since a child's default anxious response is to avoid a fearful situation, *any* interaction a child has with a feared situation is a step in the right direction, even if it seems to you far afield.
- Make a hierarchy or "stairs of learning" for the steps your child will take to reach the goal of overcoming his fear (see Chapter 5).
- After doing research on the fear, have the child teach a parent, grandparent, or sibling what he has learned about the facts of his phobia. He will feel proud and will be reinforcing the "right" messages about the object or situation.
- Have your child practice approaching the feared situation— using stuffed animals, role playing, drawing cartoons—or observe others in the same situation, taking mental notes.

- Children should always approach any exposure with calm breathing and boss back talk ready.

- In the midst of an exposure, do a role reversal: *"Is the bee afraid of you? What is the bee saying—'please don't trap me, then I'll die.'"* Or have your child be a scientific reporter, taking down neutral "data" about the situation. *What do you notice about the dog (color, tail, behavior), or the basement (number of windows, doors, lights)?* This keeps her in smart mode instead of worry mode. She can teach someone else what she learns.

- Make sure your child really has a chance to remain in the situation until his anxiety comes down significantly. An exposure is successful when a child's fear temperature has dropped about 50 percent. Don't leave early. If your child is having trouble, take a few steps back from the immediate situation, but don't leave the premises, or, go back to an earlier challenge first, then see if you can move forward.

- Repeat each challenge on the stairs of learning until it no longer evokes anxiety, and practice several times a week. Daily practice is even better. Celebrate your child's success, and move up to the next step.

- Practice frequently with small exposures and role plays for best results. If there are long intervals between exposures, the child is likely to forget that he managed the exposure and revert back to anxious anticipation.

- Keep track of progress on a chart with stickers or points. Give incentives and rewards (see Chapter 5 for guidelines).

With all phobias, use the steps outlined above. Here we take a closer look at specific strategies and potential challenges of the five phobia subtypes.

The Five Subtypes of Specific Phobia

American Psychiatric Association:
Diagnostic and Statistical Manual (DSM-IV)

ANIMAL TYPE: dogs, cats, bees, snakes, birds, mice

NATURAL ENVIRONMENT TYPE: storms, heights, water

BLOOD-INJECTION-INJURY TYPE: seeing blood, injection, medical procedures

SITUATIONAL TYPE: tunnels, bridges, elevators, flying, driving, enclosed places

OTHER TYPES: choking, vomiting, contracting illness, loud sounds, costumed characters

ANIMAL PHOBIAS

Cognitive glitches. Animals are dangerous, they are nearby, and they *want* to hurt me.

Rewire. Learn how to be safe around (and even enjoy) domestic animals, understand that they aren't vicious but loving. Learn how far away wild animals are, and that we will not have contact with them unless we go looking for them in the zoo or on safari.

Boss back talk. *I am bigger; they are more afraid of me than I am afraid of them. It isn't fair to have to stay inside. Not everyone who goes outside gets hurt. That's rare! I know what to do—if I stand still, I won't get hurt.*

Sample GUTI Exercises

BEES

- Have someone catch a dead or live bee and put it in a jar, work your way up the steps till your child can hold the jar in his hands. Put the offender in its jar across the room, and play "Mother May I" or "Red Light Green Light" until your child gets across the room.

- Increase amount of time spent in proximity to bees. Vary

the difficulty by trying exposures with varying amounts of sunlight and flowers. Keep count of number and types of bees observed.

DOGS

- As with bees, increase duration of time spent near dogs. Have your child watch a dog from a window or door or behind a fence when it is sleeping, see if he can stand closer and closer when it is asleep, then tackle approaching the dog when it is awake. Interact with the dog even from a distance, say "hi," or, "nice doggy," get points for closer encounters.
- Smaller dogs may seem less scary, but they jump more and are noisy. Try a small, quiet dog, or an older, very sedate dog. Golden retrievers are great teachers.

NATURAL ENVIRONMENT PHOBIAS

Cognitive glitches. Weather is dangerous. Things are moving; I can't stop them, and I need to. I don't know what will happen next, and I need to know what happens next in order to feel okay. Bad things always happen in storms.

Rewire. If this were really dangerous, my parents or the other adults in my life would not let me be here. Rain is necessary for plants to grow, and for animals to survive. Rain has been around since the beginning of time. Thunder and lightning are just the soundtrack to the rain. It can feel uncomfortable when things are moving around fast, but I don't need to know what will happen next. That's nature's job.

Boss back talk. *I'm okay, it's noisy but it won't hurt me. It's a surprise and I don't like surprises, but it's just a loud noise, because of electrical charges in the air. Thunder, you are just a big burp in the sky! I'm not planning my life around the weather! It's not my job to know about the weather all the time. Even if I get wet, I can deal with that. I'll change my clothes eventually. The adults in charge will let me know if something isn't safe.*

Sample GUTI Exercises

- Listen to CDs of rain and thunderstorms available from many music stores. Help your child make the sounds of a storm. Use a strobe light or flashlights turned on and off to re-create the experience of lightning.

- Get closer to watching a storm. If your child hides, closes the shades, runs to the basement, or avoids the windows, gradually progress toward looking at the storm from the window. Have your child bring his slow breathing and smart thoughts with him and do an activity while he's watching the storm. He can count the trees and notice if they are moving, and in what direction the rain is blowing. Is the sky all the same color or are different areas different colors? Move up to standing outside during a storm, then going to a friend's house, and going to the movies or some other activity in a storm.

- Sometimes museums have exhibits about the weather, where a child could learn and gain exposure in a safe environment. Your child may need to stand at the back of the exhibit until he gets more comfortable, or he may not be able to stay for the whole thing; focus on what he can do.

BLOOD-INJECTION-INJURY PHOBIAS

Cognitive glitches. It will hurt . . . a lot . . . and forever!

Rewire. Though they may not be sweet, most routine medical interventions for kids are over quicker than you can say . . . this sentence.

Many children (and adults) with a blood/injury phobia experience what is called a vasovagal response—fainting at the sight of blood—a response which often runs in families. There is an initial rise in heart rate and blood pressure, followed by a sudden dramatic drop that leads to sweating, light-headedness, and sometimes nausea and fainting. This response is physiological, not psychological. It may be helpful for these children to look away when blood is being drawn.

Sample GUTI Exercises

- Make it fun if you can. Let your child be the doctor first, and then reverse roles. Practice taking a throat culture by using a lollipop and moving it back along the tongue till you or your child gags. Then your child can enjoy the lollipop.
- Have the child practice on a toy doctor's kit, or (with supervision) actual medical supplies if your doctor will help— let her see that the needles are very thin; with supervision she could "inject" a stuffed animal, use a tongue depressor, or take a blood pressure reading.
- Practice with ketchup or water with food coloring to get used to seeing a little "blood."

Because medical procedures are often necessary, the following suggestions can be used to reduce the child's anxiety. If a child needs to get shots or have blood drawn, or go through a dental or medical procedure, help her to do her easy breathing. Encourage your child to match your breathing rhythm, and look out for hyperventilation, which can also lead to feeling faint. Tell your child's dentist or doctor that your child is feeling a little uneasy about the visit. Many pediatric dentists and doctors have developed a style that is sort of hypnotically distracting—goofy or chatty so that the child feels more at ease and may even be unaware of what is happening. Parents can do their part by staying calm and being emotionally available, but not hovering or focusing on pain. Think of yourself as the container for your child's emotion. You don't want to be shaking the jar.

- Ask the doctor or nurse to tell the child to breathe in *just before* and exhale *just as* the needle goes in. This is an acupuncture technique that reduces the experience of pain. The doctor can just say, "Can you take in a nice breath in, and now out."

- Use planned refocusing to mark the passage of time: have your child imagine progressing through another activity until the end of the procedure. For instance, she can imagine running the bases in baseball—let her know as she rounds each one; a young child can picture feeding the cookie monster cookies. *"The first one is chocolate chip, then comes peanut butter fudge, then oatmeal raisin, almost done!! Just two more cookies and you're done."*

- Use positive visualization: with dental and medical procedures, help your child imagine more padding on the nerves so that it doesn't hurt. Have your child choose the "thickest skinned" animal—a whale, or a bear. *"Okay, put on your whale skin, now your extra pillows. What color are the pillows, how many would you like?"*

- See if doctor or dentist will use a video or music headphones during procedures.

SITUATIONAL PHOBIAS

Cognitive glitch one. Uncomfortable sensations from being physically constricted in small places mean big trouble.

Rewire. *This is okay, it's just a change in setting that my brain is warning me about. Just because I feel uncomfortable doesn't mean I'm in danger.* Some children with these fears are reacting to physical symptoms (the stomach drop on an elevator) and giving them a frightening meaning. Let them know that their stomach feels funny simply because of gravity, and that those sensations are strange but completely harmless.

Cognitive glitch two. If something bad *can* happen, it *will* happen, and I need to know how to stop it.

Rewire. I'm okay, this is safer than crossing the street: My brain is focusing on how awful the danger could be but not letting me remember how unlikely it is. I don't have to know how to fly the plane or run the elevator in order to feel safe. That's not my job. Elevators are for convenience, not for worries!

Boss back talk. *Just because I feel funny, doesn't mean I'm in danger. If elevators weren't safe no one would use them! I'm not listening to the worry talk. Just because something could go wrong doesn't mean it will. I'm not going to walk up five flights just because the elevator could break. If it happens, I'll deal with it!*

Sample GUTI Exercises

- Have your child practice riding the elevator at a department store; he can get points for every floor, and trade in points for a small treat at the store.

- Try changing the station: *"What song is playing in your elevator? If you're thinking about the elevator getting stuck, then you are going to have an unpleasant ride. You can choose what CD to listen to in your mind. Change the station, you don't have to listen to "all fear, all the time!" Sing the worries, say the facts.*

- Tell your child he can compete with anxiety—be silly, do goofy things in the elevator, make funny faces, blow bubbles, sing a song.

- For airplanes: if there are noises and sensations that are frightening to your child, practice taking an imaginary ride, complete with sound effects, and correctly identify the source of the noise. *"That's just the wheels, that's just the engine accelerating—it's louder than our car because the engine is much bigger."*

- For tunnels: your child can practice taking an imaginary ride, going somewhere she wants to go. Have her do her breathing. Mark the passage of time by thinking about something fun, rather than focusing on feeling afraid. For the first part of the tunnel, have her think about her birthday, part two about Christmas, and part three about the last day of school. Then take the ride for real.

GAGGING, CHOKING, OR VOMITING PHOBIAS

If I could devote a whole chapter to any phobia, it would be to vomit. It is the most common fear in my practice, and perhaps not surprisingly, also a very common fear among parents. The fact that it's common does not in any way diminish how disabling it can be. Many adults fear throwing up so intensely that they may delay pregnancy because of a fear of morning sickness (imagine fearing that over labor!!). Fears of throwing up develop because the child doesn't want to be caught off guard by something so terrible. Meanwhile, worrying about vomit can actually make kids feel queasy. There is nothing more nauseating than thinking about throw-up all the time. Think back to the brain train and the power of suggestion. If you start thinking about craving french fries, you want them (even though you didn't want them two minutes ago). If you start thinking about throwing up, you feel nauseous. Some kids have had very unpleasant experiences with vomit, such as throwing up in a public place, or on themselves without a change of clothes, or having a child at school throw up right in front of them. Others have memories of being whisked down the hall to the bathroom by concerned parents, tripling the scare value of throwing up itself. For kids who have had a past negative experience, review it with them. Tell the worry story and make sure you can help give it an ending—where the child is okay.

Cognitive glitches. Eating is risky; I may choke and panic, or even die. If I think about throwing up, that means I'm going to throw up. Once I start vomiting, I'll never stop. If someone else throws up, that means I'm going to throw up.

Rewire. Separate the feelings from the facts. The fact is that chewing and swallowing are automatic; your body is built to keep you safe. Throwing up only happens if you're sick. People always stop throwing up. It is unpleasant but brief, and not dangerous, and your body feels better afterward.

Boss back talk. *My body knows what to do; eating is part of life, it's the easy part, it's not rocket science! These thoughts aren't a sign of nausea, they are a sign of worry! Worrying takes weeks, throwing up takes a few minutes: I'm quitting my worry job—it doesn't protect me anyway!*

GUTI Exercises for Gagging and Vomiting

- Have your child put a lollipop on the roof of her mouth or in the back of her throat—it shows that she can manage that sensation. The gag happens and then the throat relaxes again.
- Practice making gagging sounds; put oatmeal or mashed potatoes on the back of your child's tongue if you need some assistance!
- Let your child watch and listen to her therapist or a parent gag and pretend to throw up. Watch videos that show someone gagging or throwing up *(The Princess Diaries, Snow Dogs, Spy Kids 2, Space Cowboys, Sweet Home Alabama)*. Replay the segment until there's no distress, only normal disgust.
- Your child can rehearse the sights and sounds of vomit (with fake vomit you can buy at any novelty store—or make your own with various creamy soups and frozen veggies), have a gagging contest with the whole family. Play catch with fake throw-up.
- Eliminate safety measures: don't carry around a plastic bag (just in case) or antacids. These tactics only keep the fear alive in your child's mind. It's like bringing your umbrella on a beautiful sunny day.

GUTI Exercises for Choking

- Have your child wear a turtle neck, or a scarf around his neck, or have him hold his neck gently.
- He can swallow small candies (jimmies, Mini M&M's, mini-Chiclets) to relax while swallowing.
- Have your child chew dry foods (pretzels, potato chips) without water.
- Reduce the amount of time your child chews foods (some kids overchew to overprotect from choking).
- Your child can try to talk or read while eating, in order not to overfocus on chewing.

- Make a hierarchy of foods your child avoids—e.g., tough food such as meat and dry food such as chips and nuts—and *wants* to eat again.

For Kids Who Are Afraid of Choking on Pills or Vitamins. Use jimmies, Mini M&M's, or mini-Chiclets to build up a child's GUTI confidence with something tasty first. Do the following exercise with your child: take a bite of food out of your mouth and compare it with the size of the pill. Your child will see that his throat can handle it—he just has to learn that pills are okay. Probably, his throat is in overprotection mode because he thinks that the pill is a "foreign object." With enough practice and good thinking, he will be able to override that danger message and swallow his pills.

FEAR OF FIRE DRILLS

Cognitive glitches. The startle feeling from the fire drill is unbearable. I don't like to be surprised, I have to know when the drill will happen.

Rewire. What kids need to do is to change the message about fire drills, and teach their brain that it is only brief, it is manageable, and they can cope. This way they don't need to be on the lookout all the time. Tell your child that it's his nervous system saying "I don't like that startle feeling." It's just a startle; it's normal, and it will pass. The startle feeling lasts only a minute or less, then it's done. Worrying about the fear just makes it worse.

Boss back talk. *Fire drills are about safety, not danger! I can deal with the loudness, it's only a brief jump, then I can relax! This is to protect me, not scare me! The worry is much worse than the drill! I can live with this kind of surprise!*

Sample GUTI Exercise

- Practice with a kitchen timer, a dryer buzzer, a whistle, or a smoke detector. Take turns being in charge of the sound—

sometimes you can start the alarm, and sometimes your child can. She will notice that the startle is brief, then she feels fine again. Train your child to take a deep, slow breath, and to say to herself, *it's just practice* whenever she hears the loud sound. She can imagine having earphones on so it won't be such a shock to her system.

FEAR OF THE DARK

Cognitive glitches. If I can't see, there must be something there to hurt me.

Rewire. Yes, I can't see well, but I am safe. Nothing has changed. I need the dark to help me sleep. Our bodies don't sleep well if it is light.

Boss back talk. *I am brave, the house is safe, I can take care of myself, I am fine. Worry Bug, stop making me think about scary things! It's sleeping time, not scaring time. Go away, I know I'm safe, and you're being mean!*

Sample GUTI Exercises:

Children from ages 2 to 102 can be afraid of the dark. Likely the ones at the older end of the spectrum didn't have a chance to get used to the dark when they were younger. There may be other, related fears about sleep or falling asleep (see Chapter 13). For older kids the fear of the dark is combined with feelings of frustration and embarrassment that they can't "get over it." The recipe for fear of the dark is usually a combination of two separate fears: being alone and being in the dark. That's why when we're working on fear of the dark, it is usually best to start *during the day* with brief forays into being alone for increasing periods of time.

- Start during the day: do brief errands retrieving items or doing research (how many light switches or windows, upstairs or downstairs). *Walk, don't run!*
- Do a scavenger hunt, hiding items upstairs. Do this first

during the day (to practice being alone). Next, at night, do a scavenger hunt with a flashlight. Hide a few items in different rooms, play flashlight tag, read or have a snack by flashlight, forge new connections between the dark and pleasant experiences.

- For desensitization to the dark itself, gradually reduce the amount of lighting in the child's room. Use glow-in-the-dark stars or stickers to ease the transition to darkness.

- For young children whose fear of the dark is about what is hiding there, GUTI is about playing with the idea of monsters or ghosts. Don't avoid the topic, play with it. Once you have established that monsters aren't real, have fun being monsters. Draw a monster, make monster noises, name the monster, tell a story about it. You've just demonstrated to your child that monsters are imaginary, not real. Make up a silly song about the boogeyman, or a silly story, for example about how he got a cold and couldn't scare anyone, all he could do was sneeze . . .

A WORD ABOUT COSTUMED CHARACTERS

For some anxious children, anything new or unfamiliar registers as frightening. A clown that is supposed to be pleasant or humorous may not be for these children. Normally people don't have painted faces and strange hairdos, so even though the purpose of the clown is entertainment, the experience is scary for the child because it is foreign and he doesn't know what to expect. Looking at costumed characters puts kids on sensory overload—they are huge to the child, often loud, and active—it's too much to process at once. Mascots, children dressed up for Halloween, adults dressed up as cartoon characters, even Santa Claus can be very distressing. A child's senses may be processing the experience as if he were seeing monsters coming alive, which would be frightening for anyone.

The solution is to take a few steps back so that your child gets more distance. Hold her tight, follow the *scenic route* of her experience, and model coping. *Barney does have big eyes—he's like a big doll—Barney is a nice big doll. Barney is waving hello! Hello, Big Barney, I know you are nice but you are so big, I'm not used to you.* When parents explain directly—*Barney isn't real, it's just a person in there*—it may be more scary to the child. Young children even as old as four or five can't distinguish real and not real, so if you explain that there is a person in there, that may be frightening too: *Did Barney swallow that person—are they stuck? Will they get out?* Over time you can work on the idea of masks and costumes, trying them on stuffed animals and then on people, but in the meantime, short and sweet exposures may be preferable.

On the Homefront:
Fear and Phobia Prevention

Don't be surprised if your child finds new things to be afraid of, but be prepared. Rather than swooping her out of what she perceives as harm's way, help her learn that the situation is safe. Back away from the situation as little as possible, but as much as you need to in order for your child to learn this lesson. Fear is about being frozen, faced with what you *can't* do; working on fear is about generating options for what you *can* do instead. With so much to discover about the world, there is much that may at first seem scary. Kids don't know how to understand it all. Understanding is about making connections with things. Help your kids connect with new and unfamiliar experiences by role playing, drawing, imitating, making silly voices—taking the small steps to climb the stairs of learning to success.

- Slow and steady sets the pace. Don't rush—remember that high levels of anxiety are not conducive to overcoming fear.

- Go back to the "scene of the crime." Re-create the situation that generated the fear or phobia, first through talking or role play. Correct the errors, look for *coincidental learning*, finish the story, and then approach the situation in person to see that the "once = always" rule doesn't apply.
- Always try to end the experience on a good note, finding the accomplishment even if the exposure is only a partial success. Keep in mind that there is always the opportunity for more practice.

Don't hope against hope that your child won't develop a fear after something traumatic happens—a dog knocks over your preschooler, or your eight-year-old falls off the waterslide and into the pool, or your fourteen-year-old gets stuck in an elevator. Give it some time, and don't force your child right back on that horse, but try to end the interaction on a positive and constructive note. Have the child verbalize what happened, and see how much she is able to participate in the same situation again. If she is not, this is a clear signal that she needs your help processing and synthesizing what happened and learning about how to handle her thoughts if she is in that situation again.

Renee's Story

Renee had always been fearful of dogs. Her mother remembers that they were trick or treating when Renee was five and she heard a dog barking and ran right in front of a moving car. Fortunately she was not hurt. The family worked around the fear for many years, but Renee began missing out on many social activities because she couldn't go to people's houses if they had dogs. Renee's parents suggested that the family get a puppy to help with her fear. Though Renee was able to go and help pick it out, rather than getting rid of her fear, it made her feel worse because she was afraid *and* she couldn't enjoy her puppy.

Renee came to treatment, and we set up a hierarchy of situations where she could work on thinking straight and breathing calmly as she looked at her dog first from a distance (another room), progressing eventually to "playing" with her from behind a screen door. She would also just look at the dog when it was sleeping. This gave her a chance to know what she thought about the dog without being so scared. She started being able to see that Spice was a sweet dog and was jumping up to play, not to hurt her. She also worked on her command voice so she could say "No" firmly to teach Spice not to jump up. Renee kept a journal each day of how she got closer to her dog, and how her fear level was going down. Seeing the results in black and white really helped her confidence. With a combination of exposures, great support from her parents, and Renee's support from her religious faith, she was able to interact with Spice more and more, and today she is Spice's best buddy. Renee believes that her experience has made her a stronger person. "I am able to go to pet stores and actually admire the dogs. I go to people's houses with no problem, and I am enjoying it so much." She also learned how to speak up for herself because of this fear—for example, asking her friends to hold back their dogs if she wasn't comfortable yet. Her advice to parents, "You always have to push, but some things need a little more time. Be patient, frustration doesn't help!"

✳ Idea Box ✳

- Write down challenges on slips of paper and put them in a jar, or write them on a cootie catcher. Have your child choose daily challenges to work on his fear.
- Have your child become an expert on her feared object—competency burns through fear.
- Have your child interview others about how they cope with the feared situation—and take notes!

CHAPTER 8

✳

From Shyness to Social Anxiety and Selective Mutism

I don't mind helping my daughter break the ice with play dates and birthday parties, but we're not getting anywhere. She gives me such a look of terror and desperation when I mention that it's time for me to leave, how am I really helping her?

Michael can't even make eye contact with kids at school. He is so uncomfortable around other people, he could be the poster child for "painfully shy." When I ask him about friendships he asks, why would people want to hang out with me? I'll probably do something totally dorky and then they'll laugh. He won't give himself a chance, and I don't know how to either.

In the Thick of It: Here Comes the Judge!

To see Rachel at home with her family, you might think she had political aspirations. Jumping into the middle of every argument, expressing herself with the righteous indignation of her teenage credo, she doesn't hesitate to let her feelings and thoughts be known. But as soon as Rachel steps out her front door, *that Rachel* is nowhere to be found—a different person has emerged.

I lose my confidence, I suddenly overthink everything—well, I don't even know if I'd call it thinking. I'm racing, my face feels hot, I'm afraid my words will come out all jumbled, I just feel like I'm in the spotlight, I can feel it. I freeze. I can *feel* people's eyes on me—it's too intense. It gets so unbearable I run to the bathroom. As soon as I'm out of there I feel like I can breathe again, but then I feel like a jerk because all I was doing was talking to friends—not, like, giving a big speech or anything. What is wrong with me?

What makes Rachel suddenly not be herself outside the confines of her house and family? Clearly this is not something she wants to be feeling. If anxiety is about overestimation of risk and threat, then social anxiety is the threat of being scrutinized, judged, or embarrassed. Social anxiety may stem from ancient circuitry that allowed us to scan, not for poison berries or wild animals, but other human beings—and to read, by simply looking into someone's eyes, whether or not they were a threat to us. In fact, explaining social anxiety this way to kids can be very reassuring, even humorous. *Your old brain can't stop looking for danger, and invaders to your tribe. The reason you feel so nervous and sweaty, why your heart races, is that your brain is sending the signal it would if someone were going to bite your head off. What you need to do is reset the radar so that you bring the risk down to size—all you are doing is talking to classmates or approaching the playground, not approaching enemy territory. Keep your body quiet by doing your breathing; keep your thinking neutral, and soon your brain, instead of readying you for an impending attack, will help you just be yourself.*

As many as 5 percent of children suffer from social anxiety. Being around others or anticipating contact with others can make them break out into the equivalent of mental hives. A rush of worries, rules, cautions, criticisms, and catastrophes blows through their mind leaving little room for any other, more composed brain activity. Left untreated, social anxiety in childhood limits opportunities and can lead to difficulties academically, socially, and professionally in adulthood. Fortunately, social anxiety is highly treatable, and kids can learn how to become socially competent and confident.

One of the most painful aspects of social anxiety is how it backfires. As much as these children would like to disappear into the woodwork, their efforts to hide may make them even more visible and their fears more transparent. They feel painfully self-conscious, as you might feel when you are sure that all eyes are on a barely visible cold sore. While any of us may feel our anxiety ramp up a few notches when we are in the spotlight, for kids with social anxiety, it is a traveling spotlight. There is no backstage, everything is in public. Talking or singing in the car, being seen in your front lawn—in any ordinary moment your child feels that he is being constantly scrutinized. If he goes into a situation expecting to mess up, he will be watching every move and will trip over his own feet. If instead he tries to refocus on the interaction and practice social skills in small steps, he will stretch his comfort zone outside the boundaries of his own home and will find that social moments are not only survivable but even enjoyable.

What is especially disabling for kids with social anxiety is the vicious cycle that develops. Anticipating or overestimating negative reactions from peers leads to more withdrawal, which then may lead to real changes in how peers include or don't include the child. Anxious children may be significantly less popular for this reason, and while not actively disliked, their social status may be defined as neglected. This leaves them fewer kids to connect with. They may also feel that their interests are not similar to those of other children, and this may be a rationale for social avoidance. That it interferes with academic functioning is just one more reason for these children to be seen as different from their peers. Afraid to raise her hand in class, speaking so quietly that no one can hear, becoming visibly flustered when called on—all of these situations are toxic to the child, in terms of her own cognition, but also in terms of the child's accrued social history with his or her peers. Left untreated, social anxiety can have devastating effects on a child. With the coordinated help from treatment and from the school, a child will be able to rehearse for *success* in school, rather than being subjected to another round of failure each day. It is not surprising that a large proportion of adolescents with social anxiety simply refuse to go to school.

Red Flags for Social Anxiety

- Anxiety, worry, physical tension about unfamiliar people, places, situations
- Paralyzing concern that she will do something embarrassing or humiliating in a social or performance situation
- Avoiding eye contact even with familiar people (relatives, classmates)
- Speaking in a very quiet voice, or not speaking at all, e.g., unable to order in a restaurant, talk on the phone, raise hand in class, may even get sick on days when required to do an oral report
- Clinging, hiding at school, birthday parties
- Chills, shakiness, feeling hot, blushing in social situations
- Painful self-consciousness about appearance, hair, clothes, face
- Hesitant to respond to other children's social overtures, unable to initiate social contact
- May withdraw at unstructured times—lunch, recess, group activities—rather than risk rejection

Key Treatment Interventions: Fire the Judge, Lower the Stakes, Practice Small Steps!

There are three major components to working with kids with social anxiety. The first step is to turn off that internal judge. This is accomplished by explaining to kids where the judge comes from—what's going on behind the scenes in the brain—and then creating the thinking choices that we saw in the Master Plan. First, they need help challenging and bossing back the negative thoughts they have, and arming themselves with more realistic and adaptive ones. Although establishing a more accurate view of their behavior and others' reactions to it will help reduce the physiological symptoms of social anxiety, the second step is addressing these symptoms directly through breathing and relaxation. The third component is practicing social interactions first through role play, and then for real.

In preparation for GUTI challenges, kids may need some skills brush-up—understanding that communication is always a two-way street and learning some tricks and "lines" to keep conversation going. Once you determine the starting point—whether it's making eye contact, smiling at someone, saying "hi," or calling a friend on the phone—the child needs to practice these small steps until he can approach them with confidence rather than with dread. Another practical matter that must be addressed is the fact that many children have become so avoidant of social situations that other kids may see them as aloof and disinterested and stop trying to include them.

PSYCHOEDUCATION FOR SOCIAL ANXIETY

For Young Children. Everyone gets a little nervous going somewhere new or meeting someone they don't know well. It's like a Worry Mosquito is buzzing around saying the same thing over and over: "It's scary, you can't say hi, don't look at anybody, you might feel silly, it's not going to be fun." We need to teach the Worry Mosquito to quiet down and learn that birthday parties can be scary at first, but after a few minutes you get used to it and find fun things to do. So let's practice what happens at birthday parties—how to say hi, how to decide what you want to do first. That will show the Worry Mosquito that you're the boss!!

For Older Children and Adolescents. Although our nervous system is primed for danger, in today's world, despite some uncertainties, our day-to-day encounters are predictable and safe. But when you have social anxiety, it's like the brain hasn't caught up with the times and prepares your body and mind for a life-threatening encounter when you're just standing in front of the class or walking into a party. Is the boy in front of you going to bite your head off, the class suddenly going to wage an attack on you? The idea of this sounds silly, but that's why your heart races and your palms sweat. The other brain glitch in social anxiety is distorting the risk and the consequences of your actions. You are living under a microscope—the brain is set to analyze every tiny move that you make, every word you say, and every inch of your appearance. Living under that kind of microscope would make anyone feel too nervous to talk. It's like you are heading to school and in your disc-man there's a CD playing, "You suck at this, you're going to make a fool out of yourself, that's a dumb thing to say, that person thinks you're weird." In treatment, you learn how to burn a new CD with more accurate, appropriate (and encouraging) lyrics.

THINKING CHOICES

Develop a realistic assessment of your behavior and people's reactions to it.

For Young Children. While some children will actually express fears about being laughed at or other kinds of social criticism, most children simply demonstrate general feelings of discomfort (freezing, disorganization, feeling scared and embarrassed) and uncertainty in social situations ("I don't know what to do"). For that reason, when working with youngsters you may need to focus less on correcting distortions, and more on inputting self-talk that is calming and also strategic—scripting the normal steps and stages to follow at a birthday party, with relatives, on a play date, or at the playground. Using role plays and cartoon thought bubbles, children can first tell the worry story, then counter it with what another child might think in that situation, and finally, the way they want the story to go. Write the smart thoughts on index cards and have the child rehearse them in front of the mirror or in the car before going to an event.

For Older Children and Adolescents. Using the variety of metaphors in the Master Plan, kids can work on the idea of correcting the worry wrongs and creating a more realistic soundtrack for their life. Have your child run any situation down the brain train track, look at it with the worry glasses and the good glasses, write out the "what ifs" and the "what elses." Ask your child, "What's the worst thing that could happen, and how would you deal with it?" Encourage her to challenge fears like *I might say something weird.* Would she really say something like *aliens have landed on the planet?* "Would a thinking person like you actually say something so random, or is your brain giving you false information? Ask yourself, if you didn't have anxiety, how would you look at this situation?"

Situation: Calling a Friend on the Phone

What if she doesn't know who I am?
What else: Of course she'll know me.
What if she thinks I'm weird for calling her?
What else: Calling people is normal, she'll likely be happy.
What if I mess up when I'm trying to talk?
What else: I could write the words out, but even if I make

a mistake it won't be bad, and I can say, "Sorry, brain freeze," or "Take two." Normal people mess up all the time. They just don't make a big deal out of it.

Have your child write down on index cards some of the neutral or positive self-talk that he finds in his worry investigations. He can practice saying those phrases to himself every day: *"I can do this, people aren't watching my every move, slow down, give yourself a chance. Just because I feel weird, doesn't mean I'm acting weird—it's my anxiety."*

GETTING THE BODY ON BOARD

Often children with social anxiety, especially adolescents, hold tension in their bodies. Diaphragmatic breathing (Chapter 4) gives them an instant solution for the racing heart and other discomfort they feel around others. With regular practice, relaxation training (Chapter 4) allows them to support their breath, amplify their voice, and ameliorate tension in the upper body, face, and hands.

Tape recorders, video cameras, or even mirrors can be powerful tools in helping children to take charge of the social messages they send through their body language and tone of voice. They can use these devices to see what they look like when they smile and experiment playfully with creating different impressions—confident, serious, worried—noticing what it feels like in their muscles. Participating in activities like the martial arts, yoga, drama, or dance are fun ways to help kids feel more confident in their bodies.

SOCIAL SKILLS BRUSH-UP

Making Eye Contact. Young kids can be given the challenge of saying hello to someone and reporting back on their eye color;

they can do research and see how many green-, blue-, and brown-eyed children or adults they see. This way you know they are making eye contact. Older kids and adolescents should know that eye contact is another way of conveying interest in a person or in what they are saying. When you don't make eye contact, people might conclude that you are shy, but they also might wonder if you are being sort of rude or uninterested. If you don't want to send that message—look them in the eye!

Working with Your Child on Conversation Skills. Encourage your child to listen and watch others to see how conversations work. Remind him that conversation is a 50/50 venture and he's not responsible for the whole thing. He can listen for typical conversation topics, hear how conversations start and end, and see the ways that others deal with awkward silences. Other suggestions your child can try:

- Making conversation can be like selling a product on TV. By your tone of voice you can suggest to your audience that what you are saying is interesting and important—"Did you see that great cartoon in the school newspaper?"
- Keep the conversation going: Tell something about yourself, then put out a *hook* in the form of a question for the other person, "I just saw the new Eddie Murphy movie, did you see it? Did you like it?"
- Have a short list of topics that you can bring up if conversation lags—complaining about parents, discussing school, recent movies or CDs, upcoming projects for school, plans for vacation, what's happening in sports.
- Practice conversation in comfortable settings—with other kids in youth group; relatives; a same-sex peer; an opposite-sex peer.

GUTI Exercises

As with all exposures, take the time in advance to plan out the script, playing out possible scenarios of what could happen and generating with your child his choices for responding. Write down the phrases that your child likes and have him practice them in front of the mirror or on video or audiotape. If your child is ready, rehearse those scripts with role playing. If he is not ready, have your child imagine the various scenes from beginning to end, while doing relaxed breathing and inserting coping talk, such as, *"I am ok; I can do this, stay calm."* These new associations of relaxation and competency in a given social situation will replace old feelings of anxiety and dread. To further decrease the anxiety, add some humor: can your child do the role play acting like a favorite cartoon character (*"How would Superman say hi here?"*) or Valley-girl style. Experimenting with different voices often warms up the child so he can find his own.

GUTI exercises are often best conducted with people your child doesn't ever have to see again, like store clerks, deli counter staff, or waiters. Children can practice phone skills by calling businesses from the phone book. These are legitimate calls, not prank calls—ask the store for their hours or location. Encourage your child to make several of these calls in a row until she feels more at ease. She can also casually listen in on other kids' "small talk" before class or in the cafeteria or the bus line and report back three or four things that kids were talking about. Then have her generate conversation topics—movies, homework, siblings, teachers—and come up with two ideas to share about each. Remind your child that if she is not ready to increase her verbal contact with others, she can work on decreasing her anxiety level in social settings, practicing her breathing, relaxed body posture, and nonverbal communications such as nodding or smiling.

Make sure that you reinforce all of your child's efforts at

communicating with praise, stickers, and incentives. Broaden your definition of communication: eye contact and a smile from a child who previously always looked away qualify as a major step in the right direction. Always look for the ways your child has coped as compared with *his baseline,* not as compared to other children.

Sample Exercises for Younger Children

- Smile at a friend at school.
- Say hello to your teacher.
- Tell your teacher one news item (weekend plans, lost a tooth, dog threw up)
- Say hello to two children at school.
- Bring in something from home, such as a long jumprope or special toy to share—this can be an icebreaker.
- Ask a child to play a game with you.
- Join a group of kids on the jungle gym.
- Ask for a movie at the video store, answer the phone at home, place an order in a restaurant.

Sample Exercises for Older Children

- Call a store and find out their hours.
- Call the library and ask if they have a particular book.
- Order a pizza by phone (with parent's permission!).
- Answer the phone at home.
- Ask a student in the cafeteria what time it is.
- Raise your hand and answer a question.
- Compliment a classmate on something.
- Order a sandwich at a convenience store (in person).
- Call a classmate and ask about an assignment.
- Call a classmate and invite her to the movies.

On the Homefront: Eliminating Inadvertent Reinforcement of Social Anxiety

Explaining that a child is "shy" is something that we all naturally do when we see him shrinking back from a welcoming overture or being rendered speechless and unable to reciprocate a friendly hello. The problem with "shy" is that it is a role, and once cast in it a child begins to identify with it. It boxes him in. It's not that shy kids don't want to be around people or don't want to socialize. If this were case, the distress wouldn't be there. More likely kids who are uncomfortable with social contact want very much to connect, but several problems are getting in the way—either they don't know how, or they anticipate very unfavorable reactions from others, or they feel so physically anxious even thinking about it that they feel they have no choice but avoidance. "Shy" also suggests that the problem is not a big deal—either the child is stuck with it, or he'll outgrow it one day. As one mother put it, "When people say shy, it minimizes the issue. It's really much more than that. Social interaction is very painful for him and he needs help."

Begin to see your socially anxious child not as stuck in shyness, but as working slowly on a continuum toward connection. When your child seems frozen with fear at family gatherings or birthday parties, rather than saying, *"He's shy,"* say, *"Oh, Justin will be ready to play a little later, he just needs some time to warm up."* Or for your older child, find a way of welcoming him into the conversation, even if he is not ready to talk: *"Michael is our thinker, you'd be surprised with the things he comes out with after he's taken it all in."* To help start your child over the bridge to socializing, decide before you go to an event whom he feels most comfortable saying hi to first, and role play that hello. Whatever the starting point—find that first step, practice it, and be ready to try it.

SLOW AND STEADY WINS THE RACE

Though you may be tempted to rush your child into social situations, resist. Your child's history, and her imagination, are filled with social failures, embarrassments, and humiliating experiences. You want to choreograph her recovery to ensure that she is logging experiences in the "success" category. Think small. Push your child to keep working on some aspect of increasing participation and decreasing withdrawal in social situations—a precipitous leap forward may backfire and have your child refusing to even try. Be patient with the small steps, such as saying hi, and practicing with non-peers. Better to bloom late than to have her social future nipped in the bud.

SCRIPTED ROLES: A REPRIEVE FROM
PERSONAL RESPONSIBILITY

A welcome inconsistency in some children with social anxiety is how wonderfully they can do in class plays or concerts. It's as if they are able to leave their doubts and hesitations at the door when they step up on stage. For these children, their anxiety is about saying something stupid, or not knowing what to say, or being stuck with silence. A scripted role removes the responsibility for those "unknowns" and allows kids to relax, knowing that they have memorized "the right thing to say." In fact, acting classes can sometimes provide adolescents with the opportunity to get the practice "in groups" that they can't get by themselves. If your child has any inclination in the direction of the performing arts—pursue it.

Summary of Interventions for Social Anxiety

Cognitive Glitch	Fix
Excessive self-focused attention: looking at your behavior under a microscope, micromanaging	Widen the view, back up; keeping such close track would mess up anyone
Overthinking responses	Simplify: there is no one right answer to a question (other than in math!); everyone's entitled to their opinion
Body preparing for an emergency, sudden onset of criticism or attack by others	Reset the panic button to normal by doing breathing, muscle stretching, refocusing on the real situation in front of you

Julie's Story

Julie, now fifteen, has always been on the quiet side. Since she had been with the same group of kids since kindergarten, Julie established a good group of friends over the years. But when she started junior high in a much larger school, Julie was getting lost in the crowd. She wanted to fit in and be noticed, wanted to be part of what was going on in classes, but her heart would race just thinking about talking. Over the course of the year, she faded into the woodwork, blaming herself for not being confident, spending most of her time in class trying to muster the courage to say something. She felt so frustrated with herself—what was wrong with her that she couldn't do a simple thing like talk while everyone around her was gabbing away?

Things got worse when girls started to go to mixers with the all-boys' school. Julie felt like it was so hard to get the boys' attention already—let alone if she was a nervous wreck. Following the lead of friends who seemed outgoing and popular, she tried liquor from her parents' cabinet a few times and liked the effect—she felt free from her doubting thoughts. An honest girl with good judgement, Julie didn't want to hold back from her mom, but she was also scared that this would lead to alcoholism. She also worried that even though she was freer from worry, she didn't really trust herself. She wanted to feel calmer but also wanted to stay in control. Julie's mom did find out and was shocked and upset at the lying, the sneaking, and of course the use of alcohol. Fortunately Julie's mom wanted to hear why this had happened. When Julie told her how hard it was to sit in school or look at people, let alone go to a dance, she knew that her daughter's pain was real and needed to be addressed.

In treatment, Julie was relieved to know that social anxiety is more than just shyness, that all of those nervous feelings and confusion result from the brain processing the situation as a very high risk and readying the body for a major attack. She saw that instead of helping her, this protective mechanism was getting in the way of her acting normally. She wanted to learn how to dismantle that thinking process herself. She worked hard to counter her worry thoughts—she realized she wasn't a freak, but that her mind was making her feel that way. She decided to take some risks when she realized that nothing she would say could be that bizarre. She practiced doing breathing exercises at home and used them when she was talking to kids at school. Tired of people saying "what?" when they couldn't hear her, she worked on relaxing her body so that her voice didn't sound like it was trapped inside her throat. She practiced in front of a mirror, relaxing her face and upper body so that she wouldn't look so tense. Talking more in class, and finding kids smiling or spontaneously saying hello gave Julie the confidence to ask other kids to eat lunch with her and even trade e-mail addresses so she could converse with them online at night.

Within weeks Julie saw great progress. Though her heart might race when she stepped into the spotlight, asking a boy to dance or raising her hand in class, it was less intense over time, and she was able to calm herself more quickly. She still would initially hear the old thoughts (*you're going go mess up, you'll say something stupid*), but her second thoughts (*you can do this, smile, just start, it will get easier*) began to come to her without so much effort. Today Julie feels more confident in her own abilities, feels less tense going to school, and naturally smiles more because she no longer feels like she's auditioning on stage all the time—she has the part, this is her life.

Selective Mutism: When the Words Get Stuck in Your Child's Throat

If your child talks comfortably at home, but is unable to talk as soon as she steps outside the door to school or a birthday party, no matter how much you may coax, she may have selective mutism. While well-meaning adults may find the discrepancy in the child's speech baffling, the way the brain is wired in people with anxiety, it is not hard to imagine that the child is getting signals that home is safe and not-home is not-safe. The child is mortified by taking the risk of speaking (and after not talking for a while it gets scarier and scarier—what will his voice sound like?), so in self-defense, he speaks only in selected situations—at home, at school only with peers or only with teachers, or neither. For some kids it begins as purely physiological—they freeze up. For other children there are faulty but understandable assumptions about the risk of participation, and the task is to correct them and give them multiple opportunities for practicing speech of some sort. Left untreated, selective mutism, like other types of social anxiety, only becomes more debilitating. However, with systematic cognitive-behavior therapy, patiently delivered, kids will begin to participate verbally more and more.

Red Flags for Selective Mutism

- Does not speak in certain situations, such as at school or social events
- Can speak normally in settings where they are comfortable, such as in their home
- Child's inability to speak interferes with his ability to function in educational and/or social settings
- Child appears to freeze up, becoming stiff and statuelike in target settings
- Mutism has persisted for at least one month

TREATMENT FOR SELECTIVE MUTISM

As with other anxiety disorders, a child with selective mutism is not simply a little uncomfortable, and will not just outgrow it. Children grow increasingly isolated, frustrated, and angry, and feelings of low self-esteem are inevitable as they experience daily negative attention from others waiting for them to talk. They are vulnerable to other psychological difficulties. Fortunately, according to the leading spokesperson on selective mutism, Dr. Elise Shipon-Blum, the prognosis is excellent with proper diagnosis and treatment.

Anxiety Management Strategies

- Correct distortions in people's reaction to the child's lack of speech
- Teach realistic, supportive self-talk
- Begin systematic desensitization to the target setting—help the child gain comfort in school

- Positively reinforce any approximation of communication in the target setting—begin with smiles, notes, playing a simple instrument, eye contact, reading a one-word script, eventually spontaneous speech.

ENVIRONMENTAL ACCOMMODATIONS

Provide dry-erase boards, or index cards with commonly asked questions that the child can present when needed. Sometimes children will be able to speak with one or two peers but not with a teacher; if this is the case, the child can be linked with a buddy to deliver whispered messages. Allow oral presentations to be taped at home. Teachers should not call on the child unless this is something within the child's repertoire or comfort zone. Sometimes answering questions they are sure about, with some warning ahead of time, can help kids to feel that they are participating at their comfort level.

✳

CHAPTER 9

From Clinginess to Separation Anxiety and Panic Disorder

An Inside Look at Separation Anxiety:

I want to think that Nikki is a happy child, but every night she's afraid that someone is going to die and wants me to reassure her. Do other families talk about death every night? This doesn't seem normal.

Josh is eleven and still sleeps in our bed. I know it's a problem. I keep thinking he'll outgrow it. He'd be mortified if his friends knew. Is it a fear, or more like a habit now? Either way, I don't know how to help him.

An Inside Look at Panic Disorder:

Maria came down the other night looking like she'd seen a ghost. She had these strange feelings like she was in a dream or a movie. She said it felt weird to look at her hands, they felt like they were someone else's; she was terrified that she was going crazy, and now she doesn't want to leave my sight because she's afraid it will happen again. This sounds like a panic attack to me, but I don't know how to explain that to a teenager.

The tough thing about panic is that it hits without warning and it is immediately at a 10 on the anxiety scale. It's hard as a parent to give up the illusion of power—that I could or should be able to make it all go away. I've learned that if I can help her just think about breathing—just breathing—then I get her back.

Separation and Panic: Born of the Same (Dis)Connection?

CLINGING FOR DEAR LIFE

At somewhere between eighteen and twenty-four months, toddlers learn to climb the stairs and run around the yard, and just then, with the winds of freedom whistling at their backs, an interesting phenomenon occurs—they panic and want Mom! This acute but developmentally expected separation anxiety is necessary for their survival—ensuring that they won't break the ties to their source of protection—and resolves itself within several months. The young child learns through practice back and forth from home base that even though she runs away to pursue an interesting bug, friend, or trip with Grandma, she can come running back into Mom's welcoming arms . . . Mom's still there. Over the next several years this lesson—that separations are survivable, that freedom is good, and that reunions can be trusted—is tested and reinforced and serves as the foundation for children's confidence in independent exploration of the world. Though some children will master these separations earlier, typically by age five or six most children are able to separate confidently.

In contrast, children with separation anxiety disorder (SAD) have a glitch in this connection process, and rather than building confidence with successive separations, they experience each separation as a crisis. Children with SAD do not *feel* safe unless they are actually with a parent, and even then they may be troubled by future potential threats to their parents. Worries—is the parent ill/happy enough/going to die/too tired/upset?—consume much of his time. SAD is a debilitating condition for both parent and child, often limiting mobility for both.

Panic disorder, less common in children, is characterized by sudden surges of anxiety, and accompanied by unexplained and uncomfortable physical symptoms—experiencing dizziness or a racing heart, becoming hot, tired, or faint, or feeling detached or unreal. Though these symptoms are entirely harmless, the child doesn't understand what is happening to him. These sensations are experienced as signs of danger and lead instantaneously to thoughts of being out of control, and fear of dying, suffocating, or going crazy. Children become fearful that this surprise attack will occur again ("fear of the fear," or fear of the uncomfortable feelings of fear) and to play it safe (in order to survive), they begin to avoid situations where panic *might* occur. They may feel the need to stay close to home, which may look like separation anxiety disorder, but they are not concerned with their parents' well-being, they are afraid for their own.

This experience of feeling safe only within a certain distance from parent or home is one that SAD shares with panic disorder, and one reason why current theory posits that separation anxiety (most common in seven- to nine-year olds) is an early manifestation of panic disorder (most common in teenagers and adults). Further support for this hypothesis comes from the finding that nearly half of all adults with panic and agoraphobia (not venturing out because of fear of a panic attack, literally "fear of the marketplace") report having had separation anxiety in childhood.

FROM BEING IMMOBILIZED WITH FEAR TO CREATING A MOBILE SENSE OF SAFETY

For children with both these disorders, the experience of just feeling safe in day-to-day life is a full-time job. These children despairingly ask *"am I okay?"* and that question is not in reference to the distant future, or even the near future—it's the immediate present. It's as if kids with panic and SAD are gripped by an animal from which they need to wrestle free. In both panic and SAD, children hyperventilate, feel dizzy, and can become hysterical and out of control, which is not necessarily characteristic of social anxiety, GAD, or OCD. There are, however, important differences in the treatments for panic and separation anxiety disorder.

Children with separation anxiety need to tolerate increasingly longer separations and need to replace the "away from Mom = danger" circuits with "I can be safe even when I'm alone" and "alone is temporary" circuits. Children with panic need to relabel the sudden onset of physical symptoms as a misfiring or faulty signal and learn to reset their body's alarm system when it goes "testing 1–2–3." This is accomplished physically by breathing and relaxation exercises, and mentally, by relabeling the panic messages as false alarms, then venturing into situations where there is a fear that panic may occur, such as school, the mall, a supermarket, or movie theater.

The rest of this chapter will address these two disorders separately, with solutions for creating a sense of safety both in the home and outside it by addressing both thinking errors and physical symptoms. With these strategies in mind, parents will be able to nurture their child's safe launching into life. If your child has symptoms of both disorders, as do many, familiarizing yourself with the strategies will help you cover all your bases. If your young child is showing signs of difficulty with separation, or is feeling unsafe because of physical symptoms (feeling dizzy or too hot) you may be able to prevent a larger problem by teaching him or her how to manage these harmless but frightening experiences, using GUTI exercises to shore up the lessons.

SEPARATION ANXIETY DISORDER

Some children may be slow to warm up, and need extra coaxing and time to get used to changes. Though they may cling and be cautious at first, they *benefit* from extra time to transition. Their hesitation is about what they are approaching when they venture out, rather than whom they are leaving behind. On the other hand, children with SAD are often upset if they just imagine separating, even when they are with their parents, or even when the parents are just out of sight. Your child may begin to limit her mobility—and yours—by following you to the bathroom, keeping track of you at all times, calling out every few minutes, "Where are ya?" or more covertly, calling out unnecessary questions just to get a signal back to locate Mom or Dad's proximity. For the child with SAD, the perception and experience of separation is traumatic, as is her anticipation of it. Children with separation anxiety may feel that a bedtime "good night" is good-bye forever, that leaving them at school in the morning is forever, or that finding their parents in the school carpool line is a "Where's Waldo?" challenge.

Saddled with an overestimation of risk—ordinary separations feel monumental—and an underestimation of coping ability—a basic feeling of being unsafe unless they are with the parent—children with SAD are unable to adapt and habituate to the stress of separating. A child's lack of confidence in the safety and predictability of life can sometimes result from real traumatic experiences such as Mom being in the hospital, being in the hospital themselves, or being faced with a series of stressors such as the death of a grandparent, illness in the family, or a car accident. Other children may be born with a system primed to have difficulty with separations in the absence of any acute stressor.

The Challenge of SAD:
When Things Get "Excluciating"

Children with separation anxiety hang on tighter in an effort to allay the awful thoughts and feelings they have about being apart from their parents or losing them. It is not manipulation, it is desperation. The problem is that one can never feel safe when one is feeling that threatened or desperate. The two feelings are diametrically opposed. Parents are placed in a corner—they want to comfort but see that no amount of hanging on seems to help; they want to facilitate independence, but this is registered as abandonment by kids who then clutch closer. It is hard to find words to describe this pain born of love and the threat of abandonment. My twelve-year-old patient Sarah coined a phrase that described the excruciating feeling of being excluded by or pushed away from a parent when you feel the desperate need to hang on for dear life—"it's excluciating!"

Freeing your child from separation anxiety and panic requires that you understand your child's no-fault faulty processing of separations so that you can reinforce the idea that he is safe. The brain is playing the trick of having the child focus on how *awful* it would be to never see a parent again and manipulating his feelings terribly, all the while withholding the information on how *unlikely* that would be. Anyone presented with that version of the separation story would cling. The solution is not more reassurance, but recasting the issue—*the picture of separations being forever was never right in the first place.* Relabel the experience: *Brain Bug thinks this is forever; we've got to teach it what good-byes really mean!* Once new healthy circuits have been forged for separations, the risk is brought down to size, and kids and parents can begin the process of practicing successful separations. Imagine that by teaching your child how to separate you could transform a fearful moment into a

confident one twice a day, 365 days a year, for eighteen years—
that's over thirteen thousand transactions that could go well.
What better motivation to embark on this work?

Does Your Child Have Separation Anxiety Disorder?

SAD is diagnosed when several of these symptoms are present
for at least four weeks and interfere with the child's and family's functioning (going to sleep, school, work).

Red Flags

- Extreme distress upon actual or imagined separations
- Crying, clinging, tantrums, vomiting upon separation
- Nightmares about harm to parents
- Reluctance or refusal to leave the house or be apart from parents
- Frequent checking, reassurance-seeking about safety of loved ones
- Discomfort or inability to be in a separate room, or on a separate floor from parent
- Frequent calling out to parent (at home) to establish his or her whereabouts
- Frequent phone calls home or insistence that parent stay home when child is out
- Difficulty or inability to sleep in own bed
- Difficulty attending school, frequent calls home, trips to nurse's office
- Unable to go on play dates, field trips
- Desire for parents to drive in separate cars as a safety precaution
- May report unusual experiences like eyes staring at them, discomfort being in a room alone

Primary Treatment Interventions for
Separation Anxiety: Connecting the
"Good-bye" Circuit to "See You Soon"

COGNITION: CHANGE THE THOUGHTS AND THE FEELINGS (AND ACTIONS) WILL FOLLOW

The first step in working on SAD is to compassionately relabel your child's fears as resulting from misinformation from the brain. He needs to understand that he is operating on the signals his brain is sending him, but the signals are false. Few of us would be willing to jump off a cliff, but if we found out that it was really just a curb, that would change everything.

This is accomplished by using the many interventions described in the Master Plan to increase realistic thinking. With younger children, parents can relabel the worry voice as Meany Brain playing tricks, and then role play how the child would teach Meany Brain new lessons: namely that the child doesn't have to worry, that parents come back, and that thinking bad things only makes a child *feel* more scared, it doesn't make the bad thing more true. Through role playing and drawing pictures of separations, the child can then generate brave and smart statements to rehearse when preparing for separations. Older children can consider how they would look at the situation if they didn't have anxiety, list their "what ifs," counter them with "what elses," and look at separations through the two different tracks of the brain train. They can also identify which tricks the brain is playing (see Chapter 4)—looking at how awful versus how unlikely something is, or focusing on the feelings, not the facts. Thought-Likelihood Fusion, or TLF, described in Chapter 4, is another common trick in SAD: *if I thought about an ambulance, that means my parents are going to get in an accident.* Help your child see that the mere presence of a thought doesn't in any way increase the likelihood it will come true.

Boss Back Talk

- Just because I can imagine something bad happening, that doesn't make it true.
- My parents are going to be fine, they always come back, stop bugging me!
- I know how separations work! This is a small risk, I'm not jumping over a lake—it's just a puddle—stop making this a big deal!!
- My friends don't want anything bad to happen, but they don't have to worry about it all the time. Well, neither do I!
- Stop preparing me for something awful—the worst thing that is happening is listening to you!

PHYSIOLOGICAL INTERVENTION:
COMPASSIONATE LIMIT SETTING FOR THE NERVOUS SYSTEM

Slowing Down a Runaway Train. Kids with SAD can get out of control emotionally very quickly. The mere mention of a separation sends them spiraling. A child with SAD has difficulty reigning in emotion because his nervous system delivers more intense distress than do those of his non-SAD counterparts. Sometimes crying can help a child move through a situation, but often kids with SAD only escalate with crying. When they see themselves falling apart, they get increasingly out of control. Because being out of control isn't good for anybody, therapists, parents, and teachers need to compassionately direct these kids to slow the body down. You don't want to inadvertently *reinforce* the deterioration by talking with them through their tears. Say things like "in a minute when your breathing slows down, you'll feel a little better and we can talk about this." Or, "hold my hands and breathe with me, then we can talk." The directions below can be used with children with SAD and panic if they are in the throes of an episode. Teaching children how to do balloon breathing (see Chapter 4) can proactively help them keep their anxiety from escalating. They can be instructed to use breathing techniques in challenging situations such as falling asleep on their own, or going to school.

Voice	*Try to just tell me in a regular voice when you are ready; slow down the crying; wait till you've calmed down, then you can explain—don't try to talk now*
Breathing	*Slow down your breathing, breathe with me, hold my hands, look at me, do balloon breathing, breathe slowly into a paper bag*
Body Position	Help child sit in a chair, try to have him hold your hands rather than clinging or lying on the floor
Thinking	Orient child to the present, let her know that she is in no danger, that the feelings of fear will pass soon if she can stay calm. *Your mind just gave you a bad signal that you aren't safe; you are fine, these feelings will pass if you turn off the alarm*

BEHAVIORAL INTERVENTIONS

Once you have established a more realistic picture of separation and reunion, your child is ready to begin *acting* on that new belief. Kids need lots of GUTI practice, at a manageable level, to get confident that they can handle separations. Though parents, especially frustrated parents who have been stuck at home for months or even years, may be tempted to book tickets for the weekend getaway at the first chance, it is important to remember that small steps are essential to lasting success. General guidelines follow, then sample exercises for young children and older children.

General Guidelines for Working on Separation Anxiety

- Establish a hierarchy for separations, from the easiest to the toughest, using your child's fear thermometer as a guide. Remember, separation is in the eye of the beholder: ask your child what step he is ready to take first. Though the goal is stretching the amount of time that parent and child are successfully apart, it may be preferable to accomplish this through stretching the amount of time that the *parent is away*, as opposed to increasing the time that the *child is away*. If the child can remain on the familiar territory of home (with a sitter), he only has to cope with the challenge of separating; if he ventures out he is coping with the dual demands of a new situation *and* separation. Look at the Anxiety Equalizer figure in Chapter 5 to consider the impact of different factors, such as time of day or familiarity with the setting, in planning exposures for your child. The challenge list you generate becomes the risers for the stairs of learning.

- Remember that nighttime coping is generally the toughest; work in earnest on daytime separations first—this will give your child confidence to master the night.

- Get your boss back talk ready. Your child should have "cue cards" to help him remember what to think (e.g., *this is fine, don't think how awful, think how awfully unlikely, Mommy loves me, she'll be back soon, Worry Bug go away!*).

- Role play or rehearse what the child will say or do when the parent is away. Switch roles so that your child gets to be the parent. It is often enlightening for parents to hear how kids think you should be responding to them.

- Time flies when you're having fun. Make a schedule of activities that your child can do during a separation exposure. Even teenagers will benefit from this structure. *What would you do with this time if you weren't nervous or worried?*

- Use sticker charts to keep track of young children's courage challenges. For older kids, points can be logged to trade in for extra computer time, a CD, or other treat.

GUTI EXERCISES: VERY YOUNG CHILDREN (4–7)

- Make a "good-bye book" that your child can read when you go out or when the child goes to preschool. Have your child draw or dictate the story. In the beginning of the story, the child is saying good-bye to the parents; in the middle are pictures and directions for what she can do while the parents are out (play games, color, read books) and what she can say to herself if she is worried (*Mom always comes back; shoo, shoo, Worry Bug!*). The last page of the story is the happy reunion.

- Make a picture or list of things for your child to do while Mom and Dad are gone. Your child can illustrate and decorate the list.

- Drawing on ideas generated through role playing, make a list of brave statements that your child can say if he's feeling scared.

- Practice brief separations.

- Make good-byes short and sweet (see discussion in "On the Homefront" later in this chapter).

- Role play good-byes. Let your child play the parent role—you'll hear what he wants you to tell him. When you play the child, don't overdo the drama; it will frighten and overwhelm your child.

Sample Hierarchies for Young Children

Establish independence in the house

Parents should work on two factors simultaneously: increasing physical distance between child and parent, and increasing the time the child is able to engage in independent activities.

- Child sits next to parent, not on lap
- Child engages in independent activity such as reading, not shared activity
- Child follows parent to the bathroom but sits outside door and reads a book or draws a picture
- Mom leaves room to get laundry or make a phone call for increasing periods of time
- Child leaves Mom to do brief errands—gathering toys or books, getting on pajamas—in different areas of the house

Establish independence outside of the house

- Parent goes to pick up mail, child stays busy (supervised) in the house
- Parent goes out for increasing periods of time (during the day)
- Parent goes out for increasing periods of time (at night)
- Child goes to play date with Mom there—in same room, then in separate room
- Mom leaves play date (or birthday party) for increasing periods of time
- Child goes to play date or birthday party alone

Establish independence at bedtime

- Parent tucks child in, then increases physical distance from child; if starting point is parent lying in bed, move to sitting in bed, sitting on floor, sitting by door, then outside the door

- Reduce the amount of time spent in room at bedtime, checking on the child every few minutes instead
- Child is reinforced for staying in bed

GUTI EXERCISES: OLDER CHILDREN AND TEENS

- Derive list of "courage errands"—going to separate room, then separate floor to pick up items, get a snack, etc. Work toward *walking,* not running on these errands. Have sibling or the family dog go with child if she's not ready to go it alone.
- Increase time spent at school, decrease number of phone calls home.
- Establish bedtime routine where parent checks on child, child doesn't check on parent. For seven-to-ten-year olds, have child write in a journal or leave notes to Mom in a special mailbox rather than calling out.
- Use Anxiety Equalizer in Chapter 5: Find the steps your child is ready to take—going to a good friend's house in the daytime, in good weather, etc., move up to stretching the amount of time spent at a friend's, including nighttime.

Sample Hierarchy for Older Children and Teens

- Stay inside with parents outside in the yard
- Stay home while parents go for a walk around the block
- Go to friend's house in afternoon, parents stay at home
- Go to friend's house till 7 P.M., parents stay home
- Go to friend's house during the day, parents not home but at agreed-upon location
- Go to friend's house without knowing parents' specific plans
- Go to friend's house until 10 P.M.
- Do a sleepover at friend's house

On the Homefront:
New Steps in the Pas de Deux

Families aren't happy to find themselves in the separation anxiety dance, but what can be reassuring is that in changing this dance both parent and child can lead. Your child will be working on the courage challenges above, and you can make sure that you are giving your child appropriate opportunities to practice separating. Many parents who have been dealing with SAD for a long time speak a language of defeat—*I couldn't go to the party, she wouldn't let me.* Shift your response to a strategic one. Pose such questions as: *How can we make this easier for you? What part of this are you ready to do? What would you like to do while we are out?* You must take the distress seriously and respond empathically, but with a plan to help your child move past the distress. When parents don't rush to the rescue, but instead give it a few minutes, kids have an opportunity to see what they can do. It's like leaving a crying child at the sitter or at school—the tears are more likely to stop when the parent *leaves,* not when the parent *stays.*

Sometimes parents themselves have separation anxiety. If you are in this situation, use the strategies in this chapter on yourself first—what's your worry story about being alone? What's the smart story you want to think instead? If you are finding it hard to address these issues in your child because of your own lingering separation anxiety, please seek help. It will make a world of difference for both of you.

TO SLEEP ALONE, OR NOT TO SLEEP ALONE: THAT IS THE QUESTION

Many kids with separation fears have difficulty sleeping in their own rooms. They may sleep in the parents' bed, on a sleeping bag in their room, or sometimes even camped outside the door. Deal with this in steps. For one youngster, eight-year-old Kelly, we made a map from her parents' door to her room and divided the route into steps that she thought she could take each week, inch by inch. Just making the map helped Kelly see the challenge as more manageable, and she came in the next week saying that she was back in her room. Not all kids will be so eager, but put out the expectation that your child will be able to sleep alone someday soon. See more in Chapter 13 for specific strategies on dealing with nighttime fears.

IS IT MANIPULATION?

Kids don't try to manipulate, but they may not take the initiative to say no to what they think is a good thing. When you lie in bed with your child for forty-five minutes, or linger at preschool for a half an hour each morning, your child won't remind you that the experts say brief, solid good-byes are better than long drawn-out ones, but you need to know best. If you always stay forty-five minutes, your child won't ever learn that he or she can actually handle five minutes even better.

Making the Clean Break: Dealing with Clinginess and Encouraging Confident, Healthy Separations

- Find good ways to say good-bye from early on. *Don't sneak out without saying good-bye*—kids don't do well with disappearances. It doesn't give them a chance to build confidence and trust. Have the courage to take a good look at your child so he remembers your smile, rather than the sight of you sneaking away.
- When you say good-bye, don't add fuel to the fire—"I wish I didn't have to work either, I'm going to miss you all day too." Instead say, "It's always hard at the beginning, but the scared feelings won't last. We'll have a happy reunion when we get home. We'll talk about our days."

- Help your child transition to another adult (teacher) or to an activity before you leave.
- Be positive and encouraging about new situations: Help your child look through the smart glasses and see what might be fun or interesting in the new situation.
- Give opportunities for your child to practice small separations.
- Use transitional objects—pictures of family, stuffies, favorite snacks, favorite books to bring a little bit of home to the new situation.
- It's often easier for the parent to leave on brief outings for GUTI exercises (so the child stays in familiar surroundings) rather than having the child venture out.
- Don't even joke, ever, about not coming back, or calling the police to pick them up for bad behavior. These words, however lightly delivered, can be devastating to a child with anxious wiring. Joke about funny things, not about scary things.

✳ Parent's Cheat Sheet for Separation Anxiety ✳

- Remember, your separation-anxious child needs *more* practice with separations, not less.
- Go for frequent practice with small separations, rather than occasional separations with a higher degree of difficulty.
- Help your child get his thinking straight—separate the thoughts from the feelings.
- A watched door never opens . . . schedule activities for your child to do while waiting for your return.
- Keep your part of the good-bye short and sweet. Be brave and confident—you'll show your child that this is safe. Staying longer keeps you stuck in suspended animation and just defers the moment when your child can begin to cope.

Do's and Don'ts

- Do watch your own emotions—be brave. Your child will be watching your face for cues and will get more upset or frightened if he reads distress on your face.
- Do make good-byes short and sweet. Remember that your child will adjust within a few minutes of your leaving.
- Don't sneak out—show your child that good-byes are manageable.
- Don't get angry if your child is having difficulty letting go. Try to keep the emotional temperature low—just firmly say that you need to leave now.
- Do get your child involved in an activity before you leave the situation.
- Do tell your child ahead of time how long you'll stay and then stick to it.
- Do see the good-bye as a creative mutual work-in-progress. Make a simple good-bye routine that gives you both a second to enjoy each other.
- Do take into account such variables as time of day, proximity of parent, and familiarity of setting when creating your separations hierarchy.
- Don't overshoot the goal by underestimating how challenging separations can be for your child. Try to stick to a hierarchy of practice separations. For longer good-byes—a parent who travels or won't be home by bedtime—have a phone call or leave a note. Make a special calendar with words or pictures to show how many days until Mom or Dad come home. Plan special activities each day to help time fly.

Lena's Story

Lena, a teenager with extreme separation anxiety and panic disorder, was unable to attend field trips at school or even let her parents out of her sight at home. She couldn't go to friends' houses, had great difficulty when her parents left her with a sitter, and didn't want her parents to drive anywhere together—the idea of losing them both in an accident was overwhelming. In treatment she learned about panic and separation anxiety and relabeled those thoughts as the work of "Fuzz Guy." She fought back with "Smart Girl." In treatment Lena began taking small risks, walking to school, having her parents walk around the block while she stayed home, reducing the length and intensity of her good-byes. She was improving but had several challenges ahead. Then one day Lena's mother announced tentatively that there was an out-of-town business conference she'd like to attend for a week. Having braced for a difficult reaction from her daughter, Lena's mother was completely taken aback when Lena said, "Mom, I want you to go, I know how important this is to you"—this from a child who just a week earlier was still clinging to her mom in tears when she was going to go out for the evening. Lena had turned a corner. What this confirmed for the entire family is that as much as Lena may have *wished* that her mom would not go—because that would be easier—the real Lena *wanted* her mom to go and do what she needed to do in her own life. Not only did she survive this trip, which might have been a strain even for a non-anxious child, Lena began to take more independent steps—taking a train into the city, walking to Sunday school, going to friends' houses. She was on her way!

Isabel's Story

At age seven, Isabel had been sleeping with her parents from her earliest days. Among other difficulties, this left no time for her parents to get anything done in the evenings or spend any time together. Isabel had been making progress in treatment. She latched on to the idea of worry bubbles and happy bubbles and was able to successfully use this strategy to manage field trips at school. The day we discussed making the stairs of learning for Isabel to sleep alone, she cried. In fact, according to her mom, she was upset for three hours after the session! Very distraught with the idea of change, Isabel was unable to even think about having her dad lie on the floor next to her, then by the door, then outside the door. Thinking that Isabel's reaction had frightened her family off this plan for good, I was thrilled to hear what happened next. About a week after that fateful session, Isabel said, *on her own,* "Let's try that plan that Tamar talked about." Within a month, Isabel was sleeping on her own for the first time in seven years. From her previous successes with the gradual approach, Isabel was willing to start her climb to success. What Isabel's parents have learned is not to fear Isabel's strong initial protests, because despite this, they see she really wants to be free of anxiety. They need to continue creating manageable opportunities for Isabel to challenge herself and gain confidence. Not only are her parents ecstatic to have their evenings back, Isabel has had a major boost in confidence. She is going to birthday parties and field trips on her own, she has had several sleepovers at friends' houses, and she's ready to try out a new camp where she doesn't know anyone—something she *never* would have done in the past. Mastering her nighttime separation anxiety has opened up doors for Isabel all day long.

PANIC DISORDER

Panic: Fear of Fear Itself

Panic can be one of the most crippling anxiety disorders to manage because there is no specific triggering situation to be avoided and the possibility of a surprise attack is omnipresent. For parents panic can be the most baffling disorder to understand, not only because the object of the fear cannot be identified, but because attacks often happen during an otherwise perfectly calm moment. In a panic episode, children are hysterical and flatly refusing to go places because they are afraid that they *might* get afraid. When pressed for a reason, kids just feel embarrassed, angry, or simply unable to put their finger on anything other than a fear that they will feel mortally uncomfortable and need to come home.

A panic attack can best be described as the nervous system running a drill, a simulated attack—*testing one-two-three*. Reacting as if under attack, the sympathetic nervous system prepares to defend itself and creates frightening, albeit completely harmless, physical symptoms of dizziness, racing heart, and feelings of unreality. In Chapter 4 we saw that there is a logical explanation for these physiological symptoms—readying the body for fight or flight. But when they surge for no reason and escalate in a manner of seconds, they are terribly frightening. The problem is that when these drills occur, there's no flashing sign that says—*just testing*. If only the brain could announce, *"Fight-or-flight drill,"* then kids would be able to relabel those surges as false alarms and not be afraid that they signal a real danger. We don't know what causes panic attacks, but one factor may be a genetically low threshold for setting off the fight-or-flight reflex.

Red Flags

- Sudden, unexpected surges of intense fear that are unrelated to any specific worry or fear situation
- Surge of physical symptoms—overheating, dizziness, racing heart, feeling detached or unreal
- Attacks occur out of the blue and peak within ten minutes
- Subsequent to first attack, children fear venturing away from home for fear of having another attack and avoid perceived triggers and locations of previous attacks
- Child appears to be seized by fear of dying, being unable to

breathe, or losing control and may be inconsolable or hysterical.

In the Thick of It: Chicken Little Meets the Sympathetic Nervous System

For parents who haven't experienced a panic attack first hand, it may be difficult to understand how misreading a signal could lead to such chaos. Imagine that you're driving in your car and an unfamiliar icon suddenly starts flashing in red on the dashboard. What does it mean?—should you pull over? what's next? is something awful going to happen? In those seconds before you figure out that it's a harmless warning light letting you know that a bulb is out, your heart may be racing from the possibility that it's a signal the engine is going to ignite in the middle of the highway. Like the childhood story of Chicken Little, who believed the sky was falling when it was only a stick that fell on his head, we tend to misinterpret signals in the absence of clear information, and jump to conclusions. Some children may identify a "bad feeling," others may be frightened by an unfamiliar cramp, feeling overheated or slightly dehydrated. Their interpretation of these symptoms as very dangerous is what sets off the panic spiral.

In addition to the uncomfortable physiological sensations of panic, kids can have unfamiliar cognitive experiences of feeling detached from their body, feeling like they are watching a movie, not real life. Lena, whom we met earlier in the chapter, made an acronym that captures nearly word for word the DSM (*Diagnostic and Statistical Manual*) description for this phenomenon: the "SOUR" feeling—for "sense of unreality."

By learning that panic *feels frightening* but is 100 percent harmless, your child can stop the chain reaction. *It's just my heart beating fast, it's okay. A false alarm was set off for some reason.*

My body is testing its emergency response team. This can't hurt me. If I slow down my breathing and keep telling myself that it's panic and it will pass, then it will. If I don't add to the excitement by freaking out, the excitement will die down and all will return to normal.

Intervention: What to Do When Your Body Is All Stressed Up with Nowhere to Go

THE PANIC STOPS HERE: IF YOU CAN MANUFACTURE THE SYMPTOMS, THEY CAN'T HURT YOU

Until your child understands how panic works, she can't protect herself from panicking. The treatment for panic involves teaching your child about the quirks of the brain, much like a mechanic might alert you to the ins and outs of your car. When your child learns what all the signals mean, what happens when certain metaphorical buttons get pushed and how to deactivate them, she will be confident that the uncomfortable feelings are not signs of danger at all and will pass on their own. Because parents become alarmed to see their child thrown into such a state, they too need to learn how panic works so they can facilitate the deactivation process rather than getting pulled into the contagion of fear.

The most effective way to demystify panic is to manufacture the symptoms on purpose. If you can make the same sensations happen—turn the switch on, then off—then children learn that they aren't dangerous and can be controlled. What happens in panic is that we look for an explanation, an external cause for the feeling of danger, which in and of itself adds to the panic, but none is there. Once you know this *secret* you can rein in your reactions and teach your brain to correctly interpret the signals. Teenagers may see a parallel scenario in how computer-illiterate parents react when their computer freezes. The parent panics, fears that all is lost, that they've crashed the system, but the teenager may confidently be able to read that signal properly as a need for a simple reboot. Kids may even get a good chuckle at their parents' expense because they see parents overreacting when they know clearly that all is well. Kids need to learn that panic is a similar system misfire. Rebooting comes in the form of breathing, self-talk, and focusing.

This new working model of how panic operates will help your child feel back in control, savvy that he is not in danger. The *sensations* of panic—that unnecessary amping up of the adrenaline system—will still be uncomfortable until they are brought under control a few minutes later. But it is like the deceleration of an airplane—all that energy has to be discharged. One aspect of panic that is especially frightening to preteens and adolescents is the feeling that they are going crazy. They feel both so hyper in their bodies—and yet at the same time so detached physically that this feels like going insane. Again, set the record straight: this is garden-variety panic. What kids may fear is being psychotic or schizophrenic—this is what they imagine it may feel like. Those disorders, serious and painful in their own right, do not have sudden surprise attacks like this but are chronic and progressive. They are, fortunately, treatable but are in no way related to panic attacks.

LEARNING TO MANIPULATE PANIC

While it may seem counterintuitive to want to bring on anxiety symptoms when you are trying to reduce them, think of it as tripping off a circuit breaker on purpose so you can learn how to flip it back and not be helplessly in the dark. Once your child sees first hand that panic symptoms can be simulated, he will be convinced that they are harmless, and panic attacks are nipped in the bud. Therefore in treatment your child will simulate those symptoms to practice not getting "faked out" by them, using calm breathing and realistic anti-panic thinking. What follows is a step-by-step recipe for how to "create" panic symptoms. Before attempting any of these exercises, a child *must* know how to do diaphragmatic breathing so that he can calm back down after doing the exposure. See Chapter 4 for specific instructions.

Children should know that they may not be able to stop a panic attack from *starting* (it just starts on its own), but they can put a stop to it, and make it a brief *limited symptom attack*. These brief attacks show kids that even after they start to panic, they have the power to stop it. This is even more reassuring and liberating than a panic-free period where they're wondering when the next attack will happen and how they will react. These simulations allow the child that "aha!" experience: nothing bad happens when you get dizzy—it doesn't keep escalating, you don't go crazy, you just feel dizzy until that feeling passes. In other words, they get to see for themselves that there is nothing to fear.

Panic Symptom	Recipe for Simulation
Dizziness	Spin in a chair several times
Hyperventilation	Run up and down stairs several times till winded, or pant on purpose for 10–15 seconds
Derealization	Use hyperfocus to create feeling of detachment or unreality: keep saying the same word over and over until it sounds so strange you start to doubt it's a word
Disorientation	Lower your head, look down, lift head up quickly

When your child practices a panic recipe, he uses his breathing and his coping thinking (see scripts that follow) to help the sensations dissolve and the fears dissipate. Your child can also be instructed to say *"Stop—this is panic!"* and begin focusing his attention on his environment: what colors does he see, what textures does he feel, what smells can he notice. This routes him back to the present and derails the panic train. If your child begins to experience a real panic attack, his breathing, coping, thinking, and focusing skills will be most effective when used at the *earliest* sign of panic. Panic, more than any other disorder, escalates quickly, within minutes, therefore immediate intervention is essential. Don't give panic the advantage. Children need to be ready to recognize their particular telltale signs. Younger children may be given a "map" of the body and asked to circle the parts that get scared or feel funny when they have an episode. Older children can think about past attacks and track what symptom they noticed first.

THE POWER OF ACCURATE THINKING: SELF-TALK FOR STOMPING OUT PANIC

What follow are sample scripts for young children and teenagers. Once your child generates his own *anti-panic script,* he can write the messages on index cards and keep them with him to use at the onset of an attack.

For Young Children (Under Age Seven) Parents will need to guide their child through the panic by saying, for instance: *Hold my hands, it's just that busy dizzy guy, we'll breathe those feelings right out. Slow down, look at my face, match my breathing. I'm going to count. Nothing is wrong. You're just fine, everything is okay. These scary feelings are going to pass, we'll blow them away by breathing together nice and slow. We'll fill up balloons with air—here's the red one, now the blue. You just got dizzy, it gave you that uncomfortable feeling. You're okay, dizzies go away!*

Fighting Panic in Children Age Seven and Up

Panic Script	*Anti-Panic Script*
Something is wrong	Nothing is wrong. I feel like something is wrong, but I'm in no danger—everything is the same as it was two seconds ago.
I'm losing it!	This is a false alarm: my brain sent the wrong signal.
I'm going to die!	This is harmless, it can't hurt me.
I have to get out!	I need to slow my body down—there's no danger, nothing is happening, nothing has changed.
What if I faint or suffocate?	If I breathe slowly, I'll reset the system. My body will get a new signal and everything will go back to normal.
What if I go crazy?	I feel like I'm going crazy, but I'm not. No one ever dies or loses it from panic. It's not comfortable, but it can't hurt me. These feelings will pass if I don't add to them with my fear. Don't fuel the fire, put it out!

REAPPROACHING LIFE:
CARRYING THE "ALL CLEAR" SIGNAL IN YOUR POCKET

While panic is by definition a surprise attack, there are certain situations or sensations that may bring on the fear of a panic attack: class trips, cars, elevators, auditoriums, open spaces, high ceilings (as in church or auditoriums), getting overheated, open fields, stores, crowds, theaters, sporting events, or just being away from home. After children are armed with the truth about panic and have their de-panic self-talk and their breathing ready, they are then ready to make their stairs of learning and reapproach, step by step, the situations that have been avoided because of fear of panic.

On the Homefront

Panic is very difficult for parents to manage because even when they understand the mechanics and how to manage the attacks, panic attacks continue to be surprise attacks. The more you understand how panic works, the more you will be able to label what is going on. Rather than get pulled into the fray, you will be able to instruct your child on the steps she needs to take and confidently let her know that she will be fine. This takes the attack out of the crisis category and turns it into a manageable situation whose resolution is not a matter of life or death but just a matter of time. Because of the physicality of panic, it is important to immediately guide your child toward slowing down her body. Though you may feel mean redirecting your panicking child, when it is done compassionately, you are really rescuing your child from much anguish.

Working with your child's therapist, redirect your child toward panic-triggering situations that have been avoided. Rank the situations on a hierarchy and begin with the least anxiety-provoking. Get creative about breaking down a situation into small, manageable challenges. If your child wants to go to a play or basketball game but is afraid of having a panic attack, set a goal of staying for half of the event, or even a quarter. Your child will feel less overwhelmed by a smaller goal; once there he may find that it is easier than he thought. The anticipation of the event is often much worse than the event itself.

TRY TO END ON A GOOD NOTE

If your child does have a panic attack at an event, try to leave the immediate situation (his seat at a play), but not the event. Stay in the building or parking lot. Go to an area that feels safer to your child, help him to breathe, and reassure him that his panic will pass. Often children are able to return to the event once they have been assured that this will pass. Staying in the vicinity of the situation until your child's anxiety is reduced will help him to feel successful, but will also prevent the reinforcement of escape or avoidance as a coping strategy.

Kayla's Story

Ten-year-old Kayla described her panic as "the weary feeling." She knows the very day it started. While out for a walk with her brother on a hot summer's day, she began to feel tired and overheated and wanted to stop, but her brother, being a bit older, wanted to keep moving. Kayla felt faint, dizzy, and "spaced out," and very afraid that something bad was happening. She wanted her brother to carry her home—she was afraid that if she walked she might die. Following that day, Kayla was very afraid that the weary feeling would happen again. Because it seemed so terrifying and life threatening to her, she started to limit her walking. She couldn't go anywhere—even going to school was tough. Her family was getting frustrated. They didn't understand how normal activities—trips to the mall, to the Fourth of July fireworks, gym class, and even the short walk to the bus stop—could suddenly be so overwhelming to Kayla. In therapy, Kayla learned about how her brain was sending her a faulty message that she was in danger of collapse when she really wasn't—that this was called panic and she could overcome it. She named her anxiety "Shadow" because

---

Parent Coping Talk for Panic

- I'm going to help you through this.
- It feels like something is wrong, but these feelings are harmless—you are absolutely fine.
- You are not going crazy, you are not in danger, your brain is sending the wrong signal—you'll be fine.
- You got scared about what the feelings meant; the anxiety will pass in a couple of minutes
- Breathe with me, let's slow it down.
- You can move on even if the anxiety is there.

---

it always followed her. When it came to walking even the smallest distance, Shadow warned her that she would get the weary feeling and that she shouldn't try. Kayla soon learned how to devalue Shadow's false alarms, to do deep breathing, and use good boss back talk: *Worry isn't going to make the choices, I do! Shadow—stop making me look so far ahead, if I'm tired I can stop; I'm not climbing Mount Everest, I'm just going to the bus stop.* By doing exposures in treatment Kayla had the opportunity to face the fear and see that she could survive.

A turning point for Kayla was a trip we took to the mall together during a treatment session. At first Kayla was terrified to go in, but we just set small goals. Walking from shop to shop, she began to see that the "weary feeling" was in her head, not in her body—that it really was a false alarm created by panic. Kayla's parents also learned how to work with her so she could fight back the panic, rather than fighting with them. They understood that she was not trying to control them, but that *she herself* was feeling controlled by panic and that she was angry because she was so afraid that she'd get stuck feeling out of control or missing out on things. Her mother realized that kids feel strong and confident when we remind them they, not their anxiety, are in control.

Turning things around to Kayla's advantage, her parents would ask her what she wanted to do in the situation and how they could help her get there. Kayla has been panic-free for over six months now, and needless to say, with their preteen back in commission, the family is spending a lot more time at the mall!

Matt's Story

Eleven-year-old Matt suffered from panic attacks. For months Matt's parents were unsure how to handle these attacks, which occurred at sporting events and swim team practice and in school. They were very concerned for Matt, but also felt they were held hostage by these unpredictable attacks. After a couple of months of learning how to handle panic, they had a turning point when Matt had a panic attack while his mother was driving him to camp. Feeling unable to bring him to camp in that condition, Matt's mother went on to her next stop, a doctor's appointment, with Matt in the car. As Matt's panic was amping up, his mother calmly directed him on what to do: "If you need to lie down you can, but I need to go to my doctor's appointment." While Matt's mom was on the phone letting the doctor know that she was going to be a little late, Matt, who had essentially been curled up in a ball and crying, suddenly began to calm down. It was as if Matt could take Mom's lead and life could come back to normal. This wasn't the terrible disaster scene that his brain had presented to him. When his mom got off the phone, Matt said, "You know, I think I can go to camp, I can handle this." By not getting swept up in the drama, not being afraid herself of what was happening, Matt's mom was able to show panic the door, and let the real Matt step forward. Soon after this occurred, Matt, who had been unable to go to the movies because one of his first panic attacks occurred after leaving a theater, left the following phone message on my machine:

Hi, Dr. Chansky, It's me—Matt; you'll never guess where I am. I'm on my mom's cell phone. I'm at the movie theater with my mom. I did it, I made it to the movies! I felt a little iffy at first, but I waited it out. It went away. The movie was great. I'm dancing in the aisles. Wheee!! I'm glad that no one else is here, but I don't care! I did it, I can go to the movies again, and I'm not scared! Yeahh! Well, okay, bye Dr. Chansky.

Idea Box

- **SEPARATION ANXIETY:** Have your child draw an independence thermometer. Color in the thermometer in units of minutes or hours that your child is able to be apart from you, and plan a special celebration when your child reaches the top.
- **PANIC DISORDER:** Have your child draw a map, marking the *comfort zone*. Hang the map on the wall and add pictures or pushpins for each place or situation he conquers outside the comfort zone.

✳

CHAPTER 10

From Superstitions and Rituals to Obsessive-Compulsive Disorder (OCD) and PANDAS

*B*rittany is so afraid of germs, she can't get close to anyone—
even us. She is sure that she is going to catch something. This
goes way beyond good hygiene and health. She tracks every
cough, sneeze, or stomachache at school. I know more about the health
of the other kids in her class than their parents do. She yells at us if
we even exhale too close to her. It gets me so frustrated, but in my heart
I know she can't help it, and there's something very wrong.

*Martin woke up one morning and it was as if someone had taken away
our son in the night and we were dealing with a child we didn't know
at all. Nothing he did made any sense. He was confessing everything—
little things, strange things. He was worried about touching things. He
was apologizing for everything, even apologizing for apologizing. He
tells us he loves us every two seconds and keeps asking us if we love
him—it's like all the circuits just went haywire in his mind. He's a
wreck. I can't send him to school, and I'm afraid he's going to have a
nervous breakdown. How could he change so suddenly? I don't know
what to do.*

OCD: A Tyrant Whispering in Your Child's Ear

"Step on a crack, break your mother's back." For some kids, this is a game to enliven an otherwise tedious walk home from school; for others, a simple walk home becomes a matter of grave responsibility, warding off harm to a loved one. *What if I wasn't paying attention and something happened? It would be all my fault. Did I accidentally step on a crack? How should I undo it? Should I go back and start over? Uh-oh, there's another crack . . .*

Like the children we met with generalized anxiety disorder (GAD) in Chapter 6, the more than one million kids with OCD worry too much, but there are two important differences. First, unlike the everyday worries that get stuck in the nets of kids with GAD, in OCD the thoughts that get stuck are often senseless and bizarre. Take Kelly, who at age eight confessed to her mom that the reason she wouldn't watch TV in the office was because she was afraid she would swallow the thumbtacks on the cork board. Second, kids with OCD get locked into rituals to relieve the anxiety that the worries generate. These rituals or compulsions are often precise rules for ordinary behaviors—walking, talking, breathing, reading, praying, moving—that consume hours of the child's day. *I breathed out when I saw the stop sign, that means something bad will happen. I better breathe it back in, I'll do it four times for good luck.* Children with OCD may approach the world of dirt as diligently as a doctor scrubbing for surgery, hold on to used napkins like a prized possession, and fear that they have offended God simply by how their knees faced when they were sitting and praying.

Virtually anything can become grist for the OCD mill, and more and more activities must be executed according to strict rules in order to prevent harm. Since we are all creatures of habit, this chapter will show you how to tell the difference between the rituals that accompany healthy growth and development and the compulsions that can clog the arteries of your child's—and your family's—daily life. Evaluating whether the ritual or pattern helps the child feel *confident* (checking his hair in the mirror before going to school) or feel *anxious* (spending hours combing and flattening until his hair is "just right") is the primary litmus test.

Even if a child doesn't have full-blown OCD, she may have patterns, or areas where she gets stuck, that she needs help with—writing perfectly, being overly concerned with cleanliness, or being polite to a fault. OCD is a highly treatable condition, and early intervention can prevent years of suffering.

The strategies in this chapter will help you work on these behaviors at home and know what to look for in treatment for rituals such as hand-washing, checking, and perfectionism. In this chapter we first look at the diagnosis and treatment of OCD, and then briefly at red flags and interventions for the four primary subtypes of the disorder: contamination, checking, symmetry/just right, and bad thoughts. Though typically OCD has a gradual onset over months or even years, some children develop OCD symptoms virtually overnight. This subtype of OCD is called Pediatric Autoimmune Neuropsychiatric Disorders Associated with Strep, or PANDAS, and is discussed later in the chapter.

OCD puts parents in an impossible corner. Their previously reasonable child is doing things that make no sense at all—even to him—confessing to you, and even insisting that yes, he did poison the cat, steal from school, push a child into a moving car, curse at a teacher, or catch AIDS from a stain on the floor. Of course none of this is true, and though parents are tempted to reassure at first, they quickly see that reassurance has no impact on their child's worried mind. OCD is impervious to reason in the same way that supergerms are resistant to antibiotics. They don't retreat; instead they multiply. Reassurance won't treat OCD. The ticket to recovery is understanding why the thoughts are stuck there in the first place, and learning how to teach your child's brain to filter out the unhealthy, exaggerated, unnecessary messages, and amplify the healthy ones.

Parents need to understand the goal for their child: it's not about being *free from discomfort or risk*. Rather it's about relabeling and devaluing those odd, nonsensical risks as brain glitches or junk mail, and then learning to live with risk and uncertainty. As one youngster told me, *"There are all these things I have to do to get out of bed the right way, otherwise my OCD tells me I'm going to have a bad day. And even though I do it, I am thinking, all that I'm doing is getting out of my bed—how could that be so important? And it sort of feels bad to do all this tapping and counting—even though it is supposed to keep me safe, it sort of ruins my day anyway. Other kids want to have good days, but they don't have to make such a big deal out of it."*

Making the Diagnosis

What follows is a list of diagnostic criteria to help you determine if your child's habits are typical or not. If you can answer "yes" to any of these, it is time to seek professional help.

- Presence of obsessions: persistent, disturbing, and inappropriate thoughts, images, or ideas that child can't get out of his mind
- Repeatedly asking questions, and inability to be reassured by answers
- Engaging in compulsions: spending too much time doing things over and over, or avoiding ordinary activities such as

touching faucets, putting on shoes, answering questions, wearing certain clothes, or eating certain foods
- Needing parent to answer questions in a precise way
- Obsessions and/or compulsions that create distress, interfere with child's functioning, and are time consuming (take more than an hour a day)

OCD Rituals	Non-OCD Habits
Time consuming	Not overly time consuming
Child feels like he has to do them	Child wants to do them
Disrupt routine, take on a life of their own	Enhance efficiency or enjoyment
Create distress, dread, or frustration	Create a sense of mastery
Appear bizarre or unusual	Appear ordinary
Cause great distress if interrupted, child must start over	Can be skipped or changed without consequence
Become increasingly inflexible and elaborate over time	Become less important over time
Connected to a web of feared consequences, are performed to prevent harm or due to other superstitious belief	Performed for the sake of the activity itself; comforting, but have no invisible connections to feared situations or superstitious beliefs

Cracking the Code: Making Sense of OCD

The often bizarre nature of OCD symptoms can be frightening—kids and parents alike can fear that something is terribly wrong for these thoughts to be coming up in the first place. These thoughts are not a sign of danger, however; they are a sign of OCD. People across history, of all cultures and ages, have experienced the same basic four themes of OCD. Don't try to make sense of OCD by looking within your child's personality, or scrutinizing your parenting practices. Like other anxiety disorders, OCD is nobody's fault—it's due to a misfiring in the brain—but with OCD it is not the amygdala jumping to conclusions that starts the action. Instead the caudate nucleus, the filtering station for our thoughts, is malfunctioning. Thoughts that should get filtered out because they are unnecessary find their way into the "Urgent Messages" box, demanding attention. Of course there is no real urgency, but since the thoughts or images are sitting there, kids feel frightened by the thoughts themselves and the fact that they are thinking them.

Kids with OCD never act on their obsessions, but the disorder insures that they are plagued by the possibility that they could. Rather than claiming responsibility for these odd thoughts, your child should put the onus back on OCD, where it belongs. Relabeling, according to Dr. Jeffrey Schwartz, is the answer to the question, "Why am I thinking this?" "I am thinking this because of the disorder"—it's as impersonal as that. When kids look within themselves for an explanation, it's like claiming responsibility for a prank call when all you did was answer the phone. Your child can't control the intrusive thoughts he has, though in treatment he will learn how to control his *response* to those intrusions.

The cycle of OCD is a follows: First comes the intrusive

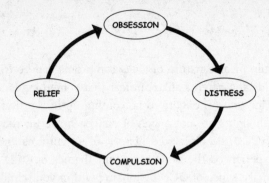

thought: *maybe I left the closets open, my baby brother will get into the cleaning chemicals.* We may all get a passing bad thought, but when we identify a "good-enough answer" for the concern, we move on. With OCD the all-clear signal doesn't come, and the compulsion (a solution that looks good at the time—*recheck the doors, rewash your hands*) fills in and relieves the anxiety *temporarily.* The problem is that the anxiety reduction from the compulsions doesn't last long, and before you know it one check turns into two or three—into checking without having any bad words or thoughts in mind, checking while standing on one foot, et cetera. What kids need to understand is that a faulty circuit is engaged, and treatment is about identifying the tricky thoughts and sticking to a plan of bossing them back.

Key Intervention in Treatment: Cognitive Behavior Therapy Using Exposure and Ritual Prevention (E/RP)—Who's the Boss?

The following are the steps that children are taught in treatment. While they bear some similarity to the Master Plan steps in Chapter 5, an important difference is the addition of exposure and ritual prevention (E/RP), our most powerful tool in overcoming OCD. In E/RP a child deliberately puts himself in the situations where OCD strikes, but refuses to follow OCD's rules. For example, a child may touch his shoes without washing his hands, or lock a door with his eyes closed rather than triple checking. Though families may be tempted to rush to use E/RP with every symptom, exposures should be conducted on a hierarchy guided by the child's fear temperature (see Chapter 5).

STEP ONE: RELABEL

The only way you can solve the problem of an OCD thought is by identifying the brain glitch that put it there in the first place. The brain filter isn't working properly so put the blame on the OCD, or the Brain Bug, Pushy Guy, Mr. Perfect. Parents and kids can join together in fighting a common enemy. Kids won't feel like they are in the hot seat, and can focus their righteous anger and frustration at the Brain Bug instead of at you. How can a child tell which is an OCD thought and which is not? Even children as young as four or five can tell the difference between "strict or pushy thoughts" and regular thoughts. For all children: Draw two boxes on a piece of paper. Label one: "What I *want* to think and do." Label the other: "Things I feel like I *have to* think or do, or else." Have your child fill in each box. The "have to" box is the OCD—your child may enjoy drawing a trashcan under it because that's where those ideas belong!

Relabeling for Younger Kids

- Give OCD a name: Brain Bug, Worry Man, Fuzz Guy, Disaster Dude, Meany Brain. This gives parents and kids a common enemy to fight against.
- Draw a picture of OCD or make a puppet of OCD, change your voice, act out how it tries to boss your child around.

Relabeling for Older Kids

- It's not me, it's my OCD!
- I am thinking this because my brain is making a mistake, not because something is actually wrong.
- Plug into the right circuit—what would I think if I didn't have OCD?
- It's the telemarketer selling me risk protection I don't need; hang up the phone!
- It's junk mail—throw it out, it's not true.

STEP TWO: RESIST WITH SHOW AND TELL

With E/RP your child is going to *show and tell* OCD who is the boss by bossing it back and refusing to do rituals. Below are many general suggestions for conducting E/RP. It is best to practice the E/RP by doing a role play first—whether with a five-year-old or a fifteen-year-old—about what tricky OCD is telling them about a situation and what they want to think instead. The role plays are moments of truth. The child *hears* what OCD really sounds like—*come on, you don't mind picking up all the litter you see; yes, you miss recess, but so what, if someone fell it would be all your fault and no one else's, you couldn't possibly take that risk!!*—and this ignites their rightful anger and frustration at the OCD and motivates them to dismiss its validity and fight back. If your child is having trouble generating the right spirit for boss back talk, ask her to use the same voice she uses on a sibling when she is really annoyed. Remind her that if her sibling or even a parent asked her to do what OCD is asking, she would flatly refuse. She has permission to refuse OCD, too—she shouldn't let it bully her.

Ritual-Busting Techniques

Once a child has constructed an OCD hierarchy using the fear thermometer to identify the degree of difficulty of breaking each ritual, he can choose from any of the strategies below to change the OCD pattern. Though ultimately the goal is to resist the ritual altogether in a given situation, these techniques create the intermediate steps that will get him there.

- Delaying tactics: Don't go to the sink; delay the ritual for progressively longer intervals; two, four, and then ten minutes.
- Early dismissal: Shorten the ritual, leave early, and you will see that the "finished" feeling will catch up with you if you move on to something else. If you stay waiting for the feeling, you will wait forever.
- What would your friends do? Try to say good night the way your friends do, or lock your locker the way another kid without OCD would do.
- Pattern change: Change the ritual in some way. Start with your left hand, do it in a different order, change the speed, use a different direction. For reassurance questions, use only the initials for a frequently asked question: WISYITM? (Will I see you in the morning?) and for the answer: YYW! (Yes you will). It will start to sound goofy and that is good. Though this is still patterned, the pattern is coming from *you*, not from the OCD, so it will be easier to break the pattern.
- Change the emotional tone: Because OCD can sound so scary and serious, even thought it's not, these techniques bring the seriousness level down. Make the voice of OCD different in some way—make it silly, make it sound like Elvis, sing the words, say them in pig-latin, or picture the voice as a silly cartoon character.
- Exaggeration: Do the ritual in slow motion, looking at yourself in the mirror.
- News reporter/sportscaster: Rather than doing the ritual, give a blow-by-blow description of what your brain is asking you to do—saying it rather than doing will give you time

and distance to choose not to heed it. Instead of saying "I have to tap three times when I see a shadow to make sure that my parents won't die," rephrase that. If you were stationed in your brain as a reporter, how would you describe it? "We now join Rich as he is walking by a shadow; for no good reason his brain mistakenly sends him a message—shadow means death. What will he do? Does shadow really mean death? What else does Rich know about shadows? Can he plug into another circuit or will the OCD win? Rich looks frustrated. This is a good sign. He is thinking to himself. We see some excellent smart brain engagement coming from Rich: 'I hate this, shadows don't mean anything, they are everywhere.' OCD shoots back, 'But just in case, tap three times to keep you and your family out of the shadows, which mean death.' Rich stops and thinks, 'This is that OCD. I can step in shadows just like anyone else. It's just a thought. I can decide what to do with it. My chemicals are misfiring. Enough. I'm going to show and tell OCD to knock it off, I'm doing the tough thing. I'm going to step in as many shadows as I can today because I want to re-teach my brain that it's safe.' There he goes! Score: Rich one, OCD goose egg!"

- Do the opposite: If OCD says start with your left foot, start with your right. If OCD says walk out the same door you came in, don't!
- Incentives: Give yourself a point for every time you walk out of a room without flicking the lights on and off or don't wash your hands after putting on your shoes.

STEP THREE:
REFOCUS YOUR CHILD ON WHAT HE WANTS TO DO

Once your child has bossed back and broken a ritual, he is going to feel some anxiety. That's because he is changing a pattern. The

OCD is in a tug of war with your child trying to pull him back into a ritual. Feeling anxiety is actually a sign that you are doing the treatment right. Remember that the anxiety will pass on its own within a few minutes, especially if your child picks himself up and doesn't count the minutes. Tell him to remember it's just like jumping into a swimming pool: it's cold at first, but then you get used to it. Have him take his fear temperature from 1 to 10. Then he should get involved in something that is more deserving of his time—play a quick game of catch, even indoors with a pair of socks. He should get active—go for a walk or a run, dance or sing—and his brain will be able to jump the groove. Notice how his fear temperature goes down a few points after engaging his brain in something of *his* choice—without doing any rituals. In a successful exposure the fear temperature should drop at least two points, but preferably 50 percent. This will help forge a new circuit. Instead of heading toward a compulsion when a bad thought barges in, he'll have set a new pattern: bad thought, re-label, go do something more important. Ask your child, "What would you be doing now if OCD weren't bothering you?"

Work with your child to write down challenges at different levels on pieces of paper, and place them in a basket. Choose from the basket several challenges a day that your child can practice. Frequent practice allows the desensitization to occur more quickly.

STEP FOUR: REINFORCE YOUR CHILD'S EFFORTS

Fighting OCD is hard work, and winning doesn't happen overnight. When your child is working on overcoming OCD it's like having an extra job, or extra classes at school—no one pays you and you don't get a grade, but your child should get credit along the way! Sometimes the relief from symptoms is enough reward, but if it's not, don't hold back. Use small, appropriate incentives to get the new circuits going. Rewards may be the reason your child starts working on reducing his symptoms; eventually, as he catches on and the work gets easier, you can fade out the rewards. You can keep track of your child's progress by using two jars—one labeled Brain Bug (or BB) and filled with beans, coins, or buttons, and the other an empty one with your child's name. Each time your child completes a challenge or blocks a ritual he can take one bean away from BB and put it in his jar. He can trade in his beans for a small prize at the end of the week.

Signs of and Solutions for Specific Subtypes of OCD

In this next section, we take a closer look at the four themes of OCD: contamination, checking, symmetry/just right, and bad thought OCD; red flags are highlighted and treatment is summarized. A detailed description of treatment is available in *Freeing Your Child from Obsessive-Compulsive Disorder*.

CONTAMINATION

Red Flags

- Fears about germs, illness; avoidance of places, people, or things that may contaminate—towels, silverware, furniture, doorknobs, phones, banisters, pens, public bathrooms.
- Extra time spent in the bathroom washing, resulting in disappearing supplies, mounting laundry, and chapped, red hands.
- Refusal to wear certain clothes because of what they might have touched; refusal to sit on certain furniture because of its possible contact history.
- Dividing the world into two different time zones—Clean Time and Dirty Time. Establishing different rules for Clean

Time (post-shower—may not go downstairs, touch family members, allow family members to touch them) and Dirty Time (during the day until child is home again).

- Excessive wiping or refusal to wipe after toileting, frequent clothing changes due to possible "drips."
- Inspecting food for foreign objects, expiration dates, ink contamination.
- Fears of contact with magic markers, cleaning chemicals, gasoline.
- Superstitious or symbolic contamination—if I touch my work when I'm dirty, I'll do poorly on the test.

Summary of Treatment A child with contamination OCD washes until he *feels* clean, or avoids common items because they *feel* dirty. Those feelings have no connection with what is actually clean or dirty, but the brain is not filtering out the contamination messages, nor is it properly delivering the "it's clean" messages. E/RP involves approaching avoided items and situations one by one on the hierarchy and refraining from washing. Bottom line message to your child: You are clean, but your brain hasn't gotten the message yet. In treatment, children construct their hierarchy of contamination situations—both those that are avoided entirely (e.g., doorknobs because they only use doors they can push open with feet) as well as those that are followed by excessive washing (scrubbing after handling money in the lunch line). Starting with the easiest challenge, children practice touching the feared object, and refraining from washing. After a quick game of catch or cards, they check their fear temperature and see how much it has dropped. Make the exposures fun whenever possible: juggle "contaminated" shoes or clothes—suspend decorum temporarily in order to retrain the brain about what is safe and what isn't.

CHECKING AND REDOING

Red Flags

- Feeling overly responsible; feeling responsible for security in the car (checking seatbelts) and house (checking doors, windows, light switches, electrical outlets, toasters, locks)
- Asking repeated reassurance questions: what did you say, are you sure?
- Rewinding a video to make sure he heard it right
- Rereading multiple times to make sure he *really* understands; if he makes a mistake, must start from the beginning
- Spending unnecessary hours redoing homework, overstudying for tests, redoing math problems, rechecking the calculator results
- Reclosing drawers, car doors to make sure they are really shut
- Going back upstairs to make sure his toys are still there

Summary of Treatment If at first you don't get the feeling of completion, *don't* try, try again! When we finish an action like sharpening a pencil, closing a door, writing a number, or putting on our shoes, we get a signal from the brain that it's done. It's like the snapping in place of a seatbelt—the sound lets us know it's done. Treatment involves gradually reducing the number of checks, having parents refrain from answering questions, or helping your child walk away from the faucet that he's not sure is really off (and so turns it off and on repeatedly). Remember that reassurance won't solve the problem because it's a brain glitch. Point out the glitch and ask your child, "Who wants to know the answer to that, you or OCD?" Help your child query the scientist in himself: ask how much of him knows that the light is off, and help him put that "smart part" in charge. Using the child's hierarchy of symptoms, begin reducing the number of items he checks and the number of times they are checked. Have your child do the following: delay the urge to check by five minutes and get busy with something else—his brain will move on; make a checking budget; make coupons and post them at the site; designate check-free zones; identify danger zones for checking, and don't go into those areas without a clear plan and purpose.

SYMMETRY, EVENNESS, NUMBERS, "JUST RIGHT"

Red Flags

- Repeatedly straightening pillows, arranging dolls, trophies, books, pencils; redoing hair; smoothing or ironing clothing, retying shoes
- Feeling like an itch on the right side needs to be "evened out" on the left
- Erasing a letter or number till it looks exactly right though by then there may be holes in the paper
- Double touching: if someone bumps into one side, needs to even it out on the other
- Homework so neat it looks typewritten; the means becomes more important than the end
- Needing to leave the room, a building, or a chair, the exact same way she went in
- Excessive slowness so that things are done in a precise manner
- Good luck numbers, bad luck numbers, chewing a certain number of times, eating a certain number of cookies, leaving TV or radio on a certain number, words or sentences need to add up to a certain number
- Having toothbrush or shoes pointing in a certain direction
- Needing to say or read syllables forward and backward
- Needing to count ceiling tiles, window panes, floorboards

Summary of Treatment Precision and neatness are qualities that we hope for in our children, but with OCD these are taken so far that they become paralyzing rather than admirable or beneficial. Because children with this "just right" OCD are flooded with the feeling of things being wrong or unfinished if certain actions aren't carried out, they often move very slowly. Nothing is automatic; they have to think through every move, see it and replay it. Did they walk through the door right? Did they put on their coat right? Every tiny action has a right way, and takes tremendous effort. The intervention is for kids to turn off their minds and just go. As former figure skater Scott Hamilton once commented while watching the Winter Olympics, you can't over think, you just do what your body is trained to do—turn off your brain and "skate stupid." When children relabel the warnings to repeat or even up as mistaken messages, they can turn off their OCD brain and just "live stupid," which in this case is the only smart way to live.

Using the hierarchy, your child can begin her adventure in unevenness. She can wear two different socks, or mismatched earrings, line up objects in the "wrong" order, place shoes haphazardly or pointing in different directions, order things with her eyes closed, have the window shades, the pillows, or the silverware on the table uneven. Tilt pictures slightly askew in the house so she can see it doesn't matter. Do things the *wrong* number of times. Use the two-jar system described above and take coins out of the Brain Bug's jar every time your child successfully refuses to even things up.

BAD THOUGHT OCD

Red Flags

- Fears of turning into a bad person
- Confessing or apologizing about insignificant or untrue things, things she "mighta" done

- Confessing bad thoughts such as "I think I hate you," "I thought that person was ugly"
- Refusing to answer questions or to say "I don't know" or "maybe" because she's afraid she may be lying (she is not)
- Repeating prayers throughout the day; fears of offending God
- Intrusive, graphic sexual thoughts or images, confessing sexual acts though innocent; intrusive fears that simple actions signify he or she is gay
- Thoughts of having pushed or kicked someone, run over or stabbed someone
- Avoidance of being near knives, driving a car, or riding a bike for fear of hurting someone
- Intrusive, disturbing images of violence, death, dismembered bodies

Summary of Treatment "Bad thought OCD" plays a cruel trick. It calls into question what your child cares most about— her very sense of herself as a decent person—and tries to convince your child that she doesn't know what she's capable of. The trick turns an uninvited, passing, unimportant thought— a "what if"—into your child's core identity. We all have strange thoughts, but for most of us they get filtered out and we don't put any import on them.

Many symptoms of bad thought are rooted in the following mistake or brain trick: *coincidence = intention. "If I happen to see a pair of scissors out of the corner of my eye, that means I want to use them to hurt someone. If I happen to swallow while looking at a girl when the teacher is talking about date rape, I must have assaulted her. If my feet are pointed to the left in church, I must be praying to the devil."* Kids with OCD—until they understand the trick—think if the thought is there, it's true, it's real. Children then begin to fall into another thinking trick that we've seen so often—

imagining how awful a situation would be instead of thinking about how *unlikely* it is. Imagine a five-year-old, all sweetness—the picture of the goodness of humanity—confessing with tears running down her cheeks that she is a very bad girl and she should go to jail because she stole something, or might have killed someone, or touched someone's private parts. This is because her "Meany Brain" OCD put these images in her mind, and she was afraid that she should be punished. Kids and parents feel unimaginable relief to learn that these awful thoughts are simply garden-variety OCD, nothing personal, and the very thoughts that millions of other sufferers have grappled with for centuries.

The primary intervention for all types of bad thought OCD is to identify where these thoughts are coming from, and by devaluing them to the level of brain hiccups, rather than true confessions, change the emotional score that is accompanying these scary scenes. Your child can turn those intrusive images of hurting people into cartoons, with little mice squeaking the scary thoughts, thus demoting them to the level of unimportance that they deserve. Fighting "scary" with "silly" or "absurd" always neutralizes the fear and puts your child back in control, e.g., singing the intrusive thought to the tune of "Row, Row, Row Your Boat," or saying it like Patrick from *SpongeBob*. Give yourself and your child permission to diminish the authority of the OCD brain glitch. As the credibility of those thoughts drops, so does your child's fear level.

On the Homefront: Cultivating Irreverence Toward the Problem and Respect for Your Child

When OCD first hits, parents are at a disadvantage. Confused and frightened, you're afraid to make a wrong move. OCD thrives on fear—yours and your child's. Showing your child that you're not afraid of OCD is the most important thing you can do. It confirms that OCD's messages are meaningless. Getting there takes some work. Parents must be ready to go out on a limb. Instinct says to *rescue* your child from pain and distress. But treatment using CBT, our most powerful intervention—with the potential to reduce OCD symptoms on average 85 percent—is about *exposure*.

When parents take treating OCD seriously, it means making the treatment less serious—using humor, sarcasm, and silliness to say, *"I trust you, and you can trust you too."* OCD is all about doubt: *if I thought about killing someone, then maybe I want to, maybe I huffed gasoline.* It would be perfectly reasonable for parents to get very alarmed by those ideas—except if their child has OCD. When parents instead take their child's distress seriously but are crystal clear that the message has no validity, then they are leading the way in their child's recovery. So at first, parents should relabel those questions or concerns: *"OCD, we see you—stop bullying my child!"* After a while parents can get a little more "edgy" and play at being unreasonable—outdoing the OCD's weirdness—then nobody is afraid of OCD.

A major caveat is to go at your child's pace. Never get ahead of your child's humor in dealing with the problem and never use the humor against him. Use it against OCD to show your child you are confident and not afraid. No one is going to be able to take risks at the beginning of treatment—everyone is frightened. With time, when OCD's patterns become predictable, parents can trust that treatment works and can begin to apply their creativity to this endeavor.

Martha really showed that she understood the idea of abandoning seriousness temporarily. Her son was struggling with the bathroom—he felt he had to take off all his clothes and shower every time he used it. We'd been working on this for several months and Nick had been progressing steadily, but he really needed a bit of a push. When Martha then gave him a ten-dollar challenge—use the bathroom without changing or showering—Nick immediately replied, "You want me to die. Is that what you're telling me—just go ahead and die? Germs can kill—anthrax, smallpox, yellow fever. You might as well tell me to jump off the Empire State Building." Jumping at the opportunity, Martha said, "You feel like you're going to die, but just because it FEELS the same doesn't make it true. Listen, I know this sounds terrible and morbid—not what a mom should say—but I'm paying you ten dollars a day to do this, and if you die it would cost me a lot more for your funeral. Doesn't that mean I think this is a risk you can take?" Nick was sort of shocked, but his mom's matter-of-fact stance sobered him, and it brought him back to reality. He was ready to make a deal. Nick's mom was able to do this because she understood that her son's fear was a false alarm and that rather than rescue him from it, she needed to teach him to fight it so he could do the normal stuff like go to the bathroom in peace.

PANDAS: When OCD Strikes Overnight

Most children with OCD experience a slow onset over the course of months, or more typically years, but in approximately a third of the children with OCD, their disorder begins dramatically and definitively overnight. Parents can practically pinpoint the moment when their child went from being a normal kid to suddenly having very serious problems, preoccupations and rituals, and becoming virtually unrecognizable. The word *possessed* has come from the lips of many very reasonable parents when describing their kids. This syndrome, which was first identified by Dr. Susan Swedo at the National Institute of Mental Health (NIMH), is referred to as Pediatric Autoimmune Neuropsychiatric Disorders Associated with Group A Streptococcal Infection, or PANDAS.

Children with PANDAS have a genetic predisposition for OCD. PANDAS is most common in children between the ages of five and nine, and generally occurs in children who have not yet entered puberty. The presence of the Group A ß-hemolytic streptococcal infection (GABHS) triggers the immune system to produce antibodies in the blood to fight the infection. In some children, the antibodies, rather than attacking the strep, attack healthy cells in the basal ganglia, the part of the brain where OCD occurs. This leads to the sudden attack of OCD symptoms, or exacerbation of existing symptoms, and other signs listed below. Within a few weeks of antibiotic treatment following a positive strep culture, children will experience a gradual lessening of OCD and related symptoms. There are usually some residual OCD symptoms, often mild, which are generally well managed by cognitive-behavior therapy. Some children with repeated PANDAS episodes are being treated with prophylactic (preventive) antibiotics, either ongoing or during strep season (winter and spring); the effectiveness of this intervention continues to be investigated.

Children with PANDAS may have none of the classic symptoms of strep—sore throat, fever, or headache—however their strep cultures are still positive. Therefore, if your child has a mild cold but a marked increase in OCD and behavioral symptoms, take him for a throat culture.

Red Flags for PANDAS

- Sudden-onset or exacerbation of OCD symptoms
- Sudden onset or exacerbation of tic symptoms—eye blinking, knuckle cracking, throat clearing, etc.
- Motoric hyperactivity
- Emotional regression
- Nighttime fears

- Separation anxiety
- Increased sensory sensitivity—clothing tags, certain textures, socks and shoes may not be tolerated
- Unusual statuesque poses and movements, choreiform movements (piano-playing movements of the fingers, writhing arms, hands, or feet)
- Worsening of handwriting
- Hyperactivity, fidgetiness, clumsiness

Tests to take if you suspect that your child may have PANDAS

- Pediatrician should do a throat swab, and if results are not positive on the quick test, have the specimen cultured (takes two to three days).
- If the culture is negative, repeat within a few days or a week.
- Blood tests for the presence of strep antibodies, called blood titer tests, can be drawn, though they may be difficult to interpret as some children may have a normally elevated baseline. These tests are the ASO titer and AntiDNase-B.

TREATMENTS FOR PANDAS

Antibiotic treatment will address the strep infection, and generally OCD symptoms will remit significantly within a few weeks after the course of treatment is completed. In some cases children do not respond to antibiotic treatment, and there are experimental procedures being investigated at the NIMH-PANDAS program—plasmapheresis and intravenous immunoglobulin (IVIG). These invasive procedures, which require a hospital stay, essentially "clean" the blood of the antibodies that are causing the symptoms. Though these procedures are promising, they remain experimental and are not widely available.

Mark's Story: Got Milk?

Mark, at age ten, was having a difficult summer. A straight A-student with a great sense of humor, an accomplished athlete in several sports, he suddenly became strangely concerned that he was breaking the rules at baseball camp. He would replay his moves and try to make sure they were right. He was concerned that he was plagiarizing on some summer reading projects. Life was not making sense to Mark or to his parents. He remembered hearing on the news about how Osama bin Laden sent messages to his cohorts through hand signals or by the items around him—a fruit basket with nine apples and eleven oranges let them know when to attack. Mark was terrified that when he held his arm out and blinked he was giving a sign to someone that would make them do something bad.

Mark and his parents were extremely relieved to learn in treatment how these bizarre symptoms made sense and were very treatable. Within a few weeks of treatment Mark was looking brighter and unburdened.

One day on an amusement park ride Mark had a Brain Bug thought that he shouldn't hold on to the seat belt or he might ruin it by leaving a mark on it. As the ride started, he panicked, but then his survival instinct kicked in: *I realized, this is dumb— do I want to die from not holding on, or risk messing up the seat belt? No question—I didn't care what happened to that seat belt, I was going to hold on!* What changed for Mark was that he was beginning to devalue the OCD message, and he realized he had a choice to make. He would have to take risks, but really they were small risks and it was worth it.

A turning point for Mark and his family occurred after about three months of treatment. Mark had an obsession at swimming practice that he might somehow leave practice and go out and kill someone. The resulting compulsion was to look at the clock after every few strokes to make sure that he could account for his time—that he hadn't in fact sneaked out of the pool to commit murder. Once he processed this with his parents he knew this was one of OCD's TLF (Thought-Likelihood Fusion) tricks. Just having the intrusive thought about it didn't make it true—at all! Mark got it—he wasn't leaving the pool, but because of his OCD he was leaving his senses! His parents, having learned the drill of taking OCD to the edge, began some creative play with Mark. They'd say, "So when you leave swimming to go out and kill someone can you stop by the store and pick up some milk for us? " This became a great code phrase for Mark in fighting the OCD—it brought the absurdity of his concerns into focus. Now when he leaves for swim practice he tells his mom, "Don't worry, I won't forget the milk!" I think you would agree that this family has found their own road through the land of OCD.

CHAPTER 11

✳

From Nervous Habits to Tourette Syndrome and Trichotillomania

*M*y son started doing this blinking thing with his eyes. He says it's nothing, but it's definitely not normal for him. Sometimes he clears his throat so hard that I think he could hurt himself—it hurts us to hear him do it. Do we ignore it or try to make him stop? I don't want him to get worse, but I would hate for him to get teased.

Lizzie came down to breakfast one morning and I knew right away that something was very wrong. I looked at her red eyes and saw—not only had she been crying, but she barely had any eyelashes left. She told me she didn't know why she did it, but she didn't know how to stop. Then we both cried, and I promised her that I would get some answers, because I don't know what to do.

In the Thick of It

When we peek into any elementary school classroom we find a sea of constant motion and a sampling of young children's typical habits. Kids exhibit lots of different behaviors for lots of different reasons. "Nervous habit" is not a technical term—

we commonly use it to describe anything from thumb-sucking to nail-biting to hand-wringing to bed-wetting. Carol may pull at her shirt because she is nervous, while another classmate may do it because he's bored and fidgeting helps him focus. Yet another child may do it because of a tic—an involuntary and nonpurposeful instruction from the brain to pull—and she may be neither nervous nor bored, but just carrying out an errant brain instruction to move.

What is most important is not what the child is doing, but what the consequences are of what he is doing. Habits can be benign or can have great social consequences for kids when they are not an occasional deliberate or mindless diversion, but are instead an automatic tic or entrenched habit that they feel unable to break. Many a child has described the beginnings of trichotillomania (commonly referred to as "trich") as just a little tension reliever that they accidentally discovered one day when they were rubbing their eyes, only to find that within weeks this innocent act has turned into a monster habit that is making them do things they can't stop or resist. Tics can be devastating for a child when others do not understand that they are involuntary, and not misbehavior—not something the child is *trying* to do.

Many children have habits that don't require treatment and can be resolved with reminders, incentives, and techniques for reducing or controlling the behavior. When needed, effective cognitive-behavioral therapy (CBT) can train children to reroute a noticeable tic such as neck-rolling or eye-blinking to a less conspicuous form, and in some cases obviate the tic altogether. Trich is also treated with CBT.

The treatment for unwanted habits, whatever their source, is a specific type of CBT called Habit Reversal Therapy (HRT). This chapter briefly summarizes the different habit disorders and describes the key elements of HRT, and how to work out a habit reversal plan for any of these habits or repetitive behaviors. Also covered are guidelines for broaching these issues with your child in a sensitive, informed, and supportive manner.

When Is a Habit a Problem?

For children under the age of three or four, habits such as thumb-sucking or ear-rubbing may represent an accomplishment in self-soothing; they are not considered disruptive and are best ignored. In fact, trying to interrupt would not only be frustrating because the child's degree of behavioral control is so limited at this time, but it would run counter to a child's development and to the trust between parent and child. Later, at about age four, with greater language ability, a greater range of distractions, and more ability to delay gratification, a child can be encouraged to take on the challenge of HRT.

While it can be difficult to distinguish a passing habit from a problem behavior, the guidelines below are a starting point. As always, don't wait for a collection of red flags; the techniques in this book can be used preventively, and some problems may be averted.

Could It Be Normal?
Red Flags for Problem Behaviors

- Child is unable to stop when behavior is brought to his attention
- Child feels frustrated by the behavior but unable to control it
- Child feels intense anxiety to perform the behavior
- Behavior is something the child feels *compelled* to do, not something he *chooses* to do
- Child feels intense frustration when he resists the behavior
- Frustration is not relieved until the behavior is performed

- Child feels sense of relief when he performs the behavior
- Behavior causes physical damage—sore neck or knuckles from tics, bald spots from hair-pulling
- Behavior interferes with functioning (in the middle of a sports event or math test, child needs to interrupt the activity to perform the behavior)
- An ordinary habit—spitting, knuckle-cracking, nail-picking—is accompanied by multiple tics or habits including vocalizations (humming, or throat clearing)

Summary of Problem Behaviors: Tics, Tourette Syndrome (TS), and Trich

TIC DISORDERS

Common motor tics include eye blinking, facial grimacing, licking lips, head jerking, shoulder jerking, chin on chest or shoulder, touching, tapping, rubbing objects, thrusting of arms, groin, or torso, hopping, jumping, clapping, dragging feet, kissing objects, touching genitals.

Common vocal tics include throat clearing, grunting, squeaking, coughing, humming, yelling, echoing of sounds, repeating phrases, clucking sound from back of throat, repeating of certain phrases.

What Is a Tic? A tic can be described as a mental itch, a partially involuntary repetitive movement that may or may not be preceded by a physical warning, such as an itch or an intense feeling of tension. Some children are at times unaware of their tics, while others may experience a feeling of tension in a particular area as if something is going to happen, akin, perhaps, to that feeling when a sneeze is coming on, and then a release of tension following the behavior. When a child tries to resist a tic, as with a suppressed sneeze, there is a feeling of tension until the action is completed. Often before the tic occurs there is a "warning" or what is referred to as a *premonitory urge*. Here your child has a window of opportunity—to resist the physiological urge using HRT and try to let it pass. Importantly, in children under age ten, simple tics (one muscle group involved) are less likely to be preceded by a warning or premonitory urge, are more automatic, and are less controllable than complex tics (multiple actions or muscle groups involved).

Children who have motor *or* vocal tics, but not both, are diagnosed with either a transient tic disorder (occurring nearly every day for at least four weeks but lasting no longer than twelve consecutive months) or a chronic one (longer than twelve months). Tourette syndrome (TS) is diagnosed when children have *both* multiple motor and vocal tics for more than a year without more than three consecutive months tic free.

There is substantial evidence that tic disorders have a genetic component. They may be caused by an oversensitivity to the neurotransmitter dopamine, which controls movement, and originate in the basal ganglia, the part of the brain that controls behaviors. One subtype of Tic Disorder, known as a *transient tic,* may be the result of an immature, though developing nervous system.

Prevalence and Course. Most children with tics begin by age six or seven with simple tics such as eye blinking. Usually vocal tics emerge by age eight or nine, followed by more tics and tic/OCD hybrids at age eleven or twelve. About 50 percent of children with tic disorders also display symptoms of OCD. Through the early years, the tics wax and wane, reaching greatest intensity in mid-adolescence and generally waning in late adolescence and into adulthood. About 60 percent will see a substantial reduction in their tics. Though estimates vary across studies, approximately 24 percent of children experience tics, but most are minor and do not warrant a diagnosis or require treatment. The estimates for a chronic tic disorder range from 0.5 to 1 percent of the population. An estimated 10 to 20 percent of boys and 2 to 10 percent of girls have a tic sometime during their grade school years.

TRICHOTILLOMANIA

What Is Trich? Trichotillomania has been around for centuries, but was not introduced into the popular media until 1989. It is considered an OCD-spectrum disorder because there are some similarities to compulsive behavior and perfectionism. Trich is a no-fault neurological condition where a child is responding to erroneous brain signals to pull hair. It may be related to ancient grooming circuitry gone awry. It is similar to the urge to scratch an itch. Imagine that a hair *calls* to the child, often beginning with a tingling sensation on the scalp. Certain hairs may have a different look or feel—longer, shorter, thicker, or with a larger root—and these call out to the sufferer like the lone dandelion in a perfect lawn. If she resists the urge, the feeling hounds her. When she pulls a hair, there is an instant feeling of relief, much as one feels when finally getting that hard-to-reach itch. But unlike the itch, with trich that feeling of relief is quickly followed by a sense of shame and guilt over the damage that has been done.

Trich is all about the moment, not about the consequences. The focus is narrowed down to the smallest unit—a kink in a hair. In the grip of a trich moment, it seems like nothing else matters. This is one of the "tricks" that trich plays on its sufferers, because afterwards, when a child has spent ten minutes getting the "perfect pull" and feels relieved, immediately the dread, guilt, and shame sets in.

Course and Prevalence. Trich typically begins in childhood, although some children outgrow what may begin as a self-soothing habit of pulling and twirling. For others, this does progress into a disorder in later childhood. Trich occurs in 1 to

2 percent of college students; it is not clear how many young children have trich. Kids with trich are more likely to have a family member with some sort of tic or habit, such as knuckle-cracking, or nail-biting.

The intervention for trich, as we'll see below, is to identify particular triggers for pulling, stretch the interval between urge and action, and use habit reversal strategies to find a replacement or incompatible behavior to interfere with the trich.

Key Interventions in Behavior Therapy

GENERAL OVERVIEW OF HRT

In this section we explore Habit Reversal Therapy (HRT), which is the specific type of cognitive-behavior therapy first introduced by psychologists Nathan Azrin and Gregory Nunn in the late 1970s for treating common childhood habits such as nail-biting and thumb-sucking, as well as trichotillomania and chronic tic disorders. This protocol has been studied for decades, and a modified version is presented here based on the research findings about the critical components of HRT. Medications may also be used in the treatment of tics, Tourette syndrome, and trich. A discussion of these is beyond the scope of this chapter, which focuses on behavioral treatments. Please see the appendix for organizations and books that will provide detailed, up-to-date information on medications.

"Blocking Moves" for Unwanted Habits and Un-voluntary Behaviors. The rationale behind HRT is that given greater awareness of habits and alternate behaviors, you can train yourself to either block the behavior or disguise it by engaging in a more socially acceptable alternative. When a child is on the lookout for that urge (to blink, to pull hair) she can take the early warning sign as a cue to perform a behavior that is physically incompatible with the undesirable one and essentially "blocks" it.

For example, a child who picks her nails may instead squeeze her hands in a fist; a child with a throat-clearing tic may learn to do a slow deep breath or a swallow, or even chew gum instead. A child with trich will pull at a koosh ball instead of her hair. For a child with a mild habit, these steps may be applied more informally, but with a more ingrained habit these steps need to be followed in a more systematic manner to "retrain" new muscles to counter the muscles used in the habit or tic. Numerous studies have documented the efficacy of HRT for a variety of habits including trich and tics. In a recent study at UCLA, Dr. John Piacentini and his colleagues found strong support for the efficacy of HRT for kids with TS. Their program emphasizes cognitive strategies to enhance early recognition, relabeling the tic urge to distinguish it from other thoughts or impulses, using competing responses to make the tic physically impossible to perform, and using a shaping procedure to decrease the conspicuousness of particularly explosive tics.

Expectations: Catch What You Can. Children and parents need to be clear about the no-fault nature of these disorders and join together to help the child have as much control as he would like. Make sure the child understands that he is not to blame in any way for these behaviors, but that if he would like to gain more control over them, there are effective techniques he can learn. Rather than focus on the tics the child performs, parents should commend him for the ones he catches. Likewise, with trich look for the times when your child interrupts pulling or fights the pulling urge.

Gaining Cooperation: What's on Their Habit Annoyance List? The best way to elicit your child's cooperation in a behavioral plan is to help her draw up an "annoyance list"—what bothers her about doing the habit, and what are some reasons why she would like to gain more control? The tics, for instance, may be interrupting her concentration, and the trich might be keeping her from swimming, because she won't be able to conceal thin-

ning hair. At this stage, discuss possible incentives or reinforcers for the new behavior.

STEP ONE: INCREASING AWARENESS

Many kids may be unaware that they are engaged in their habit
behavior. That's what gives the habit the advantage—it catches
the child unawares. When children are watching television,
talking on the phone, or sitting in class, their minds are occupied enough so that they don't know what their hands are doing. This is why one of the first steps in habit reversal is
tracking the triggers and increasing awareness of situations
where the target behavior occurs. With trich, these triggers
may be stress, boredom, anger, or fatigue. There may not be
identifiable triggers, but awareness can be increased by asking
the child to notice how the tic happens, how and where the
first signs of the urge occur, and what happens next.

*Awareness training techniques
for your child to practice*

- Notice the earliest signal of the target behavior.
- Look in the mirror to see how the target behavior happens
  in slow motion—notice opportunities for blocking moves.
- (For trich) From what part of the body is hair pulled? Are
  any tools used (tweezers, etc.)?
- Identify triggers and frequency through self-monitoring.
  Keep track on paper: the situation (bored in class, waiting
  for test, in bed after fight with Mom), the feeling, the
  strength of the urge (0 to 10), any blocking moves performed.
- Child can consult with parent nightly to review the day and
  his progress by looking at eyebrows or fingernails, or discussing tough tic moments. This should be supportive, and
  strategic—how would you want to handle that tomorrow? It

is not meant to be punitive or an occasion for parents to express their upset about their child's symptoms (this may need to be expressed, but not to your child).

STEP TWO: COMPETING RESPONSE TRAINING

When working with a habit or automatic behavior, a child will need to build up new blocking moves and muscles and find new skills outside the moment so that they are easy to reach when he needs them. Below we discuss how to identify some of the many possible competing responses and how to set up practice. Find the pattern that works best for your child. Practices should be brief—a few minutes—and can even be fun, whether it's doing relaxation training together or doing boss back plays to fight the picker. Change will not happen without this practice, but keep in mind that pushing too hard will only make conditions worse, and parents can't expect that their kids are going to whistle a happy tune about having to practice each day. Work on the spirit of practice, not the letter. Below we look at three approaches to blocking moves.

Squeeze Your Lemons. Make a fist and hold it tight, as if squeezing a lemon in your hand *for one minute;* the release can substitute for the release of tension that comes from pulling or engaging in a tic.

Incompatible Responses. Ask your child to perform a tic in slow motion in the mirror so that you can both observe the opportunities for how to block it. It's no longer an embarrassing moment, it's more of a physics project. If energy is going to move in this direction, how do we stop or redirect it? A neck roll or shoulder shrug may be interrupted by having a hand on the chin in a modified "Thinker Pose." Throat-clearing may be blocked by a slow, deep breath or a swallow, or by chewing gum; an abdomen thrust likewise may be blocked by a slow, deep breath (it's tough to breathe in and thrust out at the same time) or by having the child's arms crossed in front of him; for lip-licking he can picture his mouth as a baseball diamond, and instead of rounding all the bases, teach his tongue to go just to the corner of his mouth and back to "first base"—eventually he may be able to resist lip-licking. For tongue-thrusting, he could picture a window shade, and rather than yanking the shade all the way out, just pull it out slowly and slightly. When the urge to touch someone is inappropriate, a child can instead learn to rub a piece of sandpaper in his pocket until the urge goes away.

Staying Out of the Danger Zone. When you are on a diet, it's not wise to hang out at the donut shop—why tempt yourself? When working on changing a habit, a child shouldn't keep her hands in the danger zone. If she has trich, or a hair-twirling or nose-picking tic, as soon as her hands are above her shoulders an alarm should go off in her mind—beep, beep, beep! Because once she's up there it's a slippery slope to the target behavior. Kids can give their parents permission to do the "beep, beep"s when they see a hand heading for trouble. Parents may do better to simply throw their child a fidget tool (explained next) instead of embarking on a lecture.

Tools to Have Ready. Keep several stashes of fidgety tools near problem locations—the car, the phone, the TV—and in your child's pocket for school. These tools may include Koosh balls, stretchy toys, textured balls, Silly Putty, Gak Splat, Thera-Putty—any nondistracting, but fidget-friendly toy will serve. The ground rule for fidget tools is that they can't be *more* interesting than or require *more* concentration than the task at hand. For trich, fidget options may include fidgeting with a doll's hair, yarn, shoelaces, smooth or rough pebbles or marbles, or strands of wrapping-paper ribbon tied together, biting or breaking raw spaghetti, or pulling on dental floss.

Additional Techniques for Trich: Making It Harder to Pull. The following items interfere with pulling or let your child know when the fingers are going for the danger zone:

- Band-Aids, tape on fingers, rubber finger covers (from office supply stores), or gloves give more warning and make it harder to pull
- Bracelets with bells or charms let you know where your hands are going
- Hand lotion that makes your fingers more slippery makes it tougher to grip
- Keeping hair wet or not washing out conditioner completely keeps hair more slippery and harder to pull
- Long nails can make it harder for some kids to pull—a set of false nails can also be an incentive and reward for successful control over a given period of time
- Wearing a hat, headband, or bandanna can slow down access to hair and give your child more of a chance to fight

Practice Routines. There are various ways of practicing the competing responses *outside* the moment of the tic or other habit urge. In general, daily practice consists of your child imagining the urge and then rehearsing taking his hand away from his hair (for trich), using swallowing or calm breathing to counter the throat-clearing tic, or trying to squeeze a Koosh ball rather than picking his nails. Boss back talk can also be practiced. These rehearsals needn't take more than a few minutes but should be done regularly. In addition, you can begin to set up with your child "habit-free periods" when he will be working on blocking the problem behavior.

- Set up target times each day or night, beginning with a fifteen-minute block (it is best if it is the same every day, e.g., during your child's favorite TV show), that will be habit-free time. Make sure he has his fidget tools ready.

When your child is able to master the fifteen-minute block, then build on that foundation in fifteen-minute increments.

- Your child can identify a class period during the school day that will be habit-free. Always start with the smallest challenge, so the best class to start with would be the one where there is generally a lower frequency of the problem behavior. When your child has had at least partial success in that class, she can add another class to her challenge list.

On the Homefront

WHOSE FINGERS, HAIR, OR NECK IS IT ANYWAY?

Habits, tics, and trich can become a battleground for families. Kids may feel that their parents are trying to control them, parents feel that their kids aren't trying to help themselves. Working on these conditions requires the model proposed throughout this book—naming and blaming the responsible circuit and working to boss back the brain. As Dr. Fred Penzel, an authority on habit reversal, stresses, the more a child adopts the stance, "this is not who I am, it's what I do," the more she will feel one step removed from the powerful urges she feels. Parents can do much to facilitate this perception of the problem.

Giving your child support and tools to fight back the messages of the push-y, pull-y, or ticc-y brain can reduce tensions and power struggles because your child can reclaim power over his hands, hair, and everything else. It still leaves open the question of whether the child wants to take advantage of these programs or be left alone to do it when he is ready. In general, you don't want to become as pushy as the Trickster, nor do you want your child to see therapy as a punishment. It is best if you present your child with the techniques or give him a peek at what behavior therapy can offer, then let him decide when and how to take this on. Incentives certainly help, but ultimately the child needs to feel that the behavior is problematic enough to warrant the effort of making changes. Sometimes kids feel better when they know that it is normal to not want to have to work on this, to be mad that it's on their plate in the first place. If they meet with a therapist who understands why they wouldn't be gung ho about the treatment, that may leave the door open for them to decide willingly to pursue it.

You can't want the changes more than your child does. The most important issue is that she feels empowered. If you are *forcing* her to change by insisting she go to therapy, the only way for her to feel empowered is to resist you. If your child feels that you are on her side, then she is more free to assert her independence against the problem, not the solution. This is easier said than done, and if you are in this situation, you will need lots of support. This is a time to contact support groups online or in person to get the help you need for your own adjustment.

THE PARENT'S CHALLENGE

Seeing a child struggle causes great heartache for parents. Knowing that your child suffers with a condition that is visible to others—and more importantly, misunderstood by others—only deepens the pain. Parents add guilt to that pain when they find themselves reacting either directly or privately the way a stranger would. If you are this parent, spare yourself the anguish and know that this is a normal response. As it is uncomfortable to have those feelings, make peace with yourself first by learning as much as you can about the condition and find the *matter-of-fact* phrases that you'll say first to yourself and then to others who don't understand—whether they are family members, soccer coaches, or folks at the checkout line. You could say: *"My child has a neurological disorder, a medical prob-*

lem; it's called [trich, Tourette syndrome]. He can't help it, but he's working really hard to control it, so it would help if you didn't stare. If you have questions you can ask me." The Pennsylvania Tourette Syndrome Association has free double-sided cards available to parents for moments such as these, which explain that the child has a neurological disorder and is not misbehaving (see the resource guide for contact information). You can help your child prepare a one-liner for questions as well. Some kids may feel best saying, "It's just something I do, I'm working on it." Amy Wilensky, author of *Passing for Normal: A Memoir of Compulsion,* suggests that kids can normalize the behavior. "I have tics sometimes, like some people bite their nails or twirl their hair. It's not a big deal. Do you have any nervous habits?"

John's Story

John, a bright, creative youngster with Tourette syndrome, was trying very hard to be an advocate for himself at the ripe age of nine. Fully understanding the erratic nature of neurobiological conditions, he knew that some days things were quiet on the tic front: "A good day," he explained, "is when I don't notice myself." Other days were, in John's words, "just pickish," which meant he needed to pick—at his shoes, sometimes the rug, sometimes his scalp.

John was having a tough year at school finding room for those pickish days, but he worked with his teachers, and everyone came to a greater understanding of John's needs. He was able to go to a quiet area of the classroom when he needed to get the tics out of the way or just needed to move around. This small accommodation helped him immensely to be able to focus and participate in his educational program. John also needed some help with the other children. He didn't know how to explain to the kids that he wasn't trying to annoy them or disrespect their wishes, but that he couldn't help what he was doing. John's teacher explained to his classmates (with his permission) that John was working hard at controlling his behavior, but that it wasn't his fault, and that the behaviors were often automatic and not something he could control easily. John's school knew how to help John and his parents feel confident, knowing that as he boards the bus each day he is heading to a safe place where people understand him and are helping him along his way.

Melanie's Story

Melanie, a confident, capable, and outspoken college student reflects back on her experiences with trich, which began in junior high. She remembers that trich snuck up on her as a solution for the stress she has always felt in her life. "Everything seemed to be more than I could handle, and I guess it was. I remember one night in seventh grade when my family was on vacation I was lying in bed, thinking of all the things I was going to have to do for school when I got home. The anxiety took over my body, and I felt completely overwhelmed. It was more than I could deal with. I started feeling the upper outer corner eyelashes of my right eye. I pulled lightly, then a little harder, and out came an eyelash. Even though it hurt, it still provided me with a sense of comfort and relief. I felt again for another eyelash and continued this process. By the next morning I had no upper eyelashes. I was so embarrassed and knew people would notice. I thought about making excuses, but I decided to just avoid eye contact.

"I used to sit in my bed at night and think I was the only person who did this. That was probably the worst feeling—the loneliness. I came to hate my fingers and hands and would try to prevent myself from pulling whenever I could. When I looked in the mirror I would cry. I was devastated. Why was I doing this to myself, why couldn't I stop? When we sought therapy and found out that this wasn't a phase or a weakness but a disorder, I felt so much better. It meant that I wasn't weird and there were things I could do to control it.

"Now I've learned how to quiet and control the trich urges. I have learned techniques that work for me and know good makeup tricks to help when I need it. I try to address the reason why I am feeling upset rather than "solving" it by pulling. I have changed a lot since I first started with trich. I no longer feel bad about myself for having trich; it's not who I am, it's something I have to take care of. I know I will have to keep my eye on my trich and not let myself slip, but now I have learned to love and accept myself, to look in the mirror and be proud of the person smiling back at me."

✳

CHAPTER 12

From Acute Stress to Post-Traumatic Stress Disorder

*C*harlie was only five when we had the car accident. He was so upset that he fainted. He is really afraid of going anywhere by car, and even sometimes when he is walking on the sidewalk and cars drive by he jumps as if a car were going to hit him. It doesn't seem like the fear is fading, and I feel like we are making him worse by making him face it, but we can't just let it be.

I never meant for my son to be there when my mother died. But he saw the whole thing—her last gasps for air, the paramedics, the ambulance racing to the hospital. He doesn't want to talk about it. He can't cope with me crying. He is afraid that he's going to stop breathing. He has nightmares but won't tell me what they're about. It's like this awful experience is frozen in his mind, but he won't let us help him move on.

We'd like to believe that time heals all wounds, but as parents we know the limitations of this adage. The invisible wounds suffered by children who survive trauma can be carried throughout life if not properly treated. The darkest moments for parents are when we cannot shield our children from trauma. With the possibility of abuse, terrorism, or witnessing the death or injury of others, the potential for trauma is omnipresent in our lives and in the lives of our children. As Cynthia Monahan, Ph.D., author of *Children and Trauma,* writes, "When parents are suddenly confronted with their own child's trauma, they are forced to react to the unthinkable, as shock waves are sent through their cherished parental hopes and beliefs." But there is nothing—no therapy, no medication—more powerful than a parent's unconditional love for promoting the healing and integration of an injured child. There are so many things that parents can do to help limit the warp effect that traumatic experiences can have on children, once they understand how trauma works and discover the natural resources that children can access to cope with trauma.

Much of what we understand from trauma research is that what constitutes a trauma is how a crisis is processed and consolidated in memory. Our general approach to helping kids through trauma is both to process the trauma itself, and also to teach them how to make sense out of the very frightening symptoms of trauma, such as flashbacks, nightmares, and sudden surges in adrenaline. While a comprehensive discussion of all the specific types of trauma is beyond the scope of this book, many excellent references are available (please see the appendix for more information). This chapter is a starting point. It presents a general framework for coping with trauma—how to explain it to your child, what you can do at home, and when your child will need to get professional help.

What Is Trauma?

The American Psychiatric Association's *Diagnostic and Statistical Manual of Mental Disorders* (DSM-IV) defines trauma as exposure to an event that causes or is capable of causing death, serious injury, or threat to the physical integrity of oneself or another person. It also specifies that the child's reaction must include intense fear, helplessness, or horror, or disorganized or agitated behavior. It has long been thought that children are resilient to trauma, that their youth, like a protective shield, gives them immunity—because they don't fully understand the impact of the event, they have less to react to. However, although it is true that the majority of children survive trauma without lifelong effects, one in four will develop post-traumatic stress disorder (PTSD). The very reasons we thought kids immune—their not understanding—is the same reason we now believe they are particularly at risk.

All children exposed to trauma need to identify *what* they are thinking and feeling in order to begin to change those thoughts and feelings. Parents can be very helpful in this process because kids may be unable to articulate their distress. Think about how children indirectly show that they are hungry or tired by falling apart—so one can easily imagine that when dealing with something as unfamiliar as shock or distress, they may show how they are feeling by changes in their behavior rather than saying it in words.

Red Flags for Trauma Reactions

While each child may react differently to a traumatic incident, all children exhibit some significant changes in their behavior and mood. Very young children will not display classic PTSD symptoms, as the majority of these symptoms require verbalization of their internal state. Instead, infants, toddlers, and preschoolers react with regression in language, toileting accidents, clinginess, freezing, fussiness, lack of emotional responsiveness, generalized fear and anxiety, separation anxiety, or sleep disturbances, and likely exhibit trauma-related play. Older children may exhibit anxiety, fears about a recurrence of the trauma, hyperarousal, intrusive images about the event, concerns about personal responsibility for the event, physical complaints, sleep disturbances, eating disturbances, nightmares, loss of interest in activities, withdrawal, and, often, regressive behavior.

The DSM-IV recognizes two primary trauma-related diagnoses. Both diagnoses specify that the child's initial reaction to a traumatic event include intense fear, helplessness, or horror, or disorganized or agitated behavior. While acute stress disorder (ASD) is immediate and is characterized by a shutting down or numbing to emotional experience, post-traumatic stress disorder can begin anywhere from a month to many months after the traumatic event and is manifested by hypervigilance, emotional reactivity, and reexperiencing of traumatic material through flashbacks. What is critical in the development of trauma symptoms in children is the *perception of a life threat,* even when no one has actually been injured or hurt in a given situation. The perceived life threat explains why some children will develop PTSD or ASD even when in a very close call, the crisis is averted.

The Brain Mechanisms Underlying Trauma

Although PTSD is considered an anxiety disorder, the symptoms are in many ways distinct from those of other anxiety disorders. Clearly one major difference is the fact that PTSD is a reaction to an actual event. Consistent with our intuitive understanding of trauma—that the memories are frozen, inaccessible, but easily awoken by situations resembling the traumatic event—scientists researching PTSD have hypothesized that traumatic memories are imprinted in the senses and the emotions and remain stable over time, unaltered by life experiences, or *static, like a photograph.* This is in contrast to the brain's processing of nontraumatic memories, which are coded through meaning—schematic, narrative, and available to be amended in response to new experiences or *fluid, like stories*. Traumatic memory is fragmented, nonverbal, and characterized by vivid feelings in the body—colors, sounds, and smells.

This may be why nonverbal methods of treatment, including Eye Movement Desensitization and Reprocessing (EMDR), and play, dance, and art therapies are often used for trauma survivors. These methods are not necessarily used because a child isn't ready to talk, but rather because talk therapy may be less effective in accessing memories that are more sensory in nature. Anecdotal evidence suggests that these treatments can be very powerful and effective in unlocking the grip of trauma. Unfortunately there are insufficient studies of the use of these treatments with trauma victims to establish with certainty their overall efficacy. In my own work, I have found that using experiential therapies such as art therapy or EMDR in combination with cognitive-behavioral strategies—such as relaxation training, challenging distorted thinking, and systematic desensitization and exposure—facilitates a fast, but lasting resolution of symptoms.

Key Interventions in Treatment

A child will require professional intervention if the symptoms are interfering with his functioning and/or causing him significant distress. There are three primary goals of treating trauma. First, because the symptoms themselves can be frightening and confusing, helping children to understand—at their level—what is causing the symptoms reduces fear and anxiety. The second goal is to teach breathing and relaxation skills to give children tools for relief from the distressing symptoms that can occur suddenly and dramatically in situations that trigger replaying of traumatic memories. The third element of treatment is helping the child to transform the often disconnected and frightening memories of the trauma into a narrative that has a beginning, middle, and end. Usually the beginning and middle are vivid in their minds; the end point—that they survived, that the trauma ended, that there is some resolution—is what is elusive for people experiencing trauma. Reaching a point of closure in treatment can be critical to a child's perception that his world makes sense again, is whole again in some way, even if it is tragically changed.

HOW TO EXPLAIN TRAUMA TO CHILDREN

Children need clear explanations of the alarming symptoms of trauma and reassurance that the symptoms are normal and to be expected. While relabeling symptoms of other anxiety disorders as coming from the brain allows children to boss back their bullying worry brain, children with trauma need instead to befriend the brain. They need to understand that these pictures and flashes of information are the brain's way of trying to bring everything together because it was so overwhelmed. The traumatized child needs to stay with those pictures and allow the brain to piece together a story that makes sense, rather than having it stop in the middle or having fragments or flashbacks rush in and out.

The following script can be used to help children understand the symptoms and experiences he is having:

Our brain has a way of helping us understand and digest experiences that are difficult for us. You may try to stay away from things that remind you of the trauma, or not want to talk about it either. You may feel now like you're never going to feel better again, and it is okay to feel that way. Though you can never change what happened, with time you will be able to live with it. For right now we need to help you feel safe and strong, and when you are ready we will work on those big feelings and scary pictures. We'll take them one at a time.

We might feel upset about some things at first—if, for instance, a friend teases you, or your hamster dies—but then maybe later that day or the next day we feel a bit better, or we have forgotten about it. That system works very well for most ordinary disappointments or upsets. But when there is something very scary or very sad that happens, the feelings are so big and the memories so many that our bodies can't digest it all in a day. It is such a big job that sometimes feelings sort of shut down and we may feel numb, like nothing matters. Sometimes sad feelings may change into angry and frustrated feelings. When you think of it you may get very nervous, upset, or frightened—it's like having a video of a scary movie where you keep seeing the most scary part, and the tape seems to be stuck and won't advance. All of this is normal. After working on this, you can heal your mind so that you are in control of the remote—how and when you see those images again.

GETTING RELIEF FROM SYMPTOMS

Relaxation Strategies. At the very first session with a child who has experienced a traumatic event, the therapist should teach her skills for managing the sudden attacks of physiological symptoms that may occur; this will also help her manage the anxiety that comes up during the session. When the therapist teaches a child to do diaphragmatic breathing (see Chapter 4), a visualization of a safe place should be added. Sometimes children with PTSD can get anxious when they relax; picturing something comforting or peaceful—the beach, a mountain scene, or a big warm hug from Mom—can prevent that. The therapist will make sure that the child is competent at breathing and relaxation before embarking on exploration of trauma material. To maximize the relaxation, the child should have self-talk that redirects him to the present—*I am safe now, nothing bad is happening now, that is in the past.*

Medication. Though PTSD is the result of an external event, medication may be helpful in relieving some of the anxious arousal (reactivity, startle response), panic, sleep difficulties, and depression that are often associated with it. These medications include the SSRIs, as well as the short-acting anxiolytic medications (see Chapter 3 for discussion). Though the benefits of these medications are considered to be modest, they may enable some kids to go to school or sleep at night.

Cognitive Restructuring and Gradual Exposure. At the child's pace, therapy focuses on reconstructing a narrative of what occurred in the trauma. This process, which is ongoing in treatment, begins with the child's recollections and/or listing of difficult flashbacks or difficult intrusive thoughts he is having. The therapist's role in this process is to be a listener, never suggesting or adding material that is outside what the child himself has revealed. Children's perceptions of events often suggest distorted thinking concerning their responsibility for the adverse events—*if only I hadn't wanted that doll so bad, my mom would never have gone out to the store. I knew it wasn't going to be a good day; I should have stopped her.* It is important for the therapist to normalize this process—to explain that good kids wish so much they could control things and that taking the blame for something makes us feel like there is a reason why this happened, even if the reason is not true. The goal is to help the child work toward a more accurate explanation for events that were not under his control. Other elements of cognitive-behavior therapy (CBT) for children with PTSD include making a plan for managing flashbacks (self-talk and breathing exercises—temporarily leaving the situation), identifying triggers and reminders and making a plan for each, and ultimately creating a stimulus hierarchy for traumatic reminders that the child will gradually approach—first in the imagination and then, when appropriate, in vivo. For example, a child who was in a car accident will first undergo systematic desensitization in the office for aspects of that event, using relaxation and realistic thinking to manage anxiety that arises. Once the child has successfully been desensitized, treatment then focuses on reapproaching triggering situations, such as driving in a similar car, or on a rainy day, or at the location where the accident occurred. The treatment must go at a pace that the child feels comfortable with. As with any anxiety disorder, speed is never a factor in success.

As we will see below, the parent's role in the treatment of PTSD is essential. In a child's CBT the parent will learn the explanation for traumatic symptoms and take part in making a plan for managing symptoms, coaching the child and often accompanying her for exposures. Because parents provide containment for children's distress, parents will be encouraged to seek support and, if necessary, treatment for their own reactions to traumas that impacted them directly or vicariously.

Length of Treatment. The length of treatment varies according to the severity of the trauma and the child's readiness to work at treatment, though many children can experience significant improvement within a few months of treatment with a qualified professional.

Even after treatment is successfully completed, children can be reimpacted by PTSD at any time—for example, a child who was in a car accident may have difficulties when she begins taking a school bus, or begins to drive on her own. A child who sustained sexual abuse may have difficulties at puberty when boys show interest in her. Children who suffer severe PTSD will likely need ongoing treatment. In a 2000 review of state-of-the-art treatment for PTSD, Drs. Cohen, Berliner, and March indicate that for children who may need ongoing treatment, a "pulsed intervention" may be indicated, rather than a finite number of weekly sessions.[1] Pulsed treatment refers to the suspension of short-term treatment until the child needs further work, for example when there are increased symptoms, or at a developmental transition. The benefit of this schedule is that the child has an ongoing connection with a provider but is able to feel confident in his abilities, and return to therapy only when needed.

Eye Movement Desensitization and Reprocessing (EMDR). Although our focus is on CBT for anxiety disorders, there are other treatments that show promise in treating trauma in children. EMDR is an intervention that was developed by psychologist Francine Shapiro to treat PTSD, and, like CBT, it involves exposure through recalling aspects of the traumatic event. However, in EMDR, this recall occurs while the child is visually following specific back-and-forth hand movements by the therapist, or alternate rhythmic tapping by the therapist on the child's hands. The rationale behind EMDR is that the eye movement or tapping simulates our deep information-processing abilities that parallel what occurs during Rapid Eye Movement (REM) sleep, where we work through the difficulties of our day. There is not sufficient empirical evidence of the utility of EMDR with children, but anecdotal evidence indicates that it may be beneficial. In EMDR, a child is asked to focus on a particular mental picture of the trauma, often the most difficult moment, and with eye movement, the picture seems to progress, fade, or even change as she is focusing on it. She becomes desensitized gradually to the situation, but there is also a shift in her beliefs about the situation, or the "caption" that goes with the picture of that experience. The caption may shift from feeling helpless in a situation (a belief that is very frightening) to a belief about the child's survival—which helps consolidate the child's sense of self. In other instances the caption may shift from the child feeling responsibility in a situation to realizing that he had nothing to do with the cause. In these cases the caption, usually something along the lines of "this was very wrong, but it is not my fault," provides a fortifying end of the story, which is the reunification.

On the Homefront: General Guidelines

With so much of the work of trauma requiring professional intervention, what is the parent's role? There is a balance between modeling useful, effective efforts to manage the situation, and reassuring your child that whatever reaction he is having, he is accepted and safe. If a child is crying, or even laughing, remember that all reactions to trauma are normal. Clearly, if your child is hurting himself or others, limits must be set on him, but in a caring fashion. Help your child work out the feelings in a different way.

One of the strongest predictors of how a child responds to the stress of war is the reaction of his parents and other significant adults. By extension, in any traumatic situation, a parent's ability to model coping behavior is crucial. Important aspects of this process include the following:

- Reestablish a sense of safety, and authority. Let your child know that you are back in charge, and that you will take care of him.
- Correct misperceptions of blame.
- Attribute the trauma to its true cause accurately, but with only as much detail as necessary and developmentally appropriate.
- Provide a return to structure and routine as soon as possible, including regular bedtimes and regular meals. Though

families may feel it is best to give the child lots of room, the child may see this change in routine as a sign that life will *never* return to normal. This makes it hard for her to predict what will happen next on a given day. Though on the surface that latitude may seem appealing, it is ultimately stressful, for there is no pattern, and no semblance of order, which is necessary for a child to thrive.

See Chapter 15 for more ideas about talking to your child about trauma and other real-life stressors.

In this chapter we have identified key factors in assisting children to recover from traumatic events. Traumatic events are heterogeneous—each scenario presents its own unique challenges. The interested parent is encouraged to pursue further reading on his or her child's particular type of trauma. See the resource guide for further information.

Delia's Story: Moments of Moving On

At age nine, Delia, witnessed an unusual traumatic event. In the middle of a play performance at a community theater, a man who was sitting right in front of Delia lost control and began shouting, punching and beating up the person sitting next to him. Terrified for her life and without thinking, Delia leapt over the chairs and ran out of the theater. Her parents were also shocked by the outburst but were more concerned about their daughter's behavior and safety. Delia was in shock—irrational, crying, inconsolable. The police and an ambulance came and took the injured man to the hospital and his assailant to a psychiatric hospital. After this event Delia was terrified to go anyplace where there was a crowd—church, assemblies at school, sports events, even a small concert at a coffeehouse. Just thinking about these events, Delia would immediately get distressed and frantic that someone would lose control and try to kill her. She was unable to attend many family events or managed them with a very high level of anxiety and distress. She scanned a crowd for people who looked unstable. She would look around to see if someone was going to lose control, often jumping when someone made a small movement near her, and startling when she heard an ambulance, or someone cough, or even a small object drop or a chair moving. Delia was in a high state of alert. She walked through ordinary situations expecting to come right up against the shock of violence, and fearing for her life.

Though this event had occurred three years before Delia came to treatment, she still remembered vividly the entire sequence of events: the glasses flying off, the man being pushed to the ground, the color of his jacket, his earring, the feeling and sounds of hysteria in the crowd. She also was still unable to take part in normal activities, and had a growing realization of how much this experience had interfered with her life. In her words, "I know I can't walk away from everything."

In therapy we worked on Delia's problem from three angles. I explained how trauma works—that the pictures of the experience sort of burn into the memory and overwhelm our normal information- and memory-processing equipment, so that now whenever she came in contact with something that reminded her of the traumatic situation, it triggered the same anxious response that she had felt that night. With trauma we do remember the worst moment, the feeling of fear and helplessness. With time the memory works through that moment, and people are able to get to the end of the story, which is that they did survive. In Delia's case, she was a close bystander in a life-threatening situation and did survive. Other traumatized children may be directly impacted by the trauma, as in abuse, an accident, or a violent crime. Though they couldn't prevent those terrible things from happening, they need to think about the end of the story, which is that the trauma isn't happening now: it's over, and they are safe. I explained to Delia that the memories were following her because the event was sort of caught in her mind and hadn't been finished and filed away.

We set out to work on the treatment. I taught her how to do diaphragmatic breathing to slow down the feeling of panic when she was in a fearful situation, and we worked on relaxation and on creating a safe place in her mind. Next, I worked with her using EMDR to return to the exact original scene and facilitate Delia's desensitization to those characteristics associated with the event, and help her move through the story to the end. She was able to see that many capable people had taken charge, and that though she had been terrified that she was going to get attacked, she was in fact safe, and hadn't been hurt. Following this we began to use cognitive and behavioral techniques to change her thinking patterns about expecting danger in situations and to make a hierarchy of situations she could begin to approach. Identifying the "how awful versus how unlikely" error in her thinking, she became better able to estimate the "slim to none" chance that anything bad would happen in a situation, and worked on her breathing and self-talk to get ready for exposures.

Delia started being able to stay at church longer, and to feel less anxious there. By attending small gatherings, sitting at a distance, spending less time in the bathroom feeling upset, and more time in the event, Delia was able to climb up the stairs of relearning safety in her world. The top of the stairs, and a real triumph for Delia, was being able to attend a play— for the first time in over three years—because her best friend was performing in it and she really wanted to be there. Nervous but determined to overcome her fears, she walked in and took her seat in the theater and vowed not to scan the crowd for danger. Her friend's mother, who understood what an enormous step this was for Delia, leaned over and said to her, "Even though you are not in the play—you are truly the star!" Delia glowed and began to feel like a normal life was possible again.

PART III

Anxiety

BEYOND THE DIAGNOSES

We have just explored how the different anxiety subtypes require different types of interventions. In this next section, we go beyond the diagnoses and look at factors that affect children across the spectrum of anxiety disorder diagnoses. In Chapter 13 we address the issue of sleep—nighttime is the toughest time, generally speaking, for anxious children; included are general guidelines on how to get a good night's sleep as well as solutions to common nighttime anxieties. In Chapter 14, we look at the anxious child in the broader context of school, siblings, friends, and extended family. In Chapter 15, we address the issue of how to talk to your child about real fears out in the world. This is a difficult task for any parent, and parents of anxious children need to be especially careful to focus on safety rather than on risk when discussing such topics as illness, crime, or terrorism. Because stress is a trigger for anxiety, we also include guidelines for reducing the stress temperature of your household. In our closing chapter we witness how learning about anxiety management can effect a sea change for the entire family. There is a wonderful reciprocity where working on anxiety in your child in turn means working on anxiety in yourself. As time goes on and children become their own anxiety coach, parents may be pleasantly surprised to find their children giving them a pointer from time to time.

CHAPTER 13

✴

Things That Go
Bump in the Night

FROM NIGHTTIME FEARS TO SLEEP ANXIETIES

*H*eidi wants to sleep with the lights on—a night-light isn't enough. When we tuck her in, she follows us out of her room saying that she can't sleep. She is so upset, and we don't want her to be tired the next day, so we sleep with her, or else she crawls into our bed. How do we get out of this cycle?

Alex is seventeen and is going away to college next year, but suddenly he has this fear that he can't fall asleep. He gets so worked up thinking he'll be the last one up in the house that it turns out to be true. Now he's saying he can't go to college because he'll be up all night. Our pediatrician recommended relaxation tapes, but he's too freaked out to do that. Where do we start?

Sleep and Anxiety: What's the Connection?

Do anxiety and sleep go together? Anyone who has spent a sleepless night watching the numbers flip one by one, hour after hour, on their digital clock knows that sleep and anxiety are diametrically opposed and, for that reason, inextricably linked. Sleep is about letting go, and anxiety is about holding on.

Working out a peaceful resolution between the two is an essential life-management skill.

Much emphasis is placed on the sleep habits of infants and toddlers who are working on separation as well as fears, but older children and adolescents can be equally plagued with difficulties getting a good night's sleep. Anxiety tends to creep in when our defenses are down, when we're sick, stressed, or sleepy. Anxious kids struggle at bedtime for the simple reason that it is the first time all day when they can't distract themselves from their fears and worries—they are a captive audience. When all is quiet and the mind gets up and wanders, looking for trouble, the questions start to pop up. *What's that shadow on the wall? What was that noise? Do my friends like me? When am I going to study for my math test?* Some kids have specific fears of robbers, aliens, or monsters, but others may fear sleep itself—will they die in their sleep—or be up for hours in the middle of the night? Whatever the worry, one thing is clear—everyone in the family is losing sleep over it.

The recipe for successful sleep combines two main ingredients: 1) coping skills for kids to quiet their worries and slow down their bodies, and 2) consistent expectations and routines maintained by parents. Sleep is not something that you can *make* happen. Instead, we can make conditions optimal to *invite* sleep. This chapter will give you the tools to tuck your child in with confidence, whether he fears that bad dreams will come back if he goes to sleep or lies awake for hours, unable to turn off his thoughts. In addition to identifying key factors that facilitate sleep, this chapter focuses on solutions for common nighttime problems for all ages.

Behavioral Patterns and Routines for Sleep

GOOD SLEEP PATTERNS: EARLY INVESTMENT
REAPS A LIFETIME OF REWARDS

Though tired parents are battling their own fatigue when working on their children's sleep patterns, setting good patterns early on will reward you with easier bedtimes and hours and hours of sleep down the road. It is never too early or late to start. Researchers have found that sleep problems were more likely at ages five and ten in children who had sleep problems before the age of six months. However, don't despair: even after years of sleepless nights, you can still expect excellent results if you and your child work faithfully on creating good sleep patterns.

Many parents struggle with leaving their child awake to fall asleep on his own. Particularly when such factors as separation anxiety or phobias are present, parents may have difficulty walking out on a protesting child, but research on infants suggests that this is the right thing to do. Infants whose parents are present when they fall asleep wake up more often than those who are put to bed awake and left alone. Given the opportunity, babies learn to soothe themselves. Without that opportunity, if they wake up in the night, they will need you there in order to fall asleep again. The same is true for older children. Though you may feel like your child is too insecure to be left alone to fall asleep, he, like an infant, can acquire that competency, but first he needs to learn the skills. Once the skills of breathing, relaxation, and calming self-talk have been mastered, you can begin to fade yourself out of the picture, switching from lying in bed with your child to a tuck-in followed by check-ins.

GOOD NIGHTS CHECKLIST

The following is a list of factors that are known to facilitate good sleep. In addition to addressing anxiety issues directly, these guidelines offer strategies that will increase the likelihood that your child will sleep well.

- Allow sufficient wind-down time; plan a good wind-down activity. Extending exciting activities up to the last minute only prolongs the falling-asleep process. Stop exciting activity—rough play, television, computer games, especially those with scary content—well before bedtime. Teenagers shouldn't study up to the last minute. Establish a wind-down activity—reading, bath, quiet music.
- Keep it safe. Avoid scary material before bed—for young children, no scary books or videos, or frightening games with chases; for older kids, no scary books or movies before bed.
- Have a plan for nighttime fears. Have realistic self-talk on cue cards for the child at bedtime, teach diaphragmatic breathing, keep a flashlight on hand.
- Keep it positive. Avoid all negative associations with sleep or the child's bedroom. Don't use sleep as a punishment (going to bed early for bad behavior). Try to use another area if "time-outs" are needed. Keep the associations with being alone and being in bed positive.
- Watch the diet. Eliminate caffeine—chocolate, teas, sodas (even some root beers and clear or orange sodas contain caffeine). The effects of caffeine, which can exacerbate anxiety, may last up to ten hours after intake.
- Plan for the "ploys." Don't reward nighttime "ploy" behavior. Though nighttime conversations can be golden, if you stay an extra twenty minutes to get the scoop on school, it will likely become a new nighttime ritual. If you want that

time, push back bedtime to accommodate or encourage your child to share news with you after supper. If your child always needs a glass of water, have him get one himself and put it beside his bed before he gets in.

- Focus on readiness for sleep, not a deadline. Don't focus on expectations about when your child *should* fall asleep—she can't control that. The harder she tries to sleep, the more awake she will be.

- Avoid the problem of getting kids out of your bed—don't invite them in. Don't make more work for yourself or your child by having him just "visit" in your bed before bedtime—make your room off-limits before bedtime and so avoid the problem altogether.

- "Don't call us, we'll call you." The rule is that your child stays in bed—you will be the one checking on him, he is not to come find you. You can use incentives: happy-face charts, stickers or small prizes for young children, and more tangible rewards for older children. Without getting angry, be firm and be clear—your child needs to stay in bed.

- "Location, location, location." Settle your child down to fall asleep in the same setting (her room) and same conditions where she will wake up. For young kids, falling asleep in your room and waking up in the middle of the night in their own room will be disorienting and they'll come find you. Teenagers who fall asleep in front of the TV won't be comfortable falling asleep without the TV.

- Make parting less sorrowful—be brief. Be consistent in how long you stay in the room. You'll be supervising wind-down more with young children (under eight); with older children you will facilitate their independent "settling routine." Stay for shorter and shorter times.

- End with a pleasant interaction. In whatever way fits for your family, send your child to sleep with a message of love—singing, hugs, kisses, a funny saying, or "sweet dreams." Reinforce good cooperation with extra hugs, an extra story, etc.

Helping Your Child Sleep Well: Solutions for Common Nighttime Anxiety Challenges

NIGHTTIME FEARS

Like their daytime counterparts, nighttime fears are addressed by enlisting a child's thinking skills to turn a distorted, frightening, or worrisome situation into something that is more manageable. The fact is that just because a child *feels scared*, this doesn't mean he is *in danger*. His internal alarm system has gone off, but it was not triggered by anything real—it is hooked up to his imagination, not reality.

By asking your child what is on her worry list at bedtime (or simply noticing the kinds of questions she is asking you), you will learn what targets to use realistic thinking on. Your child can look at the shadows through the worry glasses and then the smart glasses, and get her imagination to work for her rather than working for the anxiety. Turning the frightening shadow into something silly—one of the counting sheep that lost its way, Mickey Mouse, Kermit the Frog—empowers your child to refute what Worry Bug says about nighttime and replace it with more truthful, calm thinking. It is best to start this work during the daytime when your child is not tired and therefore in better shape to think calmly.

Monsters in Closets or Under the Bed. It is very common for young children, who are still trying to master what is real and what is pretend, to be frightened of monsters, cartoon characters, or the proverbial boogeyman under the bed. While the message you need to send is that there are no monsters, use your creativity in delivering the message. Remember that gentle humor is a way to fight "fear" with "funny." You could make a silly announcement—speak into your imaginary megaphone—*This is David's mother, and I am saying that this house is officially safe, there are no monsters here.* Open the closet, look under the bed, and again make your pronouncement: *See, it's dark under there—but there are no monsters, just a shoe and some dust—oh, and my bologna sandwich from yesterday—hey, how did that get under there?* Then have your child repeat after you: *There are no monsters in my house. My house is safe.* Slightly older children can say, *I'm the boss, that's just a story. My imagination is set on "scary," but just because I can imagine scary doesn't mean I'm in danger. I'm not. I'm going to make my imagination work for me—I'm going to turn that picture into a silly cartoon.* You should lead the way with this at first but then, over time, invite your child to take increasingly more responsibility for the project. He can be the one to open the closet door, or pull back the blankets. After your child feels comfortable (this may take days or weeks), then you can transition him away from checking for monsters in the closet or under the bed to just using his brave talk. Also keep on hand a flashlight and a list of ideas (this can be a pictorial collage by the bed that your child helps to make) that your child would rather think about instead.

Fear of the Dark. Fear of the dark is most common among young children and preadolescents, but some teenagers and even adults struggle with this fear. It may be at the core of a child's difficulty sleeping alone. The fear of the dark is typically tied to the frightening ways the imagination fills in for what we can't see.

Children need to first work cognitively on looking at the dark through worry glasses and then through smart glasses—*it's just as safe, I just can't see as well, but I don't need to see, there's nothing to see.* Then they can generate boss back talk to fight the fear—*I can do this, I am brave, other kids manage this, so can I, I just have to get used to it.* Once the thinking is straight, have your child work on the fear of the dark in stages, first, during the day, taking fear challenges in the basement or attic with a flashlight, then in the early evening, going upstairs to his room in the semidarkness and doing something fun in there—reading a book, listening to music. What about flashlight tag in the dark? Or a scavenger hunt for hidden glow-in-the-dark items (the dollar store is great for these)? Finally, begin to reduce the amount of light in the room at night. If your child sleeps with the overhead light on, switch to a low-wattage lamp; if a child has three lamps on, reduce to two, and then move to a night-light or hallway light. Once you put out the idea of the stairs of learning, your child can tell you what step he's ready to take first.

Because younger children are just starting to understand the dark, be good tour guides—showing them that it can be fun, safe, and familiar. At night, start the bedtime routine with low lighting so that the transition to the dark won't be such a sharp contrast. Let your child know that at first he can't see in the dark but within a few seconds—faster than he can sing "Happy Birthday"—his eyes will adjust and then he can see. Using a familiar object of your child's choosing, such as a teddy bear, do an experiment: turn down the lights, start singing, and see how long it takes before he can make out the shape of his teddy bear. Let him also know that sometimes it feels like your eyes play tricks on you in the dark and things don't look the same, but they really are. Do another experiment by saying what things look like in the dark, and then shining a flashlight on them to see what they really are.

Fear of Sleeping Alone. Though fatigue and sympathy weaken the strongest parent, it is best not to lie down with your child, as that makes the departure tougher for her (and parents often fall asleep). Instead, sit on the edge of the bed or rub her back. Then tell your child that you'll see her in the morning, ask her how many times she wants you to check on her—two times or four times (a bargaining strategy). Make your check-ins very brief, definitely under a minute. Tuck her in and wish her sweet dreams. Make it clear that she should not call out, that you'll come back to check on her. If your starting point is that your child is sleeping in your bed, or you in hers, make a hierarchy to gradually match up the right people with the right beds.

Get to the core of the fear so it can be addressed. You need a plan for dismantling the fear before your child will be ready to take action. Have your child write his fears in a cartoon-style thought bubble, then write in another bubble what he wants to think instead. Managing sleeping alone requires a combination of cognitive tools to calm the worry, balloon breathing, progressive muscle relaxation to help the body unwind, and quiet activities your child can do until sleep arrives. Simply insisting that the child stay alone will not work. Once you've identified the source of the fear and have taught your child the thinking and relaxing skills he needs, you should begin to fade yourself out of the bedroom gradually. Or, if your child is sleeping in your bed, he can begin to head back to his room step by step.

Nighttime Worries, Last-Minute Questions. When kids have worries on their mind it is difficult to fall asleep, and it is difficult to be alone. If your child is a nightly worrier, or has ten *urgent* questions that must be answered at bedtime, schedule a worry time well before bedtime—taking five minutes to write down or say his worries, then challenging them with more realistic thoughts, using one of the analogies listed in the Master Plan. This could also be a "last call for questions time." Then at bedtime remind your child that he is the boss of his mind. Keep coping thought reminders on cards in bed, and keep a list of other thoughts or ideas that your child would like to think about.

The second line of action is addressing resistant or avoidant behavior related to sleep. Make a good-night routine and stick to it. Keep a checklist of target behaviors to reinforce: staying in bed; not calling out; waiting for Mom and Dad to check on you; coping independently through reading, breathing exercises, and writing messages or questions to parents in a worry journal to be shared the next morning.

Keyed Up, Unable to Relax. Tedium is the stuff of good sleep. If your child is too alert and awake at bedtime, check out the Good Nights Checklist above. Use relaxation strategies from Chapter 4, and tie them in with some gently "boring" mind games—along the lines of counting sheep—that will settle him down. Picture a large white canvas that you are covering stroke by stroke with a warm golden yellow, or a silvery blue; your child can invent other similar repetitive outlets for slowing down the imagination till he drifts off.

Nightmares. The majority of children will have occasional nightmares in life. The period from toddler years through early grade school is a particularly busy time for contending with fears such as separation and fear of the dark, and bad dreams may be more frequent during this time. In fact nightmares occur in as many as 50 percent of all children between the ages of three and six years. Although typically the occurrence of nightmares decreases over time, some children continue to have nightmares into adolescence and even into adulthood. Reassurance and gentle coaxing back to sleep is the best approach. Though you may be bleary-eyed, it is best to walk your child back and settle him in his room. After a few moments of gentle reassurance that the bad dream won't come back, change the channel to a new dream, flip the pillow over for a fresh start, and help your child resettle.

Refusing to Go to Bed. Bedtime resistance is defined as a child's difficulty in getting to bed three or more nights each week for at least four weeks, with the child struggling for forty-five minutes or more each night. You may think that this describes most kids, because it is the rare child who *wants* to go to bed. More often than not, even feisty nighttime fighters will surrender to the inevitable when parents hold their ground with the bedtime routine. If you are keeping to your part of the bargain but your child continues to have difficulty settling, make sure you are not overlooking any fears. Your child's compliance in getting to bed and staying there can then be reinforced with incentives—extra play time, an extra story the next night, extra computer time. Although in general incentives work best, some parents find that withdrawing privileges temporarily gets the job done.

Anne's Story

Insomnia runs in Anne's family—it is not unusual to find at least one member of the family up in the middle of the night. According to Anne's mom, Ellen, Anne has had trouble with sleep since she was an infant. But while Anne's mom learned to manage her own bouts of insomnia, for Anne one of the factors perpetuating her sleep difficulties was her worry that she wouldn't be able to sleep. Like many children with sleep anxiety, Anne is haunted by the memory of one awful night when she was up for hours and hours unable to fall asleep. Ever since that night, Anne would stay up late worrying that she wasn't going to be able to sleep. She would get so frantic and worked up that her worst fear would come true. Working on her self-talk and breathing, Anne was able to see how she could impact her anxiety level at night by what she was saying to herself and what she was doing with her time waiting to fall asleep. The more she played up the catastrophe of being awake and listened to her fears about it, the worse she did. When she was able to tell herself she was going to be okay no matter what happened and focus on breathing and listening to a relaxation tape, the worry came way down and she was able to sleep much better. As she writes, "I would feel so scared at night thinking that I would never fall asleep and that I was the only one who felt this way. I worked my way through it. Even though that night I was scared, I started to realize even if the worst thing came true and I stayed up all night again that I could deal with that. I realized too that when I didn't make that into a big deal it actually helped me stay calmer—and even if it took a while, I could fall asleep. When I saw that I could survive not sleeping well—that I could still be fine the next day at school—I knew I would be okay, and I actually worried less at night. I had seen the worst and managed it, so I didn't have to get worked up about it. I would just say to myself: *'Everything will be fine. You're not insane! You can get through anything. It will come to an end.'* Now that I've learned not to let anxiety about sleep control my sleep, I think to myself: *'Wow, I can't believe I did it! It's a great feeling.'* "

✳

CHAPTER 14

Expanding the Focus

ANXIOUS CHILDREN AT SCHOOL
AND WITH FRIENDS AND FAMILY

*I t is so difficult to get Vicki to school that I begin to wonder, is this
really necessary? Maybe she should just stay home.*

*Sometimes I think I'm the one who is losing it. My mother-in-law says
that all these problems would go away if I was just more strict. What
do I tell her?*

School: Making It Work for
Anxious Children

Children spend over 1,100 hours a year in school. Kids' difficulties with school can range from an occasional sticky situation where they refuse to attend to a serious stalemate where
nothing can get them to go. When schools tune in to the needs
of anxious kids, it can make the difference between a child attending and thriving in school or not attending school at all. In
this section we cover three school issues: assessing reasons for
school refusal; options for educational plans when your child
needs special accommodations; and finally a word about how a

school can make its curriculum more sensitive to the needs of anxious children.

REASONS FOR SCHOOL REFUSAL

When your child's struggles over attending school are not occasional, but part of daily life, it is urgent that you identify the source of the problem. Though you may be tempted to keep a child out of school until the problem is solved, total avoidance of school is counterproductive. The longer a child stays out, the harder it will be to go back. As with all other anxieties, find the starting point—how long your child can reasonably manage staying in school—and build up from there, making the necessary accommodations and bringing in the proper support.

It is best to take a wide view when investigating the reasons for your child's refusal: take in information from your child, from the school, from looking at peers, home life, and health. Is your child escaping from some unpleasant or difficult situation such as panicking about tests or unable to handle a social problem? Or is she being positively rewarded in some way for staying home, such as unlimited access to computer, television, or Mom? Once you have identified the possible source of the problem, consult the earlier chapters on individual diagnoses for strategies to address the issue. When a child is not going to school in order to avoid a perceived fearful situation (what is called negative reinforcement—escaping only reinforces the power of the fear), steps must first be taken to reduce or resolve the source of the discomfort and then to help the child reapproach school in manageable chunks. This may involve having a shortened schedule, or spending part of the day in the guidance office. When a child is inadvertently getting positively reinforced for missing school, parents must make home less rewarding and reward children for gradually attending school instead.

To find out what is at the root of a child's school anxiety, parents can ask their child what he would change at school and at home to make things better.

THE PARENT'S STANCE: BELIEVE THAT SCHOOL IS THE RIGHT THING FOR YOUR CHILD

We all want our kids to be educated and to like learning. But they won't always want to go to school. Your job as a parent is to ensure that any issues that come up are handled appropriately with the school, and to address specific concerns that you or your child may have. Once the stage has been set and a constructive plan put in place, your job is to be positive and supportive about your child's attendance. Your conviction that your child can manage the challenge of school will help him put his best foot forward. If a parent has mixed feelings about the child attending school, the child will sense this and use it to dig in. Likewise children will pick up on any conflict between the parents and the school and will side with the parents, thus devaluing the school and feeling less compelled to attend.

SCHOOL AVOIDANCE: PREVENTION AND INTERVENTION

The first step is to identify the issues and see if you can work them out with your child. If this is not sufficient, you can contact your child's teacher or, for middle or high school students, the guidance counselor or the SAP (student assistance program). A meeting may be called to address the issues. Parents are often concerned that their child will be labeled as anxious, or that the information won't be kept confidential. Discuss your concerns with the team in a positive way. *"We are working on Daniel's anxiety, but he is struggling and really needs your support during the day. We are all concerned that this be kept private and discreet. Daniel doesn't want to be treated any differently, but knows that his anxiety is getting in the way of his concentration at school."*

GETTING OUT THE DOOR

Children with school anxiety are plagued by intrusive anticipatory anxiety. This running commentary of negative thoughts is calling the shots. All revved up with images of the worst-case scenario, these children are often unreachable. This anticipatory anxiety often starts the night before. Using the strategies in the Master Plan, help them to challenge the anxiety and come up with a story about what they really think will happen at school and how they can cope with it. In addition, consider the following:

- Try to keep stress low for your morning routine.
- Even though your child may be upset, keep him moving in the morning—getting dressed, brushing teeth, having breakfast. Not only will he not be thinking about school, but he'll also be ready to go when it's time.
- If you have the flexibility, bring your child to school initially rather than having him take the bus.
- Have a teacher or guidance counselor meet younger kids at the bus or in the parking lot upon arrival. Sometimes a call from a teacher the night before or in the morning can break through the "what ifs" and remind the child that someone is on her side.
- Use tangible reinforcers (prizes, tickets to sports events, computer games) for the hard work of attending school.

HAVING A PLAN AT SCHOOL FOR TOUGH MOMENTS

In order to help your child feel more supported and able to stay in school, a teacher's or guidance counselor's office should be identified as a safe place when he needs to leave the classroom temporarily. That person should have an awareness of the child's particular anxiety issues and preferred cognitive strategies for bringing back more realistic thinking. Contact with the parents should be the last rung of the plan. Often when children talk to their parents during school, it makes it harder for them to stay at school. Individual children vary in their response, but this possibility should be taken into consideration.

FOR THE CHILD WHO HAS BEEN OUT OF SCHOOL FOR WEEKS OR MONTHS

When kids have been out of school for an extended period of time, they have a great deal of anticipatory anxiety built up, and therefore transitioning back to school may need to be even more gradual.

When Something at School Is the Problem. If there is an academic, social, or teacher–student issue, the school should get involved on the child's behalf to work out the problem. Always work closely with the child; they know best how things feel and what is likely to help.

When Leaving Home Is the Problem. Typically this is due to either separation anxiety (fear of harm befalling a parent) or panic disorder (fear of being out of a safe zone if panic occurs). A hierarchy of necessary steps should be generated using the child's fear temperature as a guide. Stay at each level until that step has been mastered, and is no longer challenging. A sample hierarchy is included below.

Challenge	Fear Level
Visit after school to talk with teachers about plan	6
Mom drives, go to class for one hour, Mom in parking lot	6
Mom drives, go to class for two hours, check in with guidance counselor, Mom stays home	8
Mom drives, go to class until lunch, Mom stays home	8

Challenge	Fear Level
Mom drives, go to classes through lunch, have lunch with guidance counselor and two friends, Mom not home	8
Mom drives, go to class for five hours	10
Mom drives, go to class for the day, Mom drives home	10
Take bus to school, stay in class all day, Mom drives home	10
Take bus in the morning, stay at school, take bus home	10
Stay after class for music lesson	10

The hierarchy above is an example of how, by taking into account the different fear variables, Matt (the child with panic whom we met in Chapter 9) was able to return to a full school day within two weeks. If there had not been the flexibility on the part of the school to welcome Matt and support his anxiety management, Matt might have simply been unable to attend because the bar was too high. Unfortunately, in the sink-or-swim method of approaching school refusal, the tragedy is that most children bail.

Do You Always Force a Child to Go Back to School? Simply forcing a child to attend school is not a treatment plan. You need to know the "whys" of the situation. Find out what has become unbearable to the child. Is it the child's perceptions that are causing the torment, or some actual situation that needs to be modified? In other words, if something is "broke" you *do* need to fix it first. Until your child can return full time, keep the connection to school going, either through partial-day attendance or, when that is not possible, homebound tutoring.

ACADEMIC ACCOMMODATIONS: YOUR CHILD'S RIGHTS

It is sometimes necessary for children to have additional supports or accommodations in school, i.e., adjustments to their schedule, curriculum, or assignments, to allow them to partic-ipate in their education given the impact of their anxiety. For some children, these accommodations can make the difference between attending school and not attending school. The law provides that all children are entitled to a free and appropriate education in the least restrictive environment possible. Like children with physical disabilities, children with anxiety disor-ders are entitled to adaptations in their academic programming so that they may be successful in school.

The Individuals with Disabilities Education Act (IDEA) pro-vides specific procedures and funding for children who require such services. Parents can contact the student assistance team to initiate the process of procuring an Individualized Education Plan (IEP) for their child. A comprehensive assessment is conducted first to establish the child's needs, and the degree of interference in his academic functioning. In order to qualify for this process, your child must be identified as having special needs. While in the past children with OCD and anxiety were labeled Socially and Emotionally Disturbed (SED), the category Other Health Im-paired (OHI) is more appropriate. IEPs can include modified schedules, one-on-one aides, and modified assignments.

For children with milder impairment, a document called a 504 plan can be drawn up by the school with parent input. A 504 plan is less formal, has no specific procedures as to assess-ment and compliance, and is based on the goodwill of all par-ties. The benefit is that it avoids the sometimes arduous assessment procedure of the IEP, but by the same token, with-out regulations, adherence can vary greatly. A 504 plan could be used to grant prorated credit for partially completed assign-ments, or allow a later arrival time at school, a phone call to parents, or similar concessions.

Remember, these accommodations can make it possible for a child with an anxiety disorder to participate and progress in school without interference from his current limitations. As children progress in their treatment and as new school challenges arise, frequent review and adjustments in accommodations will be necessary.

There are several excellent books and websites that describe in detail your child's educational rights and how to best ensure them. See the resource guide for more information.

Sample School Accommodations

Accommodations	Benefits child with:	Implementation
Excused lateness, delayed start in the morning	Multiple OCD morning rituals, medications that make child sleepy in the morning. Separation anxiety or panic: needs a shorter day	Arrange study hall or free period first so child isn't missing instruction
Tests or assignments taken orally rather than written	OCD: slowed down by perfectionism in writing	Use a scribe, tape recorder, or voice recognition computer program
Reduced homework	New diagnosis or escalating symptoms (PANDAS), holding it together at school, exhausted at home Children recovering from trauma	Set time limit for work, prorate grade on completed work, reduce number of writing assignments
Reduced public speaking; oral reports taped or conducted one on one with teacher	Social anxiety, generalized anxiety disorder, panic disorder	Work toward small public-speaking challenges, prearrange calling on child in class, work up to spontaneous public speaking

Accommodations	Benefits child with:	Implementation
Reduce in-class note-taking	OCD: perfectionism in writing, other interfering anxiety, overfocus on notes and on missing important information	Provide child with prepared notes that she can highlight in class, set child up with buddy from class who will provide photocopy of his notes
Safe place at school, free pass for brief breaks	OCD, panic disorder, separation anxiety, phobias	Prearranged signal system so child doesn't have to ask to leave (place bright-orange card on desk, wink at teacher); brief trip for water, brief 5- 10-minute check-in with identified target staff
Untimed tests	Any anxiety condition, especially test anxiety	Extended time and alternate test location (quiet office) where child doesn't see others finishing their tests quickly. Often kids don't take the extra time, but knowing it is there provides great relief and enhances concentration and performance.

Accommodations	Benefits child with:	Implementation
Preferential seating for assemblies and large-group activities	Panic disorder: needs to sit by door to leave briefly if overheated or overwhelmed; OCD: contamination fears and bad thoughts make it difficult to be around many people; may wish to sit in front where he can't see others, or in back where he can leave easily Separation anxiety	Children may need to build up their tolerance for large group events. See if child can keep increasing amount of time he is able to stay for assembly; if he needs to leave, see if he is able to return for the end, to end the exposure on a note of success.
Social skills groups	GAD, separation anxiety, social anxiety	Provides a shared experience for children who need help making social connections or help with assertiveness, expressing a differing opinion, handling teasing

BURNING DOWN THE HOUSE: PREVENTING ANXIETY-GENERATING TEACHING IN OUR SCHOOLS

Schools have been undergoing a great challenge in recent years to meet the needs of all their students. With the publication of Mel Levine's *A Mind at a Time* and other popular books on learning differences, the bar has been raised to recognize the role of individual differences in how children learn. Unfortunately in terms of our recognition of differences in emotional sensitivity, we are sorely behind. When it comes to considering the needs of anxious children in dealing with potentially frightening topics we are still operating with a one-wiring-fits-all curriculum. Specifically, there are a few very small steps that could be taken—at no cost—to reduce the amount of unnecessary anxiety exposure that occurs in classrooms every day. Parents may want to share this information, of which teachers may not be aware. Science teaching in particular seems to be problematic because of the subject matter, but offhand comments in other subjects can do unnecessary and inadvertent damage. Teachers need to be aware of the fact that anxious children, through no fault of their own, may be more affected than their peers by what they hear at school, in ways that teachers don't intend. Teachers may need to respond with some helpful processing—putting things in perspective—in order to prevent an anxious child from being traumatized.

No teacher knowingly traumatizes a child or would ever wish to, but teachers should consider the following: By conservative statistical estimates, more than 10 percent of the kids in their class are anxious and have difficulty processing risk accurately. It is not their fault, nor does it need to be their fate, if the adults in their lives are aware of what anxious children need in order to accurately understand risk. They need perspective, and the use of words like *rarely, small chance, slim to none,* or *never* will mean a great deal to them. So when teaching about how a small cut can lead to gangrene and eventual amputation, they shouldn't forget to emphasize that this is extremely rare and explain why (because people notice infections and take care of them). Otherwise kids will be coding this information as *"infection . . . blah, blah, blah . . . CUT OFF YOUR HAND!"* When talking about oxygen and using an example like *"imagine your house is on fire—how quickly would you have to get out before the oxygen would be used up?"* a teacher should consider how it would impact an anxious child—whether such an example is even necessary and if there's another way to illustrate the point that isn't so provocative. Teachers may find the following guidelines useful:

- Emphasize safety precautions as much as, if not more than, risks.
- Make sure to put the risks in perspective.
- Assume that there are anxious ears listening and correct any generic misperceptions or misunderstandings that are likely.
- Emphasize above all the appropriate and accurate take-home message.

Friends and Family: Managing Relationships

FRIENDSHIPS

Anxiety interferes with friendships on many levels. Whether your child is second-guessing what her friends think, worrying about approaching other kids, or simply spending so much time on anxiety issues that there's no time left for anything else, anxiety gets in the way. Children often feel different because of their anxiety—like they are the only one suffering—and feel not only lonely but also unacceptable because of it. Children with anxiety may be relieved to visit the websites listed in the appendix, or even to read the kids' stories in this book, to see that they are by no means alone. In Chapter 8, we discussed in detail how to help a child who is afraid of social scrutiny or embarrassment. Here we will address the additional issues of whether and how your child can talk to her friends about her anxiety, as well as offer some suggestions for how she can reenter the loop after she has been out of the social scene for a while because she was taking care of the problem.

Talking to Friends. If your child seeks your help in making the decision about whether or not to tell a certain friend, suggest that she consider how that friend has handled confidential information in the past. If a friend has shared a secret with your child, that suggests a certain level of trust. Many anxious kids don't want to tell friends until they are feeling better. This makes sense in some ways, because they are feeling too vulnerable to deal with the risk of potentially insensitive reactions and with the possibility of being seen differently. If your child does decide to talk to her friends about anxiety, she can tell them that she doesn't need any special treatment, but that it just helps if someone else knows. Some children do appreciate when their friends know that they don't like to hear really gross jokes about throw-up, or don't want to see horror movies, or that being around dogs makes them feel uncomfortable. If your child is searching for words to describe what's going on for her, here are some ideas that kids have taught me over the years:

- I worry a lot—I don't want to and I'm working on it, but my brain just comes up with tons of stuff that scares me or makes me feel like I'm not safe.
- My brain gives me the wrong messages—it's like it's stuck on the worry channel. I always think of what could go wrong. It's a pain, but I'm learning how to change the channel.
- I get nervous about a lot of stuff—it doesn't just come and go, it sticks around and makes me feel really bad.
- Sometimes I feel like something really bad is going to happen; it's scary. My brain just goes into hyper–worry mode, but I'm learning how to shut that off.

Returning to Socializing After a Break. When your child is ready to return to his social life after having been in the thick of working on anxiety management, he may worry about what awaits him. If he's been refusing invitations for a while, he may find that the phone calls have slowed down or stopped, and take that as a sign that people have moved on. It is often helpful to explain that friendship is a two-way street, and that the friends started to feel rejected when your child kept saying no—and so don't want to go out on a limb by calling. Help your child find the small steps he's ready to take to put the word out that he's interested again. Maybe that's sitting with an old group of friends in the cafeteria, instant-messaging a friend, saying hi in the hall again, or even making a weekend plan.

ALL IN THE FAMILY: MANAGING RELATIVES AND SIBLINGS

Extended Family: Advice, Criticism, Acceptance. Everyone has a role in a family—some advise, some need to be critical, and others are accepting. Identify family members who have the potential to help you with your situation, and cultivate their support. For those who are unable or unwilling to learn, you can simply suggest that with all due respect, it's not something you are able to discuss with them. They will of course counter with "I'm just trying to help" (and they are). You then have the perfect entrée to let them know that the best way they can help right now is to not bring it up. Certainly, if a relative is making unsupportive comments to your child, you need to intervene more directly. Let them know that your child is stressed and these comments will only reinforce negative feelings he is already having about himself. Suggest alternatives that would be helpful for your child to hear. For example, instead of saying, *"You're so shy! We won't bite,"* suggest that family members offer a warm hello and give your child space to warm up and adjust.

Know that you may feel some heartache, because the unkind comments that your relatives may make could echo some of your own worries about your child. Just remember the fact that anxiety is highly treatable and nobody's fault, so you have every reason to be optimistic about your child.

Siblings: Reconcilable Differences? Growing up with a sibling with an anxiety disorder can be very difficult. It is difficult to understand why things are so out of balance—the non-anxious child feels that she is held accountable for everything she does, while her anxious sibling seems to get away with murder, just by saying he's scared. Anxiety isn't a physical disability that kids can see, and the limitations it imposes aren't so easy to grasp. It is important to teach your children that their anxious sibling doesn't want to be feeling that way and is trying as hard as he can to fight it. Explain that anxiety is a normal reaction we all have, but that sometimes it goes into overdrive and problems result. Describe how your child's otherwise wonderful and normal brain is sending too many worry messages that feel real. *"It's as if you started to get a lot of crank phone calls telling you that it was going to snow tomorrow (even if it was July in Houston)—you would begin to doubt what you know to be true, and you would feel uneasy. This is what happens with anxiety. Even though anxious kids are bright and have the capacity to be realistic thinkers, the crank calls have extra power because they don't sound like crank calls, they sound totally believable."* Let your child know that everyone in the family can support the anxious sibling in learning to boss back and override his worry brain's messages. To avoid hurtful misunderstandings, children can ask their anxious sibling what they can do to help.

Strategies for Parents in Working with Siblings

- Be patient. Remember that oftentimes siblings express our own feelings in a situation—feelings we would never express. They are children too, and they deserve the opportunity to learn how to manage a tough situation. Though it hurts when they hurt, they are just doing their best too.
- Be clear that no personal attacks will be tolerated. Hold your child accountable for his actions.
- Teach your child that fair doesn't mean equal—otherwise everyone would have to eat the same food regardless of

preference, have the same bedtime regardless of age, and wear glasses whether they needed them or not.

- Don't blame—always validate your child's *feelings,* even those very sharp-edged ones (*I hate him, he's ruining our lives, nothing is fun anymore*). Help her express those feelings in a non-hurtful way. Teach your children to identify the problem in any situation because that may lead to a solution. *"You're frustrated because we can't go to the play. I know, I am too. Your brother really wanted to go, but he got overwhelmed. You're right, this does stink. We can't always control the things we want to. Let's figure out how to salvage this evening. Ping-pong and ice-cream sundaes?*

- If your child does do or say something hurtful, remember, sincere apologies are a million times better than forced apologies—and worth the wait. Think reparation—how to contribute in a positive way to the family—rather than punishment.

- Arrange special one-on-one time when possible. Friends and relatives can either free you up for this time, or if necessary can take the sibling out themselves.

- There will be times when you will need your child's help and may be asking a lot from them. Let them know that you realize you are asking a lot and instead of feeling bossed around by you, they may feel important and valued for the job.

- Try to find activities that involve humor and call on family strengths. Break some rules together, be goofy, watch silly TV shows, play charades.

✴

CHAPTER 15

Worry Prevention in the Real World

When Luke overheard that his dad has to watch his cholesterol, he came running to me in a panic—does that mean he's getting old, does that mean he's going to die?

I'm afraid to take Cheryl to the movies—it's not worth it. If anything bad happens it stays with her for weeks. She can't sleep and she makes me promise it will never happen to her.

I know I need to talk to Sean about the terrorism alerts, otherwise he'll hear about it from kids at school and that's not right. I don't want to stir things up, but I know it's better coming from me. I just don't know how much is too much to tell him.

Promise Me That Will Never Happen: Talking to Your Child About Real Fears

We would do anything to protect our children, but there are some truths that we can't shield them from. If we are mindful of this but determined, we can exercise some control over how our children are exposed to the harsher realities of life, what they learn about them, and how they live with them. These are parental privileges that can be exercised even in difficult times. Facing our limitations does not in any way leave us powerless. We are role models for coping. Under our sheltering wings, we show our children that we can take charge of our lives even though we don't hold all the cards.

Children live, like we do, in a media-saturated world that brings us a daily regimen of illness, crime, and more recently, war and terrorism. They have questions that we need to answer. All children have them, but anxious children have many more and are listening closely to the answers. These are questions that we may find increasingly difficult to answer, even in our own minds, let alone in words and concepts that they can manage. When the fears are big we feel immobilized and unprepared to handle them. But at its base, fear is fear, worry is worry, and all fears, whether great or small, real or imagined, require a return to the basics—if nothing else, when you talk to your child you are saying, *I am here for you and will do everything I can to help you.*

This chapter will guide you through the decisions you must make when talking to your children about difficult but necessary topics by first using yourself as a guide—stopping and thinking about how you would want to receive the information. Next we look at guidelines for how to build stress-proofing into your child's daily life—not overscheduling your child and trying to put boundaries around the modern-day pressures that make their way into our homes.

THE WORRIED LEADING THE WORRIED

You may think that you can't guide your worried child because you're just as scared as he is. In regard to terrorism, in particular the magnitude of the events of late has threatened to make us lose our bearings and shaken our core sense of security in the world—we've been left feeling frail ourselves, and without our usual edge of being several steps ahead of our children.

This is normal—the new normal. But in this world of changing circumstances, we must ground ourselves and revisit the same lessons we are teaching our children.

FIRST THINGS FIRST: PUT LIMITS ON YOUR WORRY AND YOUR IMAGINATION

When we are contending with something of great gravity, we may find ourselves thinking about it all the time, or feeling guilty when our thoughts have strayed. No matter how serious the matter, we need to take worry breaks or we will find ourselves depleted by the worry with little energy left to act on the reality. We can visit the chaos—imagining various catastrophic scenarios—but we must also know how to quiet it down. When worry tries to sneak back in, we can push it back as we would a child pestering us for dinner. *"No, it's not your turn yet."* Just as we coach our children to choose what tape to listen to, the worry tape or the neutral one, we need to make those choices too.

Sharing News: Consider Your Purpose

WHO ARE YOU DOING THIS FOR?

If we stop to consider why we share information with our kids, we may be surprised to see that there is a measure of guilt. If, while you are warning your four-year-old about strangers, you are thinking, *"I could never forgive myself if something were to happen,"* your distress and urgency will be the loudest and clearest message, and your words, rather than being constructive, may be confusing or even frightening to your child. As much as possible, be calm and explain what your child needs to do to be *safe*. Afterwards use phrases like *"so your job is to . . .* [let your child finish the sentence to see if he has learned the safety rule] . . . *"only go with adults I know."*

ADOPTING THE RIGHT MINDSET: IT'S NOT ABOUT RISK, IT'S ABOUT STAYING SAFE

We live with the reality of kidnappings from children's beds and yards, school shootings, violent crime, terror threats and attacks, and life-threatening illnesses. While we need to prepare our kids for these possibilities, we need to do it in a worry-smart way, rather than inadvertently borrowing our tactics from a burglar alarm or exterminator salesman. We don't want to play up the scary side of things. Although these incidents are horrific, they are extremely rare. So instead of focusing on the risks, we need to focus on safety and on what kids can do to increase their safety. This will help your child feel more in control—and feeling in control means being in control. What are the safety rules for being outside? at school? at the mall? Stating *"the family rules for safety are . . . "* feels very different from telling a child that there are strangers out there who want to hurt him, that kids have been kidnapped, and so on. The way to build resiliency is to first do no harm. Make sure that your explanations do not make the dangers seem bigger and scarier than they are. Get clear on the message first for yourself, and then begin to communicate it to your children.

MANAGING THE FLOW OF INFORMATION

Whether you are talking about war, illness, terrorism, or crime, you won't have all the answers, and much of what you can tell your child will not be good. Still, don't let your feeling that you have to have it all solved and fixed stop you from broaching difficult subjects. Even if you did have all the answers, it would not be in your child's best interest to share them all at once. In preparing you to talk with your child about fear-generating topics, the following guidelines will help you to be the rock and resource that your child needs you to be.

- Be as *concrete* as you can, not as *complete* as you can.

- Identify the people who are working on the problems that your child is asking about. There is power in numbers, and overly responsible, anxious kids need to know that others are on the job.

- Be truthful, but only in degrees. Build on your explanations slowly. Don't feel rushed or pressured to force-feed your child. Give your child a chance to digest the facts, keeping in mind what is appropriate for him or her.

- Always start with the questions that come from your child. Ask her what she thinks or knows about a situation, or what she has heard. This will allow you to build on her knowledge base. Listen for her emotional needs, and correct any misperceptions.

- Don't be afraid to state the obvious. Often very basic information, even if it is repetition of the obvious, can be very comforting. "Your grandmother loves you very much, the doctors are taking good care of her"; "We have the strongest army in the world"; "You are safe, I will always protect you."

- Focus on what your child *can* do. Give your child something to do with the information: a small job, a favor, a project. Keep in mind that the goal is to focus on competency, or what your child can do to cope or protect himself given his or her age and abilities, rather than focusing on emotional or physical vulnerability.

- Anxious children often feel responsible for situations that are not their fault. Make sure your child has an accurate understanding of the causes.

- While you don't want to *show* your distress about how uncertain these situations are, you can *tell*. Put a ceiling on how high the anxiety goes by simply saying "this is one of those situations that is not easy, where we don't have all the answers." Show confidence that we can live with some uncertainty. It's not pleasant, but we can deal with it.

Empathize over the fact that this is a situation where there aren't good enough answers.

- Reinforce realistic thinking—focus on the unlikelihood of a risk rather than how devastating it would be.
- Limit exposure to television. Turn it off yourself. Try to watch the news when your kids are not around—it is simply not appropriate for children. Though television news is informational, the content is essentially that of a PG-13 movie. Young children can't understand that the pictures they see over and over again are being replayed, rather than happening again and again. In addition, they have no sense of how far away a situation is. A five-year-old saw the news about how a man accidentally injured himself with a nail gun. That night she insisted that her mother check her whole body to make sure she didn't have any nails in her. Older children can watch briefly with you in order to process the information they have seen. If you want your child to be aware of certain appropriate topics, make use of other media—newspapers and magazines. The written word is easier for most kids to process than a constant stream of violent images, which tend to stick in their minds.

Good Housekeeping: Buffering Your Child from Our Stressful Culture

It has long been known that stress can trigger or exacerbate anxiety in children and adults. Next we'll consider the cultural factors that contribute to a child's daily stress level, and how families can take charge and counteract those influences.

In *Parents Under Siege,* authors James Garbarino and Claire Beard emphasize that parents can't regain control of their children without recognizing the social forces that exert pressure on the family. Those forces are manifold, but they include longer work weeks, tight deadlines, information overload, technology burnout, violence and sexuality in the media, commercialism, and materialism. While we all have to accommodate to these pressures to varying degrees and consider some of them integral to modern life, we can't surrender to them or they will simply steamroll through our lives.

Some experts argue that parents have little influence on their kids in comparison to peer influences and biological makeup, yet time after time we see how parents' responses, reactions, and behaviors are mirrored in the actions of their children. Children start out this way—it is their natural inclination to imitate—and they will follow their parents' lead in managing time and handling stress.

Having an anxious child can make you keenly aware of these difficulties, as your child may be even less able to accommodate the demands of our stressful culture than other children. It may be an uphill battle to contend with the external forces that work against your child, but don't concede the fight. Help your child learn to make reasonable choices about extracurricular activities—i.e., *not* letting your child play three sports and two instruments, and still expecting straight A's from her. While they may create some additional stress for you if they differ from those of other parents in your circle, decisions that favor your child's good health are only difficult until you make them. Once they are made, seeing your child happier, more productive, and less stressed will be all the evidence you need that you've done the right thing. Perhaps others will follow your lead, and communally we can reduce our supersized expectations of life to something we can actually live with.

We know that stress has physiological consequences for sleep patterns, memory, mood, health, growth, immune functioning, and cardiac and pulmonary functioning. The following are some easy-to-implement suggestions to de-stress your anxious child's life.

DO ONE THING TO IMPROVE EATING AND SLEEPING

If kids take their diet cues from television, a hamburger, fries, and coke are what *everyone* is having. We know that caffeine makes anxious kids feel more jittery and tense, and that diets high in carbohydrates or sugar do not supply kids with energy that lasts. Anxiety takes advantage of energy lows. Kids need to know that one way they can take charge of their anxiety is by reducing sugars and eliminating caffeine. Take a look at your child's diet and talk with him about some convenient ways to improve it. One change—sending him to school with almonds or mini-carrots for a snack instead of potato chips, a water bottle rather than soda—starts the ball rolling. Let your child help you make the decision. He'll be more likely to follow through on it.

Many kids—like adults—don't get enough sleep. Make a nighttime schedule; keep track of your child's success getting into bed earlier, and throw in an incentive for compliance, if needed. Eventually your child may see that feeling calmer and having more energy is its own reward.

CONNECT WITH YOUR CHILD

A predictable and supportive relationship provides the safest context for developing coping skills and reducing anxiety in children. Your child will get the clearest signal that she matters to you when you prioritize to make time for her—even if that's once a month. Young kids are thrilled when they can look forward to a date with their parents—put it on the calendar so they'll look forward to it for weeks. For teenagers, find a compromise. You might have to go to the mall in order to have a good talk on the way there. Even if you travel or work late, or work a night shift, be creative—have your nightly e-mail exchange, leave notes in a communication journal. Give your child leeway about how and how often he communicates, but let him know you are there. Spend time together as a family. Don't just coexist. Music night, game night, poetry night, family cooking night—take turns on who makes the selection. You'll find that you return to your own life less stressed as well.

VALUE AND INVITE YOUR CHILD'S POINT OF VIEW

If you want your child to grow up with a good sense of how much she matters, show her that she matters now. Inviting her opinion or input doesn't mean giving her carte blanche to do whatever she wants, but it does help her learn how to express herself effectively, lets her know that her ideas count, and builds up her tolerance for the frustration that occurs when her idea isn't chosen.

LIMIT SCREEN TIME (AND UNPLUG YOURSELF)

If your dinnertime is nonexistent or a din of ringing phones and blaring TVs, it's time to unplug. One predictor of school success is whether the family eats dinner together.

- Decide what works for your family and stick to it. The latest statistics suggest that adults are watching more TV than kids, but we know that without limits your kids can get sucked into the tube.
- Screen devices such as video TV games should be used as diversions, not full-time distractions.

Anxious children are, by definition, stressed. While parents cannot always prevent their children from experiencing stress, they can take measures to model for children how to manage stress and limit its impact on day-to-day life.

✳

CHAPTER 16

Freeing Yourself from Anxiety

YOUR CHILD WILL LEAD THE WAY

I still wish I could take away Cassie's pain, but then I pull out the tool list and remind her that she is in charge, not the anxiety. It's just my own anxiety and worry that makes me feel helpless sometimes. Actually, if I'm honest with myself, Cassie just keeps on moving ahead, I'm the one who feels more worried.

It took a long time before I could just listen to Connie's fears. Before, I would feel this incredible sense of panic and urgency to make her stop. I was worried that she couldn't handle it. Now we both know what to do. Connie's job is to work through her "what ifs" and "what elses" so she can get to the heart of the worry, and my job is to stay calm and just listen. She benefited from this approach right away; I'm a slow learner, but now I'm catching on.

As parents we all wish we could steer our kids around the inevitable bumps in the road of life. But in every life—no matter what the wiring—bumps happen. Picturing our children in the grip of fear and worry is painful and debilitating, but it's also only one side of the story—the worry side. What's missing from that picture is your child's will to be free (and every single child has it)—to fight back against anxiety, to live a good life. Believe in the strength of the protagonist in the story, and you will soon come to a page where the hero, your child, performs amazing feats and, leading the way, comes through just fine by the end. It will do you a world of good to see your child as capable and not helpless, but imagine how much it will help your child. Your belief in your child's abilities is like a great big green light—go!

I recently had the opportunity to work with a child who exemplified the idea that kids will find their way out of anxiety. Seven-year-old Julia, a spirited girl, had always been more fearful than other kids—especially squeamish about spiders, and uncomfortable with the mention of death—but she always managed just fine, and her parents weren't overly concerned. Then, one fall, Julia developed a sudden onset of OCD triggered by a strep infection. Suddenly she stopped answering questions because she was afraid she was telling lies, and she was afraid people weren't understanding her right—there weren't enough words in the English language to guarantee that she would be understood. Piles of black clothes couldn't be touched because black meant death, and furniture was off limits because of a memory that an ant or spider had been there at one time. Julia and her family came in for treatment—alarmed and despondent, completely in a tailspin, their world turned upside down. After our first session, in which I explained about Julia's "Brain Bug" (which she decided to call Jello because it always wiggled around the truth—you couldn't pin it down), Julia returned confidently to my office with a convincing action plan in hand. She unrolled a beautiful poster that she had made on her own initiative, which listed about fifty different slogans and ideas for how she was going to win the battle over her anxiety: *I'm going to do it; I'm the boss of me; Changing your mind is not lying! These questions aren't important; This isn't a chess game—it's not that complicated!; I'm going to win this tug of war game, I can do it! These are little risks, not big risks; Let the answers be free!*

Given a new understanding of what was going on in her life, Julia felt free to interact with the problem undaunted, with clarity of purpose, hope, and even a smile on her face. Although there was much work to be done, she could now draw on her creative resources to find her way out of anxiety. On the challenging path that followed, Julia would have to endure two more strep infections and one case of scarlet fever exacerbating her symptoms in a matter of seven months. The peaks and valleys of her family's roller-coaster ride during that time were very dramatic, but through every one, Julia emerged triumphant. With each fall, Julia was determined to get right back up again, and she did, kept on track by her understanding of her condition.

It was, of course, more difficult for Julia's parents, who had barely had time to recover from one episode when the next one started. They found it hard to trust Julia's smile. But it was hard to ignore Julia's progress as she jubilantly juggled her black clothes that had been off limits, decorating her hair with black ribbons, writing in black ink, saying the words, *death, die,* and *croak,* when only months before she couldn't hear those words without covering her ears and screaming.

At my last meeting with Julia, she reported that she had one issue left, but she told her mom that she didn't want to talk about it. Of course my ears perked up—was she avoiding something? We'd have to track it. No, it turned out the reason that Julia didn't want to talk about her last challenge—sitting on a couch that had been off limits worrywise—was because she had already figured out a plan for it. I told her that as a fellow colleague, I would just consult with her. Then Julia, this amazing second-grader, laid out all of the steps—*I know when something is hard I need to do it more, not less, then it gets easier. Do it a fun way, not a serious way; start small, work up, practice over and over till it gets easy.* Julia had learned her worry lessons well and was ready to graduate. Before, when things were bothering her,

Appendix

Organizations and Websites

American Occupational Therapy Association, Inc.
P. O. Box 31220
Bethesda, MD 20824–1220
www.aota.org

Anxiety Disorders Association of America*
8730 Georgia Avenue, Suite 600
Silver Spring, MD 20910
240–485–1001
www.adaa.org

The Association for the Advancement of Behavior Therapy*
305 7th Avenue, 16th Floor
New York, NY 10001–6008
212–647–1890
www.aabt.org/aabt

The Child Anxiety Network
www.childanxiety.net
Resources for parents on anxiety disorders; relaxation tapes
  and related products.

Childhood OCD Project

www.jjsplace.org

This comprehensive site has information and activities for kids with OCD, their parents, family, teachers, and therapists.

Children with Attention Deficit Disorders (CHADD)

8181 Professional Place, Suite 201
Landover, MD 20785
800–233–4050
www.chadd.org

Children's Center for OCD and Anxiety

www.childocdandanxiety.org

Information and links about diagnosing and treating anxiety disorders for parents, therapists, and teachers.

Learning Disabilities Association of America (LDAA)

4156 Library Road
Pittsburgh, PA 15234
888–300–6710
www.ldanatl.org

National Alliance for the Mentally Ill, Child and Adolescent Network (NAMI-CAN)

200 North Glebe Road, Suite 1015
Arlington, VA 22203–3754
800–950–6264

National Association of School Psychologists

4340 East West Highway, Suite 402
Bethesda, MD 20814
www.nasp.org

Resources for parents and professionals on educational and mental health issues

National Information Center for Children and Youth with Disabilities (NICHCY)
Box 1492
Washington, DC 20013
800–695–0285
www.nichy.org

National Institute of Mental Health (NIMH)—PANDAS Program
Pediatrics and Developmental Neuropsychiatry Branch
NIMH
Building 10, Room 4N 208
Bethesda MD 20892–1255
301–496–5323
www.intramural.nimh.nih.gov/research/pdn/web.htm

New York University Child Study Center
www.aboutourkids.org
A child and adolescent parenting and mental health resource.

Obsessive-Compulsive Foundation (OCF)*
676 State Street
New Haven, CT 06511
203–401–2070
www.ocfoundation.org

Obsessive-Compulsive Information Center (OCIC)
Madison Institute of Medicine
7617 Mineral Point Road, Suite 300
Madison, WI 53717
608–827–2470
www.miminc.org
A clearinghouse for articles on OCD.

OCD and Parenting On-Line Support
Louis Harkins, owner
groups.yahoo.com/group/ocdandparenting/
Subscription address:
ocdandparenting-subscribe@yahoogroups.com

PA Tourette Syndrome Association, Inc.*
132 West Middle Street
Gettysburg, PA 17325–2108
717–337–1134
www.patourettesyndrome.org

Selective Mutism Group-Child Anxiety Network
www.selectivemutism.org

The Tourette Syndrome Association
42–40 Bell Boulevard
Bayside, NY 11361–2874
718–224–2999
www.tsa-usa.org

Trichotillomania Learning Center (TLC)*
1215 Mission Street, Suite 2
Santa Cruz, CA 95060
831–457–1004
www.trich.org

*Denotes an organization that maintains names of qualified treatment providers.

Books

FOR PARENTS AND PROFESSIONALS

About Anxiety and Related Topics

Baer, Lee. *Getting Control: Overcoming Your Obsessions and Compulsions.* New York: Plume/Penguin Books, 1992.

Chansky, Tamar E. *Freeing Your Child from Obsessive-Compulsive Disorder.* New York: Three Rivers Press, 2001.

Ciarrocchi, Joseph W. *The Doubting Disease: Help for Scrupulosity and Religious Compulsions.* New York: Paulist Press, 1995.

Claiborn, James, and Cherry Pedrick. *The Habit Change Workbook: How to Break Bad Habits and Form Good Ones.* Oakland, CA: New Harbinger Publications, Inc., 2001.

Foa, Edna B., and Reid Wilson. *Stop Obsessing!: How to Overcome Your Obsessions and Compulsions.* New York: Bantam Books, 1991.

Johnston, Hugh F. *Obsessive Compulsive Disorder in Children and Adolescents: A Guide.* Madison, WI: Child Psychopharmacology Information Center, University of Wisconsin, 1993.

La Greca, A.M., W.K. Silverman, E.M. Vernberg, and M.C. Roberts. *Helping Children Cope with Disasters and Terrorism.* Washington, DC: American Psychological Association, 2002.

March, John, and Karen Mulle. *OCD in Children and Adolescents: A Cognitive-Behavioral Treatment Manual.* New York: Guilford Press, 1998.

Monahan, Cynthia. *Children and Trauma: A Guide for Parents and Professionals.* New York: Jossey-Bass, 1993.

Osborn, Ian. *Tormenting Thoughts and Secret Rituals.* New York: Dell Publishing, 1998.

Schwartz, Jeffrey M. *Brain Lock.* New York: Regan Books/HarperCollins, 1996.

Schwartz, Jeffrey M., and Sharon Begley. *The Mind and The*

Brain: Neuroplasticity and the Power of Mental Force. New York: Regan Books/HarperCollins, 2002.

About Tourette Syndrome

Bruun, Ruth Dowling, and Bertel Bruun. *A Mind of Its Own: Tourette's Syndrome: A Story and a Guide*. Oxford: Oxford University Press, 1994.

Haerle, Tracy. *Children with Tourette Syndrome: A Parents' Guide*. Rockville, MD: Woodbine House, 1992.

Shimberg, Elaine F., Oliver Sacks, and Elaine Shapiro. *Living with Tourette Syndrome*. Simon & Schuster, 1995.

About Sensory Integration Deficits

Kranowitz, Carol Stock. *The Out-of-Sync Child: Recognizing and Coping with Sensory Integration Dysfunction*. New York: Perigee Publishing, 1998.

About Trichotillomania

Anders, Jeffrey L., and James W. Jefferson. *Trichotillomania: A Guide*. Madison, WI: Obsessive Compulsive Information Center, Dean Foundation for Health, Research and Education. 1994.

Penzel, Fred. *The Hair-Pulling Problem: A Complete Guide to Trichotillomania*. Oxford: Oxford University Press, 2003.

About Sleep Problems

Cuthbertson, Joanne, and Susie Schevill. *Helping Your Child Sleep Through the Night*. New York: Doubleday and Company, 1985.

Mindell, Jodi. *Sleeping Through the Night: How Infants, Toddlers and Their Parents Can Get a Good Night's Sleep*. New York: HarperCollins, 1997.

About Educational Issues

Adams, Gail B., and Marcia Torchia. *School Personnel: A Critical Link in the Identification, Treatment, and Management of OCD in Children and Adolescents.* (Available from the Obsessive Compulsive Foundation.)

Dornbush, Marilyn P., and Sheryl K. Pruitt. *Teaching the Tiger: A Handbook for Individuals Involved in the Education of Students with Attention Deficit Disorders, Tourette Syndrome or Obsessive-Compulsive Disorder.* Duarte, CA: Hope Press, 1995.

About Psychopharmacology

Fruehling, J. Jay. *Drug Treatment of OCD in Children and Adolescents.* Obsessive Compulsive Foundation, 1997.

Wilens, Timothy E. *Straight Talk about Psychiatric Drugs for Kids.* New York: Guilford Press, 1998.

FOR CHILDREN AND ADOLESCENTS

About Worry

Henkes, Kevin. *Wemberly Worried.* New York: Greenwillow/ HarperCollins, 2000.

About OCD

Foster, Constance H. *Polly's Magic Games.* Ellsworth, ME: Dilligaf Publishing, 1994.

———*Kids Like Me.* Solvay Pharmaceuticals. Ellsworth, ME: Dilligaf Publishing, 1997.

Hesser, Terry Spencer. *Kissing Doorknobs.* New York: Bantam Books, 1999.

Moritz, E. Katia., and Jennifer Jablonsky. *Blink, Blink, Clop, Clop: Why Do We Do Things We Can't Stop: An OCD Storybook.* Plainview, NY: Childswork/Childsplay, 1998.

Wagner, Aureen. *Up and Down the Worry Hill.* Rochester, NY: Lighthouse Press, Inc., 2000.

Wilensky, Amy. *Passing for Normal: A Memoir of Compulsion.* New York: Broadway Books, 1999.

Endnotes

Introduction

1. Jean. M. Twenge, "The Age of Anxiety? Birth Cohort Change in Anxiety and Neuroticism, 1952–1993," *Journal of Personality and Social Psychology* 79, no. 6 (2000):1007–1021.
2. J. T. Walkup and G.S. Ginsburg, "Anxiety Disorders in Children and Adolescents," *International Review of Psychiatry* 14 (2002):85–86.

Chapter One

1. E. J. Costello and A. Angold. "Epidemiology," in *Anxiety Disorders in Children and Adolescents,* ed. J. S. March (New York: Guilford Press, 1995), 109–124.
2. S. M. Turner, D. C. Beidel, and L. H. Epstein, "Vulnerability and Risk for Anxiety Disorders," *Journal of Anxiety Disorders* 5 (1991):151–166.
3. D. S. Pine, "Developmental Psychobiology and Response to Threats: Relevance to Trauma in Children and Adolescents," *Biological Psychiatry 53* (9): 796–808.
4. G. S. Ginsburg and M. C. Schlossberg, "Family-Based Treatment of Childhood Anxiety Disorders," *International Review of Psychiatry* 14 (2002):143–154.

Chapter Three

1. A. M. Albano and P. C. Kendall, "Cognitive Behavioural Therapy for Children and Adolescents with Anxiety Disorders: Clinical Research Advances," *International Review of Psychiatry* 14 (2002):129–134.

2.   P. C. Kendall, "Treating Anxiety Disorders in Children: Results of a
     Randomized Clinical Trial," *Journal of Consulting and Clinical Psychology*
     62 (1994):200–210.

3.   P. C. Kendall, et al., "Therapy for Youths with Anxiety Disorders: A
     Second Randomized Clinical Trial," *Journal of Consulting and Clinical
     Psychology* 65, no. 3 (1997):366–380.

Chapter Twelve

1.   J. A. Cohen, L. Berliner, and J. S. March, "Treatment of Children and
     Adolescents," in E. B. Foa, T. M. Keane, and M. J. Friedman, eds., *Ef-
     fective Treatments for PTSD* (New York: Guilford Press, 2000), 106–138.

Phillip Stern

TAMAR E. CHANSKY, Ph.D., founder of the Children's Center for OCD and Anxiety, has helped thousands of children overcome fears and gripping mental compulsions. Author of *Freeing Your Child from Obsessive-Compulsive Disorder,* she has appeared frequently on television and radio, including National Public Radio's *Voices in the Family* and *The Parents' Journal.* She lives with her husband and daughters in Philadelphia.